samuel
beckett

Samuel beckett

Humanistic Perspectives

Edited by
Morris Beja
S. E. Gontarski
Pierre Astier

Ohio State University Press

Reprinted by permission of Grove Press, Inc., New York City:

From Samuel Beckett's *Waiting for Godot* (copyright © 1954 by Grove Press); *Malone Dies* (copyright © 1956 by Grove Press); *Endgame* (copyright © 1958 by Grove Press); *Happy Days* (copyright © 1961 by Grove Press); *Murphy* (first published in 1938; first Grove Press edition, 1957); *Proust* (first published in 1931; Grove Press, Inc., 1957); *The Unnamable* (copyright © 1958 by Grove Press, Inc.) in *Three Novels by Samuel Beckett* (copyright © 1955, 1956, 1958 by Grove Press, Inc.); *How It Is* (copyright © 1964 by Grove Press, Inc.); *Company* (copyright © 1980 by Samuel Beckett); *Ohio Impromptu* (copyright © 1981 by Samuel Beckett) in *Rockaby and Other Short Pieces* (copyright © 1981 by Grove Press, Inc.); *Collected Poems in English and French* (copyright © 1977 by Samuel Beckett); *Watt* (originally published by the Olympia Press, Paris, in 1953; first American edition published by the Grove Press, Inc., in 1959); *Molloy* (copyright © 1955 by Grove Press, Inc.) in *The Collected Works of Samuel Beckett* (1970); *Play* (copyright © 1964 by Samuel Beckett); *Rockaby* (copyright © 1981 by Samuel Beckett) in *Rockaby and Other Short Pieces* (copyright © 1981 by Grove Press, Inc.); *The Lost Ones* (copyright © 1972 by Samuel Beckett); *Film* (copyright © 1967 by Samuel Beckett); *More Pricks than Kicks* (first published by Chatto and Windus, London, in 1934; copyright © 1972 by Grove Press, Inc.); "Sounds" (first published in *Essays in Criticism*, Vol. XXVIII [April, 1978]); and "A Piece of Monologue" (first published in the *Kenyon Review*, Vol. I, No. 3 [Summer, 1979]; reprinted by the Grove Press, Inc., in *Rockaby and Other Short Pieces* [copyright © 1981 by Grove Press, Inc.]).

Reprinted by permission of Faber and Faber, Publishers, London:

From Samuel Beckett's *Waiting for Godot, Endgame, Happy Days, Play, Film,* "A Piece of Monologue," and, from *Three Occasional Pieces, Ohio Impromptu, Rockaby,* and *A Piece of Monologue.*

Reprinted by permission of John Calder (Publishers), Ltd., London:

From Samuel Beckett's *Malone Dies, Murphy, Proust, The Unnamable, How It Is, Company, Collected Poems in English and French, Watt, Molloy, The Lost Ones, More Pricks than Kicks,* and "Sounds."

*The stanza from Charles Baudelaire's "Correspondances,"
translated by Hendrik Roelof Rookmaaker, is reprinted from his
"Synthetist Art & Theories," published in 1959 by B. V. Swets and Zeitlinger,
The Netherlands, and is reprinted by permission of the publisher.*

(Continued on page vi.)

to Esther Rauch

(Continued from page iv.)

Library of Congress Cataloging in Publication Data:

Main entry under title:
Samuel Beckett—humanistic perspectives.
   Includes index.
   1. Beckett, Samuel, 1906–   —Criticism and
interpretation—Addresses, essays, lectures.
I. Beja, Morris.   II. Gontarski, S. E.
III. Astier, Pierre A. G.
PR6003.E282Z818   1982   848'.91409   82–12468
ISBN 0–8142–0334–5

contents

Preface   ix

Beckett's Theater Resonance   3
Ruby Cohn

Beckett's "Bits of Pipe"   16
James Knowlson

Beckett's Modernity and Medieval Affinities   26
Edith Kern

Beckett's English   36
Richard N. Coe

Unreliable Narrative in *Murphy*   58
Rubin Rabinovitz

The Harpooned Notebook: *Malone Dies* and the
Conventions of Intercalated Narrative   71
H. Porter Abbott

Wittgenstein, Heidegger, the Unnamable, and
Some Thoughts on the Status of Voice in Fiction   80
Allen Thiher

Neglected Biblical Allusions in
Beckett's Plays: "Mother Pegg" Once More   91
Kristin Morrison

Qu'est-ce qui arrive? Some Structural
Comparisons of Beckett's Plays and Noh   99
Yasunari Takahashi

Fiction as Composing Process: *How It Is*   107
Frederik N. Smith

"Syntax Upended in Opposite Corners":
Alterations in Beckett's Linguistic Theories   122
Judith E. Dearlove

Film and Formal Integrity   129
S. E. Gontarski

Come and Go: A Criticule   137
Hersh Zeifman

The Lost Ones: A Myth of Human History and Destiny   145
Antoni Libera

The *Company* Beckett Keeps: The Shape of Memory
and One Fablist's Decay of Lying   157
Enoch Brater

Beckett, Proust, and Burroughs, and the
Perils of "Image Warfare"   172
Nicholas Zurbrugg

Appendix: The *Ohio Impromptu*
Holograph and Typescripts   189

Notes on the Contributors   209

Indexes   213

Preface

This book grows out of a symposium, "Samuel Beckett: Humanistic Perspectives," sponsored by the College of Humanities of the Ohio State University, 7–9 May 1981, as a tribute marking Beckett's seventy-fifth year. The volume is intended as an adjunct to that conference, not as a strict record of its "proceedings." It is primarily a collection of essays in its own right, yet we hope that it nevertheless suggests the multiplicity of perspectives and approaches offered at the symposium. Only a portion of the spirit and still less of the spontaneity generated during the three days of the conference can be captured in a book. Discussion sparked by a lively paper or rejoinder tends to spill into halls and elevators, to continue into hotel lobbies, over dinner, and often well into the night over drinks (we were after all heeding the etymology of "symposium"). With sometimes as many as four sessions occurring simultaneously, participants were often faced with difficult choices. Moreover, in addition to the one hundred and forty or so academic papers and discussions, there were several theatrical performances and films, two of them premières: the American première of David R. Clark's version of Beckett's *Film*, with Max Wall; and the world première of the play Beckett wrote expressly for our gathering, *Ohio Impromptu*, directed by Alan Schneider and played by David Warrilow and Rand Mitchell.

The performance of *Ohio Impromptu* was of course a highlight of the conference. We are deeply grateful to Samuel Beckett for

writing the play, and for generously providing to us for reproduction in this volume his manuscript (including a revealing
faux départ) and three typescript versions. Although the excitement of the original production obviously cannot be duplicated
here, the various versions of *Ohio Impromptu* provide their own
different but no less genuine fascination, as we see the play
taking shape.

Similarly, while the excitement of many of the other events
also eludes the printed page, we believe that we have preserved
many of those aspects of such a conference that can be preserved—and that even gain from being put into print. Much of
what is valuable at such an event is, inevitably, passing; but
some of it can be passed *on*. For a selected collection of essays
can present arguments that merit close study and that make a
substantial contribution to our understanding of Beckett's
work. The following collection ranges from the sort of overview
of Beckett's theater and trends in Beckett studies that perhaps
only Ruby Cohn could provide, to essays on specific problems
in particular texts. Several of the essays reflect the international
character of the conference and offer perspectives that are considerably different from those usually adopted by American
and British scholars. Yasunari Takahashi's essay, for example,
compares the spareness of Beckett's drama and its pervasive
theme of absence to those features as they appear in Noh, the
highly stylized drama of Japan. And Antoni Libera's allegorical
reading of *The Lost Ones* may sit uneasily with some Western
scholars but is characteristic of much work in his native Poland,
where literature, Beckett's work in particular, has powerful
political significance—and where a relationship between art
and politics exists that is uncannily similar to that of Beckett's
Ireland.

The chief trait all the essays in this volume share is probably
the conviction that Beckett's work *matters*. That is why people
read it and go to the theater to see it. And that is why they read
about it and go to conferences to hear and talk about it—and, in
books like this one, why they write about their explorations of
it.

samuel beckett

Ruby Cohn

Beckett's Theater Resonance

In the play within the play *A Midsummer's Night Dream*, an actor plays the set. As contemporary actors can play tree or serpent, Shakespeare's tinker plays a wall that separates young lovers. The tinker Snout even particularizes the wall: "And such a wall as I would have you think / That had in it a crannied hole, or chink." Less adept than contemporary actors in sheer physical skill, Snout summons properties to enhance his credibility: "This loam, this rough-cast, and this stone doth show / That I am that same wall; the truth is so." For all Snout's assurances, however, theatrical truth is never simply "so." The tinker's Wall is at once a speaking character and a dumb artifact of loam, stone, and roughcast. Both character and artifact are concrete stage entities or signifiers or sign-vehicles, according to your ideolect. However you may designate this person-object amalgam, he/it functions as a barrier between lovers, who can communicate only through an aperture that happy Freudians will hasten to penetrate.

Samuel Beckett's dramatic characters—he calls them "my people"—never play artifacts, and one can never dogmatize: "The truth is so" about his resonant plays. I propose to examine a few harmonics of that resonance, especially for plays we experienced together at the symposium. But to show how far Beckett has traveled, I begin with his first extant complete play, the unproduced, unpublished "Eleuthéria" of 1947. *Eleuthéria*

is Greek for freedom, which is the goal of the play's oxymoroni-
cally named hero, Victor Krap. In a well-worn dramatic path to
freedom, Victor Krap has left his comfortable Passy home for an
uncomfortable Left Bank hotel room. Beckett confronts his
putative audience with both dwellings simultaneously—for two
of his three acts. No wall separates the stage rooms, but no
character crosses the invisible border from one area to the
other. The Krap living room is stuffed with bourgeois furnish-
ings, but Victor's hotel room is bare of everything but a folding
bed; and yet that nearly empty room fills three-quarters of the
stage space in act one, while the remaining quarter is stuffed
with the Krap salon. These two stage rooms are of course symbolic of two different ways of life, and the dramatic action of the
play is predicted by the change of setting. The opulent Krap
living room hosts the act one action on its quarter-stage, and
Victor's dingy space accommodates act two. By act three the
Krap living room vanishes; it would fall into the orchestra if the
stage were round. When Victor's wretched room usurps all the
space, he has achieved his victorious freedom—to do nothing
in indigence. And this will surprise no one familiar with
Beckett's other works.

In "Eleuthéria" Beckett himself is not free from traditional
symbolism of the realistic play, despite his simultaneous sets.
Each partial set bespeaks its way of life, like Ibsen's *Doll House*
or Chekhov's *Cherry Orchard*. Victor Krap has turned his back
on the Krap way of life, as lived on a quarter of the stage.
Peeping beyond realism, however, Victor finally stretches out
on his unfolded folding bed; he stretches out and literally turns
his back on the theater audience, who have absorbed the Krap
living room, bourgeois as they probably are.

Written less than two years after "Eleuthéria," *Waiting for
Godot* spurns realism, since it is set in a no-man's-land at twi-
light. The nearly bare stage, as everyone knows, symbolizes not
a way of life but the human condition, where momentary activities are wrested from the surrounding void. The printed text of
Godot designates only two items of the set: "A country road. A
tree." Both road and tree are traditional symbols of human life,
and Beckett relies on our familiarity with this convention, in

order to subvert it. His life-road does not lead to Godot, and his life-tree is linked to death wishes by hanging.

In *Godot* Beckett's scenic directions are minimal for set, but they are virtually absent for costume (except for footnoted bowlers). From the first Paris production on, however, Vladimir and Estragon have worn the tuxedos and derbies of vaudeville comedians, which prepare us for their vaudeville turns even before we hear a word. No such convention governs the costumes of Pozzo and Lucky, but when Beckett directed *Godot* in Berlin in 1975—the only time he has directed his most famous play—he designed his costumes symbolically. In act one Beckett's Vladimir wears black coat and striped trousers whereas Estragon wears striped coat and black trousers, and the reverse is true in act two. The two friends belong together, matched through mismatch. Pozzo and Lucky also belong together in Beckett's production; the tan-brown check of Pozzo's trousers is picked up in Lucky's vest, and Pozzo's gray vest is cut from the same cloth as Lucky's gray trousers. Different as the four men are, they belong in the same play through their bowler hats, at once correct city attire in Britain and international comedian attire in show business of the Western world. Perched on heads, these bowlers are related to human minds, but in no allegorical fashion that could not survive a juggling act.

Godot's bowlers may serve as transition to the resonances Beckett obtains from numbers, as few other playwrights do. Worn though the hats may be, the bowlers retain circularity— roughcast zeroes, like the setting sun or rising moon. The sun was invisible in Beckett's production, but the moon was a full round zero. In the printed scenic directions, Vladimir and Estragon *circle* around Lucky, and in directing, Beckett often had the two friends walk in small circles during the verbal canters of act two. A tradition of divinity in a perfect circle is subverted by Beckett to the zero that is never uttered in *Godot*, as it is repeatedly in *Endgame*. But zeroic circularity is nevertheless confirmed in *Godot* by thirty odd repetitions of the word "nothing"—the nothing that is both "done" and resisted.

Set, costumes, and circularity depict this version of the

human condition, or life *un*like a dome of many-colored glass staining an *un*radiant eternity, or void. *Godot* also plays *against* the void, since the drama of waiting absorbs us for over two hours, and it does so by inventive if repetitive word and gesture, sometimes geared to larger numbers than zero. The Christian number three threads through the play, which we view through three changes of light in each act. The two friends move through several triads. Vladimir probes the interior of his hat and Estragon the interior of his boot in three distinct movements—looking, feeling, shaking the prop. Vladimir shifts mood in three phases, as in the sequence: "There you are again, there we are again, there I am again." Pozzo's name is deformed to Bozzo and Gozzo, Godot's to Godin, Godet—phonetic triads. The two friends juggle *three* hats. When Estragon is wounded in his leg, the two friends hop together on *three* legs. Most striking in Beckett's direction is his segmentation of Lucky's monologue into *three* movements, the theme of the first an apathetic God, the second dwindling man, and the third indifferent nature. In three increasingly desperate degrees, Pozzo registers dismay at Lucky's logorrheal triad. In act one the two friends prop up Lucky, and in act two Pozzo, each human trio recalling the iconography of Christ crucified between two thieves.

Every critic has commented on this last trio, which troubles Vladimir in the actual dialogue of *Godot*. Three crucifixions and two thieves. The number two lacks the sacramental associations of three, and Beckett deploys two as a Janus-symbol in *Godot*. On the one face, the number two can indicate repetition, and on the other, opposition.[1] Repetitions in *Godot*—two acts, two pair of couples, two men in each couple, two entrances and exits of Pozzo and Lucky, two entrances and exits of the Boy, two brothers serving Godot, and many, many gestural and verbal doublets. For Beckett as for Ecclesiastes, there is nothing new under the sun, and these pairs hint by one repetition at an infinity of repetitions during the course of life on this muckheap.

The Gospel according to Saint Matthew presents the two thieves reviling Christ, but Saint Luke contrasts the two, the one thief rebuking Christ and the other defending Him and receiving His mercy. It is Luke's version that informs the oppositions of *Godot*. One couple is bound by serfdom, but the other by fraternity. Within each couple are contrasts: master Pozzo and menial Lucky, pensive Vladimir and physical Estragon. Even props contrast: phallic carrots and vaginal radishes, hats and shoes at opposite ends of the human body.

In the resonance of numbers, I leap from two—contrast or redundancy—to Vladimir's "million years ago" and Estragon's "billions" whom he claims Vladimir has killed, as well as "billions" who have kept their appointment. Patent exaggerations, these numbers reach out toward infinity—of years in time, of human mites in cosmic time.

In *Godot* Beckett is no traveler in an undiscovered country of symbols. Set, props, shapes, numbers, costumes, and even the bones that span prop, word, and intertextuality have all appeared in pre-*Godot* plays; but through their convergent resonance, Beckett has shaped a theater classic of our time.

Rather than rest on his laurels, Beckett ventures ever deeper into an unbaudelairian forest of symbols. Some fifteen years after *Godot* Beckett wrote *Play* and invented a new kind of theater sign with its own generative capacity—an invention that he has refined in his plays of the last decade. *Play* of 1963 requires three actors to play a man and two women confined to an eternal triangle inscribed in a vicious circle of repetitions. Each of the three characters believes himself or herself to be alone, although their urns touch. We glean their supposed solitude from their speech, which is triggered by a spotlight that Beckett in his scenic directions designates as an "inquisitor." Unlike Shakespeare's Wall, the spotlight does not speak, but all three characters speak to it. Provoked by the spotlight, the three characters first deliver a Narration of their earthly imbroglio and then a Meditation on their present situation, both frankly physical and fictionally metaphysical.

In *Play* Beckett subverts an old symbolic tradition of life as light. The spotlight of *Play* acts like an alarm, awakening the characters to their living death. This light is an instrument of a theater technician, which enables us to see Beckett's play. It is also a fictional inquisitor eliciting confession and inspiring interrogation from a man and two women in supposed isolation from one another. This light—a reality in the theater and a fiction in the drama—is what I call theatereality. Of it the man asks anxiously: "Am I as much as . . . being seen?" Since we see him, the answer is affirmative. It is small wonder that in rehearsal director Alan Schneider baptized so effulgent a light—with the name Sam.[2]

Advancing to Beckett's most recent plays, I quote Albee's George in praise of their "quiet intensity"—a spotlit quivering mouth in the darkness (*Not I*), a spotlit head with its halo of white hair (*That Time*). Paradoxically and perilously for the theater, Beckett limits stage movement in these plays. In even later plays Beckett again blends the reality of the theater into the fiction of the drama. Brecht uncovered the theater machinery, and his disciple Richard Foreman bares more sophisticated technology, but only Beckett makes a play (pun intended) of physical fact against dramatic fiction.

Brief as it is, *Footfalls* of 1975 contains four movements, punctuated by blackouts followed by chimes, but that is a structure we appreciate only in retrospect. Through the four movements we behold a long wooden board, a meter wide. The high spotlight of *Play*, *Not I*, and *That Time* falls in *Footfalls* to the floorboard. The footfalls are not, however, visible, for the single visible character is a woman with a "worn gray wrap hiding [her] feet." In the first three of the four movements, the gray ragged figure paces back and forth on the wooden board—nine steps and turn, nine steps and turn, the number of steps decreasing from movement to movement, the light dimming from movement to movement, until, in the fourth and final movement, the stage board is barren of human trace.

The first three movements of *Footfalls* dramatize mother-daughter relationships, a drama conveyed by two voices, although we see only the one gray woman. Each of the first three movements alludes to a daughter pacing back and forth—at once our visible fact and audible fiction. During the course of the first three movements, mother, daughter, and pacing woman garner details, for even as the footfalls decrease, the words about them increase. The first movement presents the pacing woman as a daughter named May, offering various ministrations to her invalid but invisible mother. Despite her own illness, the mother worries about her daughter's restlessness, revolving a mysterious "it all" in her mind. The second movement, a monologue by the invisible mother, seems to be a flashback to her daughter May's compulsion to pace back and forth on a wooden floor and to hear her own steps. The third movement, a monologue by the woman we see, begins what she explicitly labels a sequel, and thus implicitly continues the mother's account. Both women speak obliquely of the daughter's anguish at "it all," the gonglike syllable that closes each of the first three movements.

I see theatereality in an actress pacing nine steps, counted off on the board as she shudders through ghostly roles. The words of the first movement situate an aged woman perhaps in a hospital, her middle-aged daughter tending her, and revolving some matter in her mind. The words of the second movement situate a mother and her young daughter in a family home where the daughter spurned games in order to pace back and forth, even tearing up the carpet so that she could hear her own steps. The words of the third movement situate a nameless walker in a locked church where she broods about Christ's poor arm as she paces. Hospital, home, and church coalesce into a sounding-board for footfalls, visual analogue of a mind revolving the unnamed pain of "it all."

This brief but complex play fuses several harmonics of theatereality. The titular footfalls are at once actual and fictional; we hear them and we hear about them. We see a wooden board as we hear about a transept, and churches are built in the shape of a cross. The invisible woman directs our attention to the visible woman; in scene one she counts her steps, and in scene two she solicits our regard: "See how still she stands." "But let us watch her move." "Watch how feat she wheels." The third and longest movement is segmented into three: the woman we see announces "The sequel" about a ghostly woman walking in a locked church; the second part, entitled "The semblance," gradually builds a verbal self-portrait of the woman we see, culminating in the vivid phrase "A faint tangle of pale gray tatters." Without title, the third part offers to a *reader* description and dialogue of old Mrs. Winter and her daughter Amy at Sunday night supper.

Not only does Beckett fictionalize the theater facts—the sight of the woman pacing on a wooden board and the sound of her footfalls (a sound Beckett changed in successive productions from a hard knock to a grating rasp), Beckett also literalizes the old genre of mystery play through playing against what is literally hidden. One character, the fictional mother, is always hidden from our sight. In scene two her bodiless voice narrates how the fictional daughter was *absent* from the childhood game of lacrosse, how the adult daughter speaks only "when she fancies none can hear," implying *our absence* from scene three when it is apparently a daughter who speaks. She tells of a fictional daughter Amy who claims to be *absent* from a church service where her mother Mrs. Winter nevertheless heard her respond "Amen." The Winter segment is addressed to a reader, and yet book and reader are *absent* from the stage (in marked contrast to *Ohio Impromptu*). As the nothings of *Godot* become almost palpable through the several circularities, the absences of *Footfalls* haunt us through these verbal traces, but by scene four even they are absent.

Words and music of *Footfalls* harmonize in an exquisite "cascando" of steps, chimes, and light. *A Piece of Monologue*, in contrast, is a still life unveiled by the parting of a curtain (unfortunately lacking in the Columbus performance). On audience left is a figure in white—white nightgown and socks. To *his* left is a lamp as tall as he is, topped with a skull-sized white globe faintly lit. Just visible on audience right is the white foot of a pallet bed. After ten seconds the figure utters the word "Birth." Some fifty minutes later he closes this piece of monologue with the word "gone." Between start and stop of speech, the white-clad figure on stage describes a white-clad figure in a room that contains a lamp the height of a man, and the corner of a pallet bed. The monologuist barely moves, but he tells of the movements of his subject in the room—westward toward a window from which he looks out into darkness, eastward toward a wall on which photographs once hung. Between west window and east wall, continues the monologue, the white-haired figure in white gown and white socks stops at a man-sized oil-lamp whose wick he lights, sometimes with a match, sometimes with a spill. Gazing before him at wall or window, the narrated man sees below him in his mind's eye a rainy burial. My account is more coherent, more sequential than the actual monologue composed of terse phrases in semi-sentences—repeated, accreted, qualified, denied, with the delicate tonal variations of David Warrilow, for whom the play was written.

Unlike *Footfalls*, where we have a slow eclipse of theater fact by dramatic fiction, *Monologue* very soon presents an apparent coalescence. After the curtain parts but before a word is spoken, we have ten seconds to absorb the still, invariant image—two uprights and a corner; the two uprights—man and lamp—are visual reflections of one another. Through them Beckett subverts the old symbol of life as light. During the course of the monologue, we sense a man moving toward death while the lifeless lamp glows unmoving on. (At the Stanford University performance, where the audience was distant from the stage, after-images produced a symbiotic exchange between man and lamp.)

Once words are heard, counter-images are conjured against the hypnotic still life. *Footfalls* plays with an identity between the pacing woman of fact and fiction, but *Monologue* plays on the divergence between a narrative of frequent displacement and a white-clad figure "still as the lamp by his side." We count the titular footfalls—nine and wheel—but the bleached figure of *Monologue* is still[3] as he recounts how another totters, gropes, stands, turns, backs. A single gesture is mimetic; the speaker wryly describes "Making do with his mouth," as he makes do with *his* mouth.

This stage figure in his setting is both coalescence and contradiction, through theatereality. There are, moreover, degrees of contradiction; most blatant is the repeated and accreted choreography of lighting an *oil*-lamp while the *electric* lamp on-stage is untouched by human hands. Further, we see a *white* pallet, but we hear of a *brass* bedrail. Although the stage set is bare of wall and window, the narrated figure moves between them. And a rainy burial—three times described—in the mind's eye of the narrated man is summoned by words to *our* minds' eyes.

Man, lamp, corner pallet are a sounding board for words between the opening "Birth" and the closing "gone." Through words Beckett draws a faint thread of *theatrum mundi*. About halfway through the piece, we hear these phrases: "Gown and socks white to take faint light. Once white. Hair white to take faint light. Foot of pallet just visible edge of frame." What began as narration appears here to be performance. Then, a shadow review describes how, in the light of a spill, a pair of hands light the lamp with a spill. In the actual theater the light is constant to the end of the play, but periodically the narrator punctuates a narrated scene with: "Fade." Less often, "Thirty seconds" sounds to delay the funeral scene—the anonymous funeral framed to exclude the coffin. Toward the end of the monologue, we are fixed in a theater by "White foot of pallet edge of frame stage left"—where we see the actual corner of a pallet bed.

While the white-clad figure absorbs the invariant light, while the skull-sized globe glows with *its* invariant light, we listen to a piece of monologue, beginning with "Birth," ending with "gone," and oscillating between two kinds of light. One kind clings to the old light/life metaphor through an old man made of words—thirty thousand nights or two and a half billion seconds old, with both numbers belittled as "so few." His loved ones are long gone, along with their photographs in a thousand shreds. The stubborn durability of human life is hinted by those large numbers for 79 and 82 years, avatars of the biblical three score and ten.[4] Yet those huge numbers are mere specks in infinity, variously rendered in *Monologue* as "black vast," "empty dark," "dark whole," "black beyond," "black veil," whence emanates the second kind of light of a lifeless cosmos. As we in the theater "take" the steady light from the stage, death seeps through the words of the monologue: the sun is long sunk, the light is fading, and the white figure moves westward; birth collapses into a funeral scene and loved ones into ghosts. Death even plays through a pun: "Never but the one matter. The dead and gone." When all beings and their memories are dead and gone, it does not matter about mere matter. Light is finally not life, for man is finally not the measure. An unaccountable light "whence unknown" drizzles through the cosmos, but there is no one to perceive it, once the globe darkens.

A Piece of Monologue and *Footfalls*, like the thirty-second *Breath*, announce in their very titles Beckett's view of life *theatrically imaged*. Footfalls are what we hear and what we hear about as a metaphor for the mind revolving life's pain. A piece of monologue shimmers through the many meanings of piece—fragment, entity, example, play, game-counter—all synecdoches for life. In both plays moving figure or still figure sketches a verbal self-portrait that is then animated into imaginary actions. As Beckett's recent fiction *Company* proves so dramatic that he has accorded Frederick Neumann permission to perform it, so these two late Beckett plays precipitate fiction *and* drama as a new concentrate. Paradoxically, *A Piece of Monologue* abjures narrated dialogue in favor of pure description of a life spent between birth and death, groping toward western window from eastern wall.

Which leads me to deliberate circling back to Shakespeare's Wall, character and artifact. In Beckett's late plays character is etched into artifact. Feet fall on a wooden board that is hospital, home, and church; a lighted globe is man's conquerable mind and his vulnerable world. Beckett's late plays, like the early ones, theatricalize his vision of the human situation, but the late plays fuse the actual audience experience into the dramatic fiction. It is as theater experience that I cherish these plays— that weary old word *experience*—and if you see the plays as codes of signifiers that conform to a theoretical model, then you and I view the plays from opposite sides of a wall, "[But] such a wall as I would have you think / That had in it a crannied hole, or chink" through which dialogue may still be possible, within humanistic perspectives.

Addendum on "Ohio Impromptu"

Ohio Impromptu was written in English (in 1980), but in keeping with its "Latin Quarter hat," it sports a French angle to "Impromptu." I quote from a recent theater dictionary: "Pièce théoriquement improvisée et jouée sans préparation. . . . Souvent, le dramaturge y expose les difficultés de l'activité d'auteur et d'acteur."[5] Beckett again subverts, for the difficulties he asks his actors to expose are those of the creative and critical aspects of fiction-writing—in his most convoluted example of theatereality.

The stage is strictly black and white, lacking the glowing globe of *Monologue*. As in a Magritte painting, we see two images of the same figure, a black-coated, white-haired man—the one nearer us in profile, the farther one full-face, although both heads are bowed, obscuring the faces. Both actors sit in "armless white deal chairs" at a white deal table, on which a single black, broad-brimmed hat reposes. The man facing us is silent—and motionless except when he raps with left hand on the table; the profiled man reads aloud from the last pages of a large book. He reads about a man in long black coat and wide-brimmed hat who, having moved to a lonely abode overlooking the Isle of Swans, is visited by a man who reads to him throughout the night, quieting his *malaise*. Night after night, the man visits him "to read the sad tale through again." Of that second-degree "sad tale" we learn nothing, except that through it the reader and listener "grew to be as one."

Not only does *Ohio Impromptu* condense genres even further than *Footfalls*—a tale within a tale within a play—but the coalescence and divergence of theatereality is more involved than can be absorbed in performance. On stage the refracted images of old men resonate toward reflection within the tale that is read from the book—hinted through the fictional place to a swan song. Within the book-tale, however, the two men "grew to be as one" as the tale is repeatedly read, while on stage the two men diverge before our eyes. The single hat, starkly black on the long white table, may be a symbol for a single mind, for a single *creating* mind, one aspect reading the noted words and the other aspect pacing or judging the reading. Toward the end of *our* play, we hear that once the sad tale is read a last time, the two men sit "as though turned to stone." On stage, in contrast, once the book is closed, the two men raise their heads to "look at each other. Unblinking. Expressionless," and only then as still as stone. Unlike Proust's transcendent book admired by Beckett in his youth, unlike Molière's impromptu about producing a play for a king, *Ohio Impromptu* almost drains a story *of* experience in order to theatricalize the reading/writing itself *as* experience. To adapt the end of *Watt* to this occasion: "No resonance where none intended."

1. Cf. Lawrence E. Harvey, "Art and the Existential in *En attendant Godot*" *PMLA* (March 1960), 143–44.

2. "Working with Beckett," in *Samuel Beckett: The Art of Rhetoric*, ed. Edouard Morot-Sir, Howard Harper, and Dougald McMillan III (Chapel Hill, N.C.: University of North Carolina Press, 1976), p. 273.

3. Warrilow turns twice to his right: east or west?

4. I am grateful to Linda Ben-Zvi for calculating the ages.

5. Patrice Pavis, *Dictionnaire du Théâtre* (Paris: Editions Sociales, 1980), p. 213.

James Knowlson

Beckett's "Bits of Pipe"

In a letter of 11 April 1972, replying to questions more detailed, and indeed more audacious, than any that I should now presume to put to him, Samuel Beckett wrote as follows: "I simply know next to nothing about my work in this way, as little as a plumber of the history of hydraulics. There is nothing/nobody with me when I'm writing, only the hellish job in hand. The 'eye of the mind' in *Happy Days* does not *refer* to Yeats any more than the 'revels' in *Endgame* (refer) to *The Tempest*. They are just bits of pipe I happen to have with me. I suppose all is reminiscence from womb to tomb. All I can say is I have scant information concerning mine—alas."[1]

In this essay, I want to examine the status of some of Beckett's "bits of pipe," limiting myself, since the subject is a rather large one, to the quotations that are found in the English and French versions of *Happy Days*, but also seeing how this issue can be related to certain wider aspects of Beckett's dramatic technique and considering not only the play in the light of his remarks but also his remarks in the light of the play. In the letter just quoted, was Samuel Beckett, to put it a trifle baldly, merely adopting a favorite defensive stance, namely that of ignorance, whether feigned or real, or was he assuming the perspective of the worm in the core of the apple, unable to perceive the outside of the apple in the way that others can? Or does Beckett's comment (as I believe it does) say something perfectly valid about the status of quotation in *Happy Days* in particular, but also in his plays in general, that is worth examining much more fully?

The identification of Winnie's quotations now belongs to past critical history. They were identified for us in any case by Beckett himself in the fourth typescript of the English play, preserved in the Ohio State University Library.[2] Ever since, the authorship and location of Winnie's "wonderful lines" have been scrupulously recorded by Beckett in preliminary notes that he sent to Alan Schneider and in notebooks prepared for his own productions of the play in Berlin and London, sometimes situating the sources with words such as "end of speech beginning 'oh what a noble mind'" (for the "oh woe is me" quotation) and "Marcellus disappearance of ghost" (for the "bird of dawning" quotation), adding only in 1979, "sorrow keeps breaking in" as a deliberate distortion of Oliver Edwards's remark to Dr. Johnson, "cheerfulness was always breaking in."[3] Since Ruby Cohn's first book on Beckett in 1962, it has been known, therefore, that Winnie is familiar with "such good old poets as Shakespeare, Milton, Herrick, Gray, Keats and Browning"[4] and also quotes from Edward Fitzgerald, W. B. Yeats, and Charles Wolfe. The sources of the French quotations in *Oh les beaux jours* have also been clearly identified, ranging from Beckett's own translations of Shakespeare, Milton, Gray, and Keats to Ronsard's *Stances* (for "bouchette blémie") and Racine's "Qu'ils pleurent, oh mon Dieu, qu'ils frémissent de crainte," which becomes in Beckett's play "Qu'ils frémissent de honte."[5] And, of course, the different tone and associations of the French title, provided by the quotation from Paul Verlaine's poem *Colloque sentimental* ("ah les beaux jours de bonheur indicible / Où nous joignions nos bouches—C'est possible") have also been noted and explored.[6] All of this, like the presence of death in Ionesco's play, *Tueur sans gages (The Killer)*, is already "known, assimilated, catalogued."[7]

On the evidence of the manuscripts in the Ohio State University Library, the choice of these quotations was made by Beckett with considerable care and with great concern for their relationship with important themes of the play. Several scholars have examined the echoes that are set up by Winnie's allusions to some of the "classics" of English and French literature. It seems, in fact, irrefutable, as Ruby Cohn wrote in *Back to Beckett*, that Winnie's quotations comment ironically on the cruel landscape, speak of woe, and invoke the proximity of death.[8] And S. E. Gontarski has extended these ironies to discover in Winnie's use of quotations important Beckettian themes and wider mythic patterns. He writes that "the themes of the failure of love, the misery of the human condition, the transitoriness of all things, the disjunction between the real and the ideal, the misery of awareness, have been carefully reinforced in Winnie's literary allusions and reverberate through the play like a constant drumbeat."[9]

Yet there is a world of difference between noting and exploring the subtle ironies set up by the presence of these quotations and, as other critics have done, stressing the *co-presence* of both texts, that of Beckett and of the work quoted by Winnie, to the extent of reading Beckett's play as if it were a development, an ironic reflection, or, in some cases, even a parody of the original source work. One scholar, for example, has considered Winnie and Willie as echoes of Verlaine's ghosts from *Colloque sentimental*.[10] Another has written that "only if we take the whole passage [the Shakespearean "O what a noble mind is here o'erthrown" speech] and substitute Winnie and Willie [for Ophelia and Hamlet] can we appreciate the grotesque parody implied," or again, "Winnie persists as a parody Prometheus because there is nothing else to do."[11] A critical approach that may seem to be justified by the apparent openness of Beckett's technique of verbal and visual allusiveness has tended to become quite the opposite: unduly explicit, over-referential, imaginatively restrictive, and inappropriate to Beckett's handling of the theatrical medium.

There are, in fact, several good reasons why we should consider the quotations in *Happy Days* a good deal less referentially than this and acknowledge that, by focusing too hard on reference, we might only too easily be missing the much more important function. First, of course, is the obvious fact that Winnie's "wonderful lines" register in the theater only within

certain specific constraints. There is no time during a performance to formulate or to dwell on extended parallels between
Winnie and Hamlet, no time to consider the analogies between
Romeo's discovery of Juliet, lying seemingly dead, and
Winnie's studied contemplation of her own face in the mirror,
"ensign crimson . . . pale flag." Secondly, two of Winnie's
quotations at least lay unidentified for several years: the quotation from Browning's *Paracelcus*[12] and the Oliver Edwards distortion. Winnie identifies these different phrases as actual
quotations by means of her characteristically reassuring "What
are those wonderful / exquisite lines" in only four of the fifteen
quotations that are now commonly noted. The other eleven
arise far more naturally and could pass almost unnoticed in the
context, except by the scholar, probably forewarned and hence
on the lookout for such allusions. Further, there are also many
other, only half-hidden, literary or religious allusions or actual
quotations made in the course of the play: to *Hamlet*, to the
Bible, to the Christian marriage ceremony, to Dante, to
Schopenhauer, perhaps even to Daniel Defoe's *Robinson Crusoe,*
which, along with the *Inferno,* seems to have been a major inspiration for the play.[13] Winnie makes no distinction at all of
level between her various "classics." Charles Wolfe is admired
and cherished as much as are Shakespeare and Milton. All have
become, one might say, "Winnieisms," bearing on occasions
Winnie's characteristic *imprimatur,* the "something . . .
something" of a learner of lines who is more enamoured of
rhythm than she is of sense. But Winnie's questions still retain
the relevance as well as the slightly foreign flavor of the borrowings.

Even without imputing to an audience the knowledge of the
literary scholar, however, the spectator will register immediately some of the bitter truths found in the quotations that
Winnie puts forward in the guise of phrases of reassurance:
"Laughing wild amid severest woe" needs no scholarly commentary at all to echo the earlier "oh fleeting joys oh something
lasting woe" and to provide an ironic commentary on Winnie's
plight and a wider statement on the sad, transitory nature of
human existence. The opening words of the second act, "Hail,

holy light" ("Salut, sainte lumière" in Beckett's own French translation) almost provoke a shudder in the listener, so sharp is the irony between Winnie's Miltonic greeting and her newly revealed state of more radical deprivation. It is not that ironies will not be reinforced or even that further layers of irony will not be revealed, if one should happen to recognize the words and the context of the original quotations. It is, I suggest, that to regard them *primarily* in terms of reference is to diminish their important role within the play and to misunderstand certain crucial elements of Beckett's dramatic technique.

In another, and more important, sense, *Happy Days* is almost all quotation. For Beckett has Winnie confront the "hellish sun" and endure a life of growing immobility with a vocabulary of secondhand, rose-colored platitudes, clichés of middle-class piety and complacent optimism. Her speech is a kind of modernized, suburbanized *Robinsonadesprache*. Beckett's first manuscript draft was called "Female Solo,"[14] and, as a point of comparison with *Happy Days*, one may choose the dramatic monologue that Beckett most likely saw at the Comédie Française in February 1930, Jean Cocteau's *La Voix humaine*, which he condemned in *Proust* as "not merely a banality, but an unnecessary banality."[15] When, thirty years later, Beckett came to write his own female virtual monologue, he was very careful to avoid the trap that Cocteau had fallen into, namely, that of creating a banality out of banalities. For, instead of merely using cliché in *Happy Days*, Beckett makes it work for him dramatically, as part of a dense linguistic structure, which is characterized by many variations in the levels of meaning, register, and tone. The numerous borrowed clichés are, then, not only registered as such by the spectator. They are made to reverberate with a subtle blend of irony, understated human feelings, and deeper philosopical concerns. The technique is complex, but stated in the broadest of terms, this effect is achieved by contrasting Winnie's clichés and bland phrases of reassurance with the stark visual imagery of imprisonment in a barren earth and exposure to a hostile sun, and by the juxtaposition, repetition, and association of the component phrases themselves. So flat, commonplace, apparently neutral words and phrases signify at the obvious surface level, but also prompt their own wide-ranging, and often momentous, echoes: "world without end," "cannot be cured," "sleep for ever," "blind next," "running out" are just a few examples chosen from the opening moments of the play.

Yet, as I have developed more fully elsewhere,[16] common-place, worn-out words, which Winnie uses to tame and do-mesticate a mysterious, elusive reality, also lead her to the very edge of the abyss, when sorrow, regret and loss intrude re-peatedly into her busy chatter. And so the horror of her im-mediate predicament, a sense of the mystery of being, and a fear of the silent, solitary wilderness that may await her cannot be wholly kept at bay by her familiar, borrowed words. Liter-ally, "sorrow keeps breaking in," in the shape of her literary quotations (the creations of others) and her fictions (her own creations), but also in the tiny qualifications of a remark, a break in, or faltering of, the voice or the swift erasure of a smile. When Winnie draws Willie's attention to the heights that she has scaled, most often she has ironically been plumbing un-common depths of perceptiveness into the nature of her true condition: "and wait for the day to come—the happy day to come when flesh melts at so many degrees and the night of the moon has so many hundred hours";[17] "and should one day the earth cover my breasts, then I shall never have seen my breasts, no one ever seen my breasts."[18] This alternation, even inter-play, of keen insight and self-deception adds substantially, of course, to the dramatic interest and the poignancy of the play, as Winnie spins her own web of words, of which she becomes the victim as well as the creator.

Winnie's quotations come, however, in different registers and occur even in several different voices, as she indulges in a highly sophisticated form of ventriloquism. She quotes, for ex-ample, the blandly ironic words of wisdom from the toothbrush handle and the medicine bottle label—in a special tone, as Ruby Cohn pointed out, in Beckett's Berlin production.[19] The range of her voices, moreover, echoes the range of her repeated ges-tures and habits. She talks regularly to herself in many different tones: sharply, "as to one not paying attention"; cautionarily, "do not overdo the bag, Winnie"; anxiously, "and now?", and so on. The range of her inquiry and address to Willie is even more diversified still. And, at the end of the play, her voice offers a chilling impersonation of her "soul-mate," as his prenuptial pleas take the form of a piece of sardonic self-address: "Life a mockery without Win"[20] "I worship you Winnie be mine and then nothing from that day forth only titbits from *Reynolds' News.*"[21] In the Shower/Cooker story, Winnie alternates between three different voices and provides a complex interweaving of accents and linguistic registers: "Stuck up to her diddies in the bleeding ground" [first male voice] "coarse creature, fit mate" [her own voice] "Dig her out, he says, dig her out, no sense in her like that [first male voice]—Dig her out with what? [second female voice] she says [her own voice]—I'd dig her out with my bare hands [first male voice] he says—Must have been man and wife [her own voice]."[22] In the French translation, the shifts from assumed vulgarity to natural censoriousness are even more marked, providing an impressive tribute to Beckett's bilingual sensitivity. Finally, the "Milly and the mouse" narrative introduces sharp pain into a fictional world that is reminiscent not only of the child's fairy tale but of the setting of a Katherine Mansfield story (*The Dove's Nest,* for example). The vocabulary is again borrowed, this time from the literature of the nursery, with its stock epithets, and its child's perspective on the world: "big, waxen dolly," "complete outfit," "frilly frock," "legends in real print," "steep wooden stairs," and "silent passage."[23] But the real screams contrast sharply with this borrowed, rehearsed, even stilted terminology. To regard this as parody of the style of the nursery tale—even less of Katherine Mansfield—is to miss the point entirely. For it is with these delicate, stylistic borrowings, recited in a tiny child's voice, that Winnie expresses obliquely a sense of the violence of sex, procreation, and birth, and the mystery of pain and being. Primarily, these elements are used then functionally, combining important tonal variety with the oblique, thematic significance of this fiction and the Shower/Cooker encounter.

In conclusion, it is worth stressing how much this creation of a multiplicity of voices, levels, tones, and registers demands by way of active involvement on the part of the spectator. By a technique that clearly owes far more to suggestion and ambiguity than it does to reference, the spectator is able to move freely between these different levels, questioning, judging, and often supplying what is hinted at rather than stated. Reference is, then, anathema for Samuel Beckett, as it was for Stéphane Mallarmé, for whom "nommer un objet, c'est supprimer les trois quarts de la jouissance du poème, qui est faite du bonheur de deviner peu à peu; le suggérer, voilà le rêve."[24] If Mallarmé is here a potent source for inspiration for Beckett, it may be the example of John Millington Synge, whose own dramatic allusiveness followed no "sustained referential scheme,"[25] that helped Beckett avoid some of the dangers inherent in the symbolist legacy. Beckett, unlike those dramatic heirs of symbolism commonly referred to under the label of the "Theater of the Unspoken" (e.g., Maeterlinck, Bernard, Vildrac),[26] is not attempting to evoke a world of mystery or of the spirit; nor is he trying to convey obliquely or by means of silence the inner life of his characters; nor again is there any Pinteresque "weasel under the cocktail cabinet" in Beckett's theater. The silences that figure prominently in Beckett's plays are filled more by the spectator measuring what is being seen against what has just been said or following, within specific constraints, the multiple associations aroused by preceding statements or patterns of statements. For, in a very real sense, Beckett's verbal and visual imagery echoes not on the boards alone but in the mind of the spectator.

Winnie's "classics" differ hardly at all, then, from the remainder of the text. It may be said, of course, that part of their function is to add further levels of meaning. But the variations in voice, level, tone, and register that they introduce tend to predominate over the actual "references" themselves. The "bits of pipe" of which Beckett speaks do not "refer," as he suggests, therefore in this sense. To extend the plumber analogy a little further, however, they are of exactly the right shape, length, thickness, bore, even ring, for the job in hand. And inasmuch as they do point outside the play, it is as part of a dramatic technique that aims, above all, to involve the active imagination of the spectator, liberating it rather than imprisoning it with the shackles of reference.

1. Letter to J. Knowlson 11 April 1972.

2. These manuscripts and typescripts are fully discussed in S. E. Gontarski, *Beckett's "Happy Days": A Manuscript Study* (Columbus, Ohio: Ohio State University Library Publications, 1977).

3. These production notebooks are preserved in the Library of the University of Reading, England. The two German notebooks for Beckett's 1971 Berlin production are MS. 1396/4/10 and MS. 1227/7/8/1. The Oliver Edwards quotation and the other references noted here are found in the notebook for Beckett's production of *Happy Days* at the Royal Court Theatre in London in June 1979, Reading University Library, MS. 1730.

4. Ruby Cohn, *Samuel Beckett: The Comic Gamut* (New Brunswick, N.J.: Rutgers University Press, 1962), p. 253.

5. Most of the French quotations were identified by Beckett in a reply to questions by James Knowlson, n.d. The Victor Hugo quotation, which replaces Charles Wolfe's verse, was located by Richard Admussen in the *Chants du Crépuscule*. All the quotations are listed in the notes to a bilingual edition, *Happy Days. Oh les beaux jours*, ed. J. Knowlson (London: Faber and Faber, 1978).

6. See bilingual edition, *Happy Days. Oh les beaux jours*, p. 128.

7. Eugène Ionesco, *Tueur sans gages*, in *Théâtre, II* (Paris: Gallimard, 1958), p. 122.

8. Ruby Cohn, *Back to Beckett* (Princeton, N.J.: Princeton University Press, 1973), pp. 180–82.

9. Gontarski, *Beckett's "Happy Days,"* p. 73.

10. Dorothy F. Jones, "Beckett's *Colloque sentimental*," *French Review* 50 (February 1977): 460–66.

11. Anthony S. Brennan, "Winnie's Golden Treasury: The Use of Quotation in *Happy Days*," *Arizona Quarterly* 25 (Autumn 1979): 205–27.

12. The Browning quotation was identified by Gontarski, *Beckett's "Happy Days,"* p. 69.

13. These, and other, possible literary allusions are suggested in Gontarski, ibid., chap. 6, and in the notes to J. Knowlson's bilingual edition of *Happy Days*.

14. This first draft is preserved in a manuscript notebook of Beckett's entitled "Eté 56" in Reading University Library, MS. 1227/7/7/1. It is discussed in Gontarski, ibid.

15. S. Beckett, *Proust* (New York: Grove Press, 1957), p. 14.

16. In *Frescoes of the Skull: The Later Prose and Drama of Samuel Beckett* (London: John Calder, 1979; New York: Grove Press, 1980).

17. *Happy Days*, rpt. (London: Faber and Faber, 1966), p. 16.

18. Ibid., p. 30.

19. Ruby Cohn, *Just Play* (Princeton, N.J.: Princeton University Press, 1980), p. 254.

20. *Happy Days*, p. 45.

21. Ibid., p. 46.

22. Ibid., p. 33.

23. Ibid., p. 41.

24. Quoted in May Daniels, *The French Drama of the Unspoken* (Edinburgh: Edinburgh University Press, 1953), p. 24.

25. J. M. Synge, *The Playboy of the Western World*, ed. Malcolm Kelsall (London: Ernest Benn, 1975), p. xxi.

26. See May Daniels, *The French Drama of the Unspoken*, and K. Worth, *The Irish Drama of Europe from Yeats to Beckett* (London: Athlone Press, 1978).

Edith Kern

Beckett's Modernity and Medieval Affinities

Because of a circularity that defies customary logic and linearity, critics have often seen in Samuel Beckett's work an absurdity they believe to be modern and expressive of the world we live in. It is true, of course, that the author has given manifold and striking expression to alogical circularity, so that the unassuming ditty (originally a German children's song) hummed by Didi in *Waiting for Godot* may well be considered emblematic of the author's entire work as it teasingly begins again whenever one expects it to end and, indeed, cannot be brought to any logical ending.[1] In *Molloy* the protagonist's assertion that the first lines of his report were its beginning but are now nearly its end conjures up a similar mood of unending circularity bordering on the absurd.[2] In the year of the celebration of Beckett's seventy-fifth birthday, we might do well, however, to ask whether this mood is exclusively modern and meant to reflect merely the chaos known to us. It would seem to me rather that it is informed by a conception of man that Beckett's works and those of other contemporary authors share with the literature preceding both the rediscovery of Aristotle's *Poetics* and the neoclassical emphasis on rationality and individuality. Not unlike authors of the Middle Ages, Beckett conceives of the individual *sub specie aeternitatis*, and in *Waiting for Godot* this vision is brilliantly dramatized when blind old Pozzo, having fallen over decrepit Lucky, is unable to get up. His cries for help are reluctantly answered by Didi and Gogo, whose efforts end in their own loss of balance, though they reply to Pozzo's inquiry as to who they are: "We are men." Nameless and faceless, mankind is groping to get on its feet, and the same medieval notion of the insignificance of the individual is later epitomized by Pozzo when he proclaims: "One day we were born, one day we shall die, the same day, the same second. . . . They give birth astride of a grave, the light gleams an instant, then it's night once more" (57). Such a conception of man does not call for clearly outlined literary protagonists or psychological explanations. Nor is it concerned with personal confrontations or social problems. The focus is rather on mankind and its unchanging structures and needs within the universe. The individual is but the transitory and ephemeral link in Nature's unending chain of birth, life, and death.

Quite obviously, such a vision of man and the universe affects the function and form of literary dialogue. When it is not employed to develop plot or reveal individual character, dialogue becomes ludic. It is not surprising, therefore, that the verbal exchanges of Beckett's characters often seem absurd to those who approach them with attitudes that conform to neoclassical expectations. But when Didi and Gogo wonder, for instance, whether they should leave, end it all, go on, or come back tomorrow, they engage in conversational patterns of the kind we might encounter in any medieval French farce:

E: Where shall we go?
V: Not far.
E: Oh yes. Let's go far away from here.
V: We can't.
E: Why not?
V: We have to come back tomorrow.
E: What for?
V: To wait for Godot. (59)

In his study of French farce, Robert Garapon has referred to such dialogue, which reveals no facts and follows no logical pattern, as "un jeu de paume,"[3] and the verbal exchanges of

Beckett's characters resemble, indeed, quite frequently verbal ballgames—although the effect may be, on occasion, highly lyrical and poetic.[4] Beckett's own consciousness of this ballgame effect of dialogue is quite apparent. "In the meantime," Gogo suggests on one occasion, "let us try and converse calmly, since we are incapable of keeping silent" (40). Vladimir—musing why it is that of the four Evangelists "only one speaks of a thief being saved"—prods Estragon, who had remained silent: "Come on, Didi, return the ball." (9) In *Endgame*, of course, Clov's question "What is there to keep me here?" is answered by Ham with "The dialogue" (58).[5] But in Beckett's work such ludic dialogue may also assume the form of medieval *flyting*, that is, of half-playful, half-serious insults. On one occasion when Didi and Gogo have nothing to do and nowhere to go, as they wait for Godot, they begin to quarrel just to pass the time away. They are close to getting into a fist fight, when Gogo suggests: "That's the idea, let's abuse each other." Stage directions indicate that they turn, move away from each other, and begin to insult each other, one outdoing the other until Didi is utterly vanquished and Gogo calls him "Crritic!" so that Gogo concedes: "Now let's make it up!" (48). In all likelihood, such *flyting* had its origin in more ancient "slanging matches" that, in the view of Johan Huizinga, may well represent the very origin of theater.[6] The exaggerated insults that rival tribes engaged in would have led to violent war, had there not been in existence a tacit understanding that they were meant to be an impersonal game of one-up-manship—a liberation of pent-up emotions in a spirit of make-believe, not unlike that of "playing the dozens" known to black communities. It is interesting in this respect that the *iambos*, the meter of Greek tragedy, is thought by some to have meant *derision*, suggesting that theater and the exchange of insults have been linked from time immemorial.[7] In the commedia dell'arte such slanging matches were standard in the lover's pursuit of his beloved and her playful or serious rejection of him. Eugène Ionesco recently used them with great skill in his play *Macbett* (based on Shakespeare's *Macbeth*) to give expression to the snowballing effect of murder, as he has his conspirators reach the tragicomic frenzy of hatred in the course of their verbal exchanges.[8] Beckett availed himself of such tragicomic playfulness mainly in order to be able to discuss questions as serious as those of man's place in the world and his relationship to God, without sounding pompous or transgressing the limits of theater as entertainment and stage business.

In his early works, ludic dialogue and *flyting* permitted Beckett, above all, to juxtapose the sacred and the profane in a mood of the seeming absurdity known to the Middle Ages. Thus Vladimir and Estragon, wondering whether man is *tied* to God (or is it Godot?), have an answer suggested to them that is as ambivalent as it is ironically farcical when Pozzo appears upon the stage led by Lucky, to whom he is tied (or who is tied to him?) by a rope. In *The Absolute Comic*, I have discussed at some length the significance of medieval parodies that, in similar manner, juxtapose the sacred with the profane and whose popularity is attested to by the large number of Latin manuscripts still extant. Their spirit was caught remarkably well by Nietzsche in *Thus Spake Zarathustra*, which contains a travesty of a Mass, not unlike those celebrated during the medieval Festival of the Ass. A brief sampling of it will convey the flavor of such parody in all its carnivalesque irreverence that laughingly turns the world upside down:

And the litany sounded thus;
    Amen! And glory and honour and wisdom and thanks and praise and strength be to our God, from everlasting to everlasting!
    —The ass, however, here brayed Ye-A.
    He carrieth our burdens, he hath taken upon him the form of a servant, he is patient of heart and never saith Nay; and he who loveth his God chastiseth him.
    —The ass, however, here brayed Ye-A.
    He speaketh not: except that he ever saith Yea to the world which he created: thus doth he extol his world. It is his artfulness that speaketh not: thus is he rarely found wrong.
    —The ass, however, here brayed Ye-A.
    Uncomely goeth he through the world. Grey is the favourite colour in which he wrappeth his virtue. Hath he spirit, then doth he conceal it; every one, however, believeth in his long ears.[9]

Nietzsche's travesty, though used by him in the spirit of satire, would seem to be sacrilegious, unless we recognize that it belongs to that—usually more lighthearted—medieval tradition. It is in this same tradition that James Joyce parodied the litany, the liturgy, and the Lord's Prayer and that his work abounds in ludic travesties such as the following: "Haloed be her eve, her singtime sung, her rill be run, unhemmed as it is uneven." Or: "Oura Vatars that arred in Himmal," with its exuberant fusion of different languages, real as well as invented. Or: "Ouhr Former who erred," a sheer play on sound.[10] Rabelais had indulged in such exuberant and irreverent playfulness in his *Gargantua and Pantagruel,* and in his seminal study *Rabelais and His World,* Mikhail Bakhtin points out that one of the book's protagonists, Panurge, seeking advice from Friar John as to whether he should marry or not, couches his words in praise of the male sexual parts in the form of a litany repeated 153 times.[11] Rabelais used Christ's last words on the cross "sitio" (I thirst) and "consummatum est" (it is finished) in a literal sense as if they referred to food and drink, and such mingling of the sacred and the profane was so readily accepted and enjoyed in the author's time that he did not expunge it from his 1524 edition, which had to pass severe censorship.[12] It would be difficult but also idle to ascertain whether Beckett consciously adopted the spirit of this tradition, or whether it was simply germane to his own concerns. We know, of course, that, like Joyce, he had been a student of Romance literatures and that his early poetry was cast in the Provençal and medieval French forms of the troubadours tradition: the *enueg,* the *planh,* and the *alba.* This "modern minstrel," Harvey wrote, "chooses titles for seven of his thirteen poems directly out of the troubadour tradition. . . ."[13] There can be no doubt, at any rate, that in his theater and fiction Beckett perpetuates or reinvents medieval juxtapositions of the sacred and the profane—both in a sense of playfulness and of profound seriousness.

There is, for instance, the narrator of Beckett's *Watt,* identified as Sam somewhere toward the middle of the novel, who conveys to us that, one day, in the garden of his pavilion (it seems to be part of a mental institution), he espied Watt, whom he had previously and intimately known at another place. Watt was walking toward him but was walking backward. As Watt grotesquely advances—perpetually falling into the thorny shrubbery and painfully extricating himself from it—he turns his face toward Sam, who perceives him both as an image of Christ bearing a crown of thorns and as his own mirror image. The identity thus evoked between a religious image of Christ as painted by Bosch and hanging in London's Trafalgar Square, on the one hand, and the half-crazed representative of mankind Watt, who is the grotesque mirror of Sam himself, on the other, would border on the sacrilegious, were we not conscious of the fact that Watt advancing backward and perpetually falling is also a figure of medieval farce, of carnival, and of what I have designated with the Baudelairean term "the absolute comic."[14] Beckett maintains the ambivalence of that absolute comic so that, through laughter and tears, he can seriously probe the meaning of human existence without assuming the part of the philosopher. Beckett's ability and determination to pursue such serious questions under the guise of farce make themselves felt everywhere in his work and prove themselves perhaps most strikingly in a scene of the second novel of his trilogy, *Malone Dies*. There Macmann (Son of Man) is grotesquely caught in the rain, far from shelter, in an open field. Dressed like a scarecrow, he lies down on the ground in the posture of one crucified as the "rain pelted down on his back with the sound . . . of a drum. . . . The idea of punishment came to his mind, addicted, it is true, to that chimera and probably impressed by the posture of the body and the fingers clenched as though in torment. And without knowing exactly what his sin was he felt . . . that living was not a sufficient atonement for it. . . ."[15]

But it is above all in Lucky's speech, that torrent of seeming madness, that Beckett's mingling of the sacred and the profane and even the scatological assumes truly medieval aspects. In the manner of participants in medieval farce, Lucky turns traditional patterns of reasoned discourse and theological debate into farce. Yet the seriousness of his concerns becomes apparent when we strip his speech of its carnivalesque elements.

He then seems to suggest something like "given the existence . . . of a personal God . . . with white beard . . . outside time . . . who from the heights of divine . . . aphasia loves us dearly with some exceptions for reasons unknown . . . and suffers with those who . . . are plunged in torment . . . it is established beyond all doubt . . . that man . . . fades away" (28–29). A number of critics more or less agree on such a reading. Yet nothing could better illustrate the half-serious, half-playful travesties of medieval carnival and their ridicule of theological and scholarly pomposity that takes itself too seriously than Lucky's speech. It is clearly patterned after a medieval French *sermon joyeux,* a burlesque sermon of the kind preached in churches during carnivalesque celebrations and that later became part of the threesome that made up French traditional theatrical performances: the *sermon,* the *sottie,* and the *mystère* or *farce.* Rhetorically, the *sermon joyeux* was a *coq-à-l'âne,* a discourse defined as disjointedly passing from one subject to another without logical transition of any sort. "Sauter du coq à l'âne" meant literally "to leap from the rooster to the donkey," and the expression may well have its origin in animal debates. Although the sixteenth-century French poet Marot is credited with the invention of a poetic genre by that name, the concept is clearly much older. In the form of a *coq-à-l'âne, sermons joyeux* often travestied sacred texts by speaking of food, drink, and sex as if they were discussing theology or vice versa. The aim of the *sermon joyeux* was, on occasion, satire, but the genre was usually expressive of a sheer joy in verbal fantasy, often starting with Latin invocations, such as "in nomine Patris, et Filii et Spiritus Sancty. Amen."[16] It jumbled together disparate notions and languages and did not hesitate to address itself in the same phrase to Bacchus, Venus, and the Christian God. In its grotesque references and its play on sound rather than meaning, the genre represented a triumph of carnivalesque fantasy, both in exuberance and in irreverence toward all that was taboo. Unfortunately, the examples extant of such *sermons joyeux* are not easily accessible to the modern reader because of their generous mixture of medieval French with an oddly gallicized Latin, so that the genre is, perhaps, most easily illustrated by a sampling from Molière's *Don Juan*. This is how Don Juan is lectured to by his servant Sganarelle:

> . . . I can keep quiet no longer . . . , but I must open my heart to you and tell you that I think as a faithful servant should. You know, master, the pitcher can go to the well once too often, and . . . men in the world are like the bird on the bough, the bough is part of the tree and whoever holds on to the tree is following sound precepts; sound precepts are better than fine words; the court is the place for fine words; at the court you find courtiers, and courtiers do whatever's the fashion. . . . A good pilot needs prudence; young men have no prudence . . . ; old men love riches; riches make men rich; the rich aren't poor; poor men know necessity and necessity knows no law. Without law men live like animals, which all goes to prove that you'll be damned to all eternity.[17]

Lucky's mock sermon abounds, from its start, in scholarly references to authorities that bear names as grotesque and even obscene as Puncher and Wattman, Testew and Cunard, Fartov and Belcher, Peckham Fulham Clapham, Steinweg and Peterman, and Essy-in-Possy. Lucky's elaborate proof of the existence of God is put in question because it is based on the findings of these authorities. Nor do we derive assurance from the childish picture he evokes of a God with white beard, or from the animal-like sounds—quaquaquaqua—with which he accompanies the word God and which in French pronunciation become obscene references to the body and its elimination. A similarly irreverent effect is achieved by Lucky's stuttering profering of "Acacacacademy" and "Anthropopopometry." Such phrases as "labors left unfinished," "for reasons unknown," together with heaven, hell, flames, and fire conjure up a world presided over by a god as inscrutable as he is unpredictable, while the phrase "it is established beyond all doubt" ridicules the foolish and arrogant certainties of certain scholars. Like a medieval fool, Lucky truly leaps from topic to topic, as he turns the world mockingly upside down. But while he engages in *fatrasies*, the farcical play with words known to the French Middle Ages, he raises serious questions concerning man and his place in the universe—the same questions, in fact, that were raised by Didi and Gogo at the beginning of the play, namely, whether there is a God who loves man dearly and knows why he saved only one of the two sinners, or whether man's notion that "time will tell" is as absurd as the certainty of some that knowledge can be "established beyond all doubt." Such questions can be dealt with, after all, only in the ludic mode of the *coq-à-l'âne*. For whosoever raises them—be he medieval or modern man—will be listened to only if he plays the role of the fool.

Seen in this light, the play's title cannot but be recognized as one of the half-serious, half-playful bilingual combinations so often encountered in medieval French literature—regardless of what immediate experience might have suggested to Beckett the name Godot. It represents clearly a juxtaposition of the sacred with the profane as it links the Anglo-Saxon word *God* with the French suffix -*ot* that abases and makes laughable any name it is attached to, such as Pierre/Pierrot, Jacques/Jacquot, Charles/Charlot. Such "absurdity" is not an inadvertent reflection in Beckett's work of the chaotic universe we live in but rather a conscious tool in the hand of an author who sees man *sub specie aeternitatis*, who ridicules the desire of most of us, expressed for centuries in literature, to envision himself—not unlike Hamm in *Endgame*—as the center of the universe, of an author realizing that he can speak of what is most serious only in the manner of farce and the absolute comic. I am tempted to impute to Beckett a passage from Plato quoted by Huizinga: "Though human affairs are not worthy of great seriousness it is yet necessary to be serious. . . . God alone is worthy of supreme seriousness, but man is made God's plaything. . . . What then is the right way of living? Life must be lived as play, playing certain games, making sacrifices, singing and dancing, and then a man will be able to propitiate the gods, and defend himself against his enemies, and win in the contest."[18]

1. Samuel Beckett, *Waiting for Godot* (New York: Grove Press, 1954), p. 37. References to pages of this work will appear henceforth in parentheses in the text. For one of the best discussions of circularity in Beckett's work, see Rolf Breuer, *Die Kunst der Paradoxie* (Munich: Fink Verlag, 1976), passim.

2. Samuel Beckett, *Molloy* (New York: Grove Press, 1955), p. 8.

3. Robert Garapon, *La Fantaisie verbale et le comique dans le théâtre français, du Moyen Age à la fin du XVIIe siècle* (Paris: Colin, 1957), pp. 93ff.

4. See, for instance, *Godot*, p. 40.

5. Samuel Beckett, *Endgame* (New York: Grove Press, 1958).

6. Johan Huizinga, *Homo ludens: A Study of the Play Element in Culture* (Boston: Beacon Press, 1950), pp. 68–69. Cf. Edith Kern, *The Absolute Comic* (New York: Columbia University Press, 1980), pp. 31–32.

7. See *The Absolute Comic*, pp. 33–34.

8. See Eugène Ionesco, *Macbett* (Paris: Gallimard, 1972).

9. Friedrich Nietzsche, *Thus Spake Zarathustra*, trans. Thomas Common (New York: Modern Library, 1929), pp. 350–51.

10. James S. Atherton, *The Books at the Wake* (London: Faber and Faber, 1959), p. 187.

11. Mikhail Bakhtin, *Rabelais and His World*, trans. Helene Iswolsky (Cambridge, Mass.: MIT Press, 1968), pp. 417–18.

12. Ibid., p. 86.

13. Lawrence E. Harvey, *Samuel Beckett, Poet and Critic* (Princeton, N.J.: Princeton University Press, 1970), p. 79.

14. Samuel Beckett, *Watt* (New York: Grove Press, 1959), p. 159. See *The Absolute Comic*, pp. 3 ff.

15. Samuel Beckett, *Malone Dies* (New York: Grove Press, 1956), pp. 66–67.

16. See *The Absolute Comic*, pp. 64, 78.

17. Molière, "Don Juan, or the Statue at the Feast," in *"The Miser" and Other Plays*, trans. John Wood (Harmondsworth, England: Penguin, 1974), p. 245.

18. *Homo ludens*, p. 212.

Richard N. Coe

Beckett's English

Oh I am ashamed
of all clumsy artistry
I am ashamed of presuming
to arrange words. . . .[1]

Few aspects of Samuel Beckett's work are more exasperating to the cautious critical mind than the style of his early writings in English—before, in a fit of exasperation all his own, he turned to writing in French.

This is partly because, like Mr. Knott's wardrobe, this style is "very, very various." It is not one style, but many—"now heavy, now light; now smart, now dowdy; now sober, now gaudy; now decent, now daring"[2]—making it seemingly impossible to pin it down for long enough to analyze it. It is also partly because, with all its obvious faults and failings, which should, according to most of the canons of taste, render it virtually intolerable, it nonetheless holds its own. It remains memorable and quotable; and at times it achieves a quite haunting beauty. It is, on the face of it, a *perverse* style. And yet, looking back now from the distance of nearly half a century, it is possible to discern a methodical process at work behind the façade of this apparently disorganized exuberance.

Two comments by early critics may offer a clue to the understanding of the Beckettian enigma. In the first-ever-published full-length study of Beckett, *Die Unzulänglichkeit der Sprache* of 1957, Niklaus Gessner observes that he once asked the writer why he had abandoned English for French. The reply—which, characteristically, was given in French rather than in English— was "parce qu'en français, c'est plus facile d'écrire sans style."[3] And a second remark from the same period, which was roughly that of the first English production of *Waiting for Godot* at the Arts Theatre Club in London in 1956, was made to me by that well-known historian of the English novel Dr. Arnold Kettle: "it sounds like a bad translation from his own French."

Now, it is generally assumed that Beckett is a superlative translator from the French, whether his own or anyone else's. It is true that he *can* be. Robert Pinget's play *La Manivelle*, for instance, is more effective from every point of view—poetically, dramatically, atmospherically—in Beckett's version, *The Old Tune*, than it is in the original. On the other hand, there are some efforts that had best been left unpublished. Rimbaud's *Bateau ivre* is one of these. There are some passable lines in *Drunken Boat*; but there are far too many that are clumsy, amateurish, and frankly in bad taste—neither good Rimbaud, nor good Beckett:

> Et, dès lors, je me suis baigné dans le poème
> De la mer infusé d'astres et lactescent,
> Dévorant les azurs verts où, flottaison blême
> Et ravie, un noyé pensif, parfois, descend;
>
> Où, teignant tout à coup les bleuités, délires
> Et rythmes lents sous les rutilements du jour,
> Plus fortes que l'alcool, plus vastes que vos lyres,
> Fermentent les rousseurs amères de l'amour. (Lines 21–28)

> Thenceforward, fused in the poem, milk of stars,
> Of the sea, I coiled through deeps of cloudless green,
> Where, dimly, they come swaying down,
> Rapt and sad, singly, the drowned;
>
> Where, under sky's haemorrhage, slowly tossing
> In thuds of fever, arch-alcohol of song,
> Pumping over the blues in sudden stains,
> The bitter redness of love ferment.[4]

The first two lines of Beckett's translation are admirable; but thereafter the reader is torn between a kind of startled amazement at the slick skill with which the translator, like a virtuoso of the jigsaw puzzle, has taken each separate piece from Rimbaud's pattern, juggled with it, and then fitted it neatly into his own, the irritation at the ineptitudes of the vocabulary ("dimly" and "singly" jingling away in consecutive lines), the modish, post-dadaist, antipoetic imagery, and the rough and jerky rhythms taking the place of the smooth and subtle convolutions of the Rimbaldian prosody.

The unevennesses of *Drunken Boat* are revealing, if only for the fact that they are almost certainly (in a way) deliberate. For all that the Rimbaud translation was done frankly for money, Beckett betrays few of the characteristics of the polished professional translator. He is at once something less and, obscurely as yet, something more. He is less for the reasons outlined above; he is more in that quite clearly his use of English is designed to serve purposes of his own that are very different from those which Rimbaud was serving with his French. The distinction, in briefest possible form, is that Rimbaud was using language positively and creatively; Beckett is using it—in part at least— negatively and destructively. And it is this negative, destructive, or self-destructive element in Beckett's English style that we shall attempt to follow in this essay.

For Beckett the problem of a literary language presented itself in the form of an insoluble contradiction. As a metaphysician— that is, as a plain but compulsive writer with something to say about the condition of man *sub specie aeternitatis*—his concern was to get beyond language: to transmit not ideas but (in his own phrase) the more elemental "shapes of ideas"; not concepts but the logic of the failure of conceptualization; not "cogito, ergo sum" but rather some elusive echo of the Sartrian rejoinder: "non sum, ergo cogito." But to deal in language with the "shapes of ideas" without getting bogged down in the ideas themselves would mean reducing language itself to a form so automatic and primitive that it conveys no concepts whatsoever, but merely its own inherent patterns: computerized "shapes" (as in *Ping*), which may, by awakening some responsive echo through the sheer intricacy of their permutations and combinations, serve to suggest the "shape" of the idea without evoking the idea itself.

It is a problem that perhaps can be illustrated from the art of painting—the problem, say, of painting a fish. A traditionalist painter paints a fish in its context of water, reeds, and movement: the fish *plus* its essential "fishness." A modern Japanese painter will paint a swirl of reeds and water without the fish: "fishness," as it were, without the fish itself. But a modern Canadian painter will paint the fish in a bleak and disquieting void, as a *Ding-an-sich*, an arbitrary and meaningless phenomenon in a nonexistence of space and time: fish, in fact, without "fishness."[5] Beckett's ambitions would seem to be most nearly akin to the latter category: the "shapes" of ideas, stripped of any hint of the omnipresent associations and significances of the ideas themselves.

In this situation, the problem of language looms threateningly large. Setting aside for the moment the inevitable role of language in providing a context of conceptualization, the more immediate obstacle is that of "style"; for "style" in any advanced literary language, but more especially in English, provides a reverberating "context" of echoes, images, and associations—precisely the elements that Beckett wishes to avoid. "Style"—the "clumsy artistry," the "presuming to arrange words"—is the ultimate enemy, the trap, the devil's most dangerous, most insidious temptation, the sin for which there is no forgiveness: that of inauthenticity. All language distorts; stylistic language distorts absolutely. "A thought expressed is a lie," wrote the Russian poet Tyutchev over a century ago. If only it were possible to write without language at all—or, if not without language, at least without style! The problem is not new. Stendhal, in the 1820s, was already struggling with it, and came to the conclusion that the only valid model for his writing should be the impersonal officialese of the Napoleonic *Code civil*, the nearest that the language of literature could approach to the nondescriptive language of mathematics. The *Code civil*: as close as the nineteenth century could get to the styleless language of the computer.

But—and herein lies the dilemma—Beckett is not only a metaphysician, he is also a poet. And for the poet, the over-whelming and compulsive need is to convey his experience of the depth and richness of the world, its ecstasies and its des-pairs, *through* language. Probably this has always been so; but in the contemporary "Death-of-God" context, it is truer than ever. In a universe from which the traditional God-the-Father figure has been abstracted, the supreme experience is that of existential "is-ness" ("être-avec," in the phrase coined by Gabriel Marcel): the intuitive sense, in certain instances almost verging on the mystic, of being uniquely and absolutely at one, both with one's own self, and with all else that simultaneously exists, randomly and inexplicably, in a given instantaneous--external accident of space and time. This "communion with It-ness"[6] is the ultimate experience of the poem and the justifi-cation of poetry, and it can be expressed only through lan-guage. The poet's "style"—his linguistic *alter ego*, the embodi-ment in conceptual form of the miracle of his being-in-the-world—has about it nothing that is haphazard. It is the signifi-cance of his existence; it is the reason why he is a poet rather than a building contractor or a motorcycle salesman.

The outcome, in Beckett, has been from the outset a duality and a contradiction: a tug-of-war between poetry and non-poetry, between "style" and "nonstyle," which, in the early writings in English, emerges as a series of self-parodies, almost in the manner of an introspective Raymond Queneau directing his *exercices de style* against himself. Each successive style, by dint of its deliberate and baroque exaggerations, becomes a "nonstyle," or perhaps, better, an "antistyle," destroying its authenticity by the assertive self-consciousness of its own arti-ficiality. In Beckett's case "le style," quite categorically, "n'est pas l'homme même."

In the long run, however, for a serious writer, anything so artificial and negative as an "antistyle" can scarcely offer a final solution—any more than the "antitheatre" and the"antinovels" of the 1950s could be perpetuated indefinitely. An "antistyle" is at best the means to an end, and the end itself is a "nonlan-guage," a vehicle of expression in which the concepts to be signified are neither colored nor distorted by the words used to signify them.[7] In the last analysis, this could be the reason Beckett eventually turned to French. Not necessarily because French is less rich in poetic overtones and nuanced imagery than is English (although to some extent this is in fact the case); nor even because for any writer to write in a language not his own involves a degree of structured artifice that renders the self-conscious and auto-destructive artificialities of "style" superfluous; but ultimately because in the gap between one language and another there may reside that nonlanguage which it is Beckett's final aim to realize. Belacqua once claimed to live "a Beethoven pause"[8]—to have his existence in those gaps of silence more real (for "Nothing is more real than nothing")[9] and more significant than the great musical phrases surrounding them; and it is worth recalling that, in 1962, the somewhat eccentric Collège de Pataphysique, apparently following up a similar train of thought, devoted an issue of its *Dossiers* to an exploration of literature born "dans les interstices du langage."[10] Beckett's French linguistic self is not identical with his English-structured linguistic self; nor, even more significantly, are his English translations from his own French identical renderings from one idiom into another. In both cases, there is a gap; and somewhere in the gap between the abolutes of any given language—be it English or French, German or Italian, Latin or Computerese—lies that nonlanguage which is at once existential poetry, and yet "styleless" in any recognizable context except that of Beckett himself.

Returning, however, to Beckett's use of English in the earlier writings, before the transition to French, what we discover is a series of experiments in artificiality; a multiplicity, in fact, of "antistyles," each one of which contains within itself the seeds of its own negation. One of the initial problems, on Beckett's own admission, was the "poetic" quality of English—the wealth of unwanted imagery, color, allusion, and reminiscence conjured up by the simplest sentence. And Beckett's earliest attempt at a solution was to intensify the richness of this color and allusiveness, of this "poetry," to the point where the "poem" itself becomes virtually incomprehensible to anyone but the poet himself, and thus stylistically defeats its own object. To the poem *Whoroscope* (1930), Beckett, in a moment of weakness, provided some explanatory footnotes of his own; but the subsequent *Alba* (1931), *Home Olga* (1932), and *Echo's Bones* (1935) are stripped of any such primitive aids to exegesis, and in fact it took trained academic critics the better part of forty years to begin to penetrate the obscurities and to grasp dimly at the meaning[11]—and then not all of it since, as it chanced, none had happened to be living in London and Dublin and Paris and Dortmund during those precise years.

To illustrate this hermetic-solipsistic style—a "style" so inaccessible that it becomes in effect a "nonstyle"—we may take the two poems from *Echo's Bones*, entitled respectively *Enueg I* and *Enueg II*.

When these were reprinted in 1961, in the collected *Poems in English*, enlightened critics could do no better than to suggest that the mysterious word *Enueg* could be nothing more subtle or significant than an approximate anagram of the French word *jeune*. Beckett, who had studied the literature of twelfth-century Provence, knew of course that *Enueg* derived from the late-Latin word *inodium* meaning "vexation," and was a form of poetic *complainte* familiar to troubadour poets such as the Monk of Montaudon; but the majority of accredited critics, and certainly the average reader, did not possess this knowledge. Once the Provençal context is detected, then other allusions fit into place like (once again) the pieces of a jigsaw puzzle: the "Isolde Stores,"[12] for instance, with the "great perturbation of sweaty heroes" who may equally well be Arthurian knights after a battle or simply hurling players after an exhausting game. But unquestionably the elucidation of the mystery does require the services of a skilled literary detective who is prepared to devote several years of his life to the job.[13] And in the end, perhaps, the final significance of the intrusion of this antique Mediterranean element into an English poem lies precisely in the fact of its non-Englishness: a first step in the undermining of the monolithic self-sufficiency of a linguistic structural absolute.

Other equally exotic and esoteric allusions are drawn from the Bible and from classical mythology. Nothing straightforward, of course. To start with, just houses and trees: "Above the mansions, the algum-trees." There are no algum trees in Dublin, more's the pity; but they did grow once, in the highlands of Lebanon, and Solomon commanded that their wood should be transported by sea to Jerusalem for the building of his temple (2 Chron. 2:8–11)—the house or "mansion" of the Lord. So much for the Old Testament; from the New, that recurrent Beckettian obsession, the Crucifixion. But, again, one has to pick up the initial clue for the rest of the hermetic allusion to fit into place:

at *Parnell* Bridge a *dying* barge
carrying a cargo of *nails and timber* . . .
on the far bank a gang of down and outs would seem to be *mending a*
    beam. . . .
and the *weals* creeping alongside on the water . . .
de morituris nihil nisi . . .
veronica mundi
veronica munda
gave us *a wipe* for the *love of Jesus*
sweating *like Judas*
tired of *dying.* . . .[14]

and, through the intermediary of Dante ("God's Quisling on earth"), a brief vision of the River Liffey transformed into "the Pit" of Hell, with the Damned, Doré-fashion, or like the climbers of the ladders in *The Lost Ones* (*Le Dépeupleur*), attempting to crawl out:

> Blotches of doomed yellow in the pit of the Liffey;
> the fingers of the ladders hooked over the parapet,
> soliciting. . . .

The classical allusions are similar unmethodical and (apparently) scattered at random. If the "algum-trees" suggest the house of Solomon and the mansion of the Lord, they could equally evoke (for the classical scholar) the Greek word αλγος, meaning "pain," which makes much sense in the context of the woman dying of tuberculosis in the "Portobello Private Nursing Home." And then, on the road to Kilmainham,

> I splashed past a little a little wearish old man,
> Democritus . . .

introducing thus for the first time in the Beckettian canon the figure of the "Abderite" with his memorable "guffaw." And back in the Isolde Stores, he observes the hurling-players

come hastening down for a pint of nepenthe or moly or half and half

and though the most illiterate of his readers (if any) would have been familiar with "half and half" (a mixture of two brews of beer, half mild, half bitter), again only the scholar like himself would have identified nepenthe, "the drug producing forget-fulness of grief," or moly, the "fabulous herb with white flower and black root, endowed with magic properties." The picture formed by the jigsaw puzzle is easy enough to interpret once the pieces are in place, but utterly baffling so long as the key to the structure as a whole is missing.

Or, to take another element in the "nonstyle" of these poems: the use of rare, exotic, and unfamiliar words. Latin words: "Exeo," with which *Enueg I* begins, thus invoking the Cartesian "Cogito" and, like Descartes, avoiding the too-dominant subjectivity of the pronoun "I," with which two of the following sections of the poem begin. French words: *gaffe*; or "feet in *marmelade*"—not the familiar bitter-orange jam of the English, but rather any kind of Gallic or Slavonic jelly-like squishy mess. "Wearish" = OE "Werig" = OHG "wuarag," meaning "drunk." Irish: "pucking," from "puckaun," meaning a billy goat:

> a small malevolent goat, exiled on the road,
> remotely pucking the gate of his field. . . .

German: "doch doch I assure thee." Or plain English rarities such as "cang" (reference to a Chinese torture) or "Rafflesia"—the latter, named after Sir Thomas Raffles, lieutenant-governor of Sumatra 1818–23, later founder of the Regent's Park Zoo in London, being the largest flower in the world, and one of the most evil-smelling. All this constitutes not so much a language, in the normal sense of the word, as a *code*, just as the "language" of the computer is a code. And a code, at least in any literary sense, is a nonstyle.

It might be added that the formal style of the poems themselves (written ca. 1930–35) was, in its time, "exotic"; that is, it belonged to a French rather than to an English tradition. Its origins may lie remotely in the Provençal *Enuegs* themselves;[15] but more immediately, these origins are to be found in the French tradition as it had developed over the decades between Rimbaud and Laforgue on the one hand and Beckett's contemporaries Max Jacob, Pierre Reverdy, and Benjamin Péret on the other. This manner of conceiving poetic structure was absolutely foreign to English-language poets of the period, with the significant exception of those who were closely in contact with France: T. S. Eliot, for instance, or Ezra Pound, or e. e. cummings.[16] For the rest, English poetry seems to have been so dazzled by the revelation of Gerard Manley Hopkins in 1918 that for the better part of a generation it was immunized, as it were, against the whole Rimbaldian aesthetic; and even James Joyce (so often referred to as Beckett's "mentor") would seem, in *Pomes Penyeach* (1927), to have been taking an anachronistic "last ramble through Palgrave,"[17] rather than to have kept even remotely in touch with the truly original poetic idiom of his own time. Thus Beckett, in the *Enuegs* as in the other poems of *Echo's Bones*, was in fact writing English poetry in an almost entirely French poetic idiom: yet another descent into that "gap" of silence that lies secreted in the interstices of language.

If the hermetic "code" of the *Poems in English* constitutes one "nonstyle," Beckett's use of realism, paradoxically, constitutes another. This is essentially because, though never cheating, he goes to immense pains to conceal the fact that he is a realist. Not the jigsaw puzzle now, but hide-and-seek is the game: "I hid and you sook," as he observes in a not wholly irrelevant line of *Whoroscope*. So efficacious have been these efforts at concealment that few if any critics seem to have concerned themselves seriously with the immediate—as opposed to the ultimate—metaphysical reality underlying Beckett's writing;[18] yet it has been apparent for a long time that his "absurdism" (like that of his disciple Armand Gatti) is arrived at by driving the "realities" of reason, observation, logic, and mathematics to their necessary but unacceptable conclusions, and that his "surreality" never for an instant severs its relationship with the real—frequently in its grossest and most unpalatable form. Where a literal reality takes on the shape of a fantasy, a nightmare, or a plain impossibility, then "real" and "unreal" cancel each other out, and the result is another "nonstyle."

Admittedly, this technique of contradiction and cancellation is not exclusive to the writings in English; but it is more noticeable, say, in *All That Fall, Happy Days, Play, Film,* or even in *Ohio Impromptu,* than it is in *Godot,* in the *Trilogy* or in *Comment c'est;* and certainly all the fundamental techniques of Beckettian realism are well and truly laid in the early writings. It is as though the switch to French induced an additional stratum of abstraction—culminating in texts such as *Le Dépeupleur*—thus to some extent upsetting the carefully calculated balance of the "nonstyle," and allowing the artificially acquired language (just *because* it is artificially acquired) more autonomy than the natural, maternal idiom.

Once one starts to look for plain reality in Beckett's writing, the more evident it becomes. There is geographical reality—the basic guidebook promenades through central Dublin and through its remoter suburbs—in *Enueg I,* for instance ("Over the Liffey with its steep perilous bridge");[19] in "Fingal" and in "A Wet Night," and of course in *Watt. Murphy* similarly follows an accurate street plan of small but very real sections of London—of Edith Grove, Cremorne Road, Lot's Road, and Stadium Street, for instance, all of which, within less than a hundred yards of each other, can be located on the North Bank of Chelsea Reach in any edition of the familiar *A–Z Atlas and Street Guide* of that city. But undoubtedly what Beckett loves best to light upon is the existence of a real place whose name conceals an accidental but resplendent symbolism—it could well have been his acquaintance with a very *real* suburb of Dublin named Chapelizod (= "The Chapel of Isolde") that sparked off the whole "troubadour" structure of *Enueg I*. And the very summit of this amalgam of realism and symbolism is attained when (given the Beckettian vision of decaying humanity astride disintegrating bicycles) the already symbolic place-name, to those who actually know the place, is associated with a hospital: Kilmainham (*Enueg I*), where the hurling-players have been locked in mortal combat, was, first, the building in which the "crucified" Parnell had once been imprisoned, and second, one which had later become a hospital; and what better syllable for the name of a hospital to begin with (and Beckett is supremely alert to the significance of the opening syllables of names) than "Kil"? The Chelsea Reach of *Murphy* leads directly to the famous Chelsea Royal Hospital. And Murphy himself, mewed up in life if not in death in his "Mew in West Brompton," overlooked the Western Hospital, which has as its garden the immense West Brompton Cemetery. When, in the course of translation, Beckett moved Murphy to Paris, West Brompton could not go with him; but—marvel of marvels—close by the cemetery of Montparnasse, Beckett discovered a (real) "Impasse de l'Enfant-Jésus"; *and* it was overshadowed by the grim walls of the Hôpital Necker!

Thus symbol and reality interfuse; and the same is true as he walks the streets and observes the life around him. In such a manner, the "surrealist" admonition to "smoke more fruit" (*Enueg II*) combines the essence of two all-too-prevalent publicity campaigns in the London of the 1930s: the Imperial Tobacco Company's "Smoke Capstans" (on huge hoardings), and the South African Trade Bureau's "Eat More Fruit" (in delicious cardboard cutouts of oranges, lemons, pineapples, and so on, available at every greengrocer and fruiterer). Or— another example of observed reality apprehended for its accidental symbolism—the Great Ice-Cream Rivalry. In Murphy's London, two firms vied for the juvenile ice-cream market: Wall's and Eldorado. Both employed disabled former servicemen to pedal around the streets on delivery-tricycles fitted with refrigerated containers. Wall's (blue-and-white, with the slogan

"Stop Me And Buy One") was reputed to have the better quality; but it was also more expensive. Eldorado (red-and-white) was the cheaper, inferior product; and cheap ice cream was then known as "hokey-pokey." "Hokey-pokey-penny-a-lump," chanted the nannies to their charges—conjuring up visions of unsanitary Italian vendors, their product concocted in the bathtub. A laborious explanation; but it is necessary, perhaps, for the modern reader to understand the typically elaborate mixture of the real and the symbolic that underlies one of Beckett's apparently more ingenuous sentences:

> Celia [contemplating suicide by drowning herself in the Thames] walked to a point about half-way between the Battersea and Albert Bridges and sat down on a bench between a Chelsea pensioner and an Eldorado hokey-pokey man, who had dismounted from his cruel machine and was enjoying a short interlude of paradise.[20]

Observed reality—decrepitude, hospitalization, and death—*Inferno, Purgatorio, Eldorado.* Social realism also: Wall's "Stop Me And Buy One" would probably not have bothered with Lot's Road or Chelsea Reach during the days of the Great Depression. Nor is the "cruel machine" wholly to be dissociated from the later Beckettian bicycle image, which had already made its first appearance in the "Fingal" of *More Pricks Than Kicks* (pp. 33–36).

But if Beckett's eye is accurate, so also is his ear. Like Proust, he is truly a human tape recorder. The role of the tape recorder itself in *Krapp's Last Tape* is not accidental; the then newly invented machine simply vulgarizes the processes of his own mind. The rhythms, intonations, and inflections of *Murphy* and *Watt*, of the English version of *Godot*, and even of some of the later sketches such as *Footfalls* or *Theatre I* and *Theatre II*, are not the product of Mind working in the quintessential Abstract; they are the rhythms of the Dublin street and public house—as accurate as those of Stanley Holloway's Wigan and Runcorn, or of Barry Humphries' Moonee Ponds. The utterances of the Winnie of "Fingal," sparse as they are, nonetheless suffice to reverberate with the limitless vulgarities of her tiny-minded conventionality. "The Smeraldina's Billet Doux," as the pastiche of a letter written in her own brand of English by a Germanic woman-in-love, is so devastatingly accurate that it hurts. The very accent of Kassel—or is it not rather that of Wiener-Neustadt?—echoes through the written words:

> Bel! Bel! how could you ever doubt me? Meine Ruh ist hin mein Herz ist schwer ich finde Sie nimmer und nimmer mehr. (Goethes Faust.) Lord Lord Lord for god sake tell me strate away what agsactly I have done. Is everything indiffrent to you? Evedintly you cant be bothered with a goat like me. If I don't stop writing you wont be able to read this letter because it will be all ofer tears. Bel! Bel! . . .
>
> Do you remember last summer (of course he dose) and how lovely it was lieing hearing the bees summing and the birds singing, and the big butterfly that cam past, it looked grand, it was dark brown with yellow spots and looked so beautiful in the sun, and my body was quite brown all ofer and I dident feel the cold any more. (P. 166)

On the other hand, the purely parodic speech-realism of La Smeraldina, or for that matter of the Miss Coonihan of *Murphy*, or of Maddy in *All That Fall*, is superficial compared with the profound psychological reality of verbal patterns in some of the later works. What Beckett's significant personal experiences may have been is unknown to us, and will probably remain so.[21] But that he has passed through (and mentally tape-recorded) some of the most traumatic moments of a human existence is unquestionable. Psychoanalytical interpretation of great works of literature are normally futile because they are directed at the writer, who is usually far more intelligent than the would-be psychoanalyst. But in Beckett's case the result might be more fruitful, since these interpretations could only be directed at the characters. The Winnie of *Happy Days*, for instance: an uncannily accurate recording of the voice of a woman whose marriage has broken down, during the last days before she resorts to the tranquilizing pills, the psychiatrist, and the mental-home; *Play*: the word-for-word nastiness of marriage and adultery—the bestial melodrama that no modern dramatist without the genius of a Beckett would dare touch, and yet which is true nonetheless:

> W2.   One morning as I was sitting stitching by the open win-
> dow she burst in and flew at me. Give him up, she
> screamed, he's mine. Her photographs were kind to
> her. Seeing her now for the first time full length in the
> flesh I understood why he preferred me.
>
> N.   We were not long together when she smelled the rat.
> Give up that whore, she said, or I'll cut my throat—
> (hiccup) pardon—so help me God. I knew she could
> have no proof. So I told her I did not know what she
> was talking about,
>
> W2.   What are you talking about? I said, stitching away. Some-
> one yours? Give up whom? I smell you off him, she
> screamed, he stinks of bitch.[22]

Or, of course, Lucky's great monologue in *Godot* that, from the
psychiatrist's point of view, is the almost untreated, unex-
purgated version of the outpourings of any contemporary intellectual adolescent in the first crisis of drug addiction or of
plain schizophrenia.

Another nonlanguage. In almost everything that he has written (but particularly in English), Beckett is presenting a total
reality: a more-than-Zolaesque, absolute naturalism, which,
within its context, refuses to *behave* as naturalism, or even as
realism. It is the language of literal truth (to those who can
recognize it) masquerading as the language of the metaphysical, the mythological, and the absurd. Truth pretending to be a
nontruth. Truth and nontruth canceling each other out. Again a
void.

Perhaps Beckett's supreme attempt to write both in superlative literary English and, at the same time, "without style" was
achieved in *Watt*. *Watt* represents the nearest ever that a great
poet has managed to transform himself into a computer; yet
(because he *is* a poet) it remains a computer-with-a-bad-con-
science.

The objective of *Watt* is to use language *as though* there were
no positive or necessary relationship between word and concept—between signifier and signified. For Watt himself this is
both a puzzling and (since he had not then read the later struc-

turalists) a painful procedure: "Watt's need of semantic succor was at times so great that he would set to trying names on things, almost as a woman hats . . . " (_Watt_, p. 90).

For Watt's creator, on the other hand, it was a supreme, a desperate _exercice de style_; or rather (once again) _de non-style_. But the basic principle of using words in a completely random relationship with concepts—saying of a pot, for instance, "It is a shield, or, growing bolder, It is a raven, and so on" (p. 90)—is only one part of the general pattern of linguistic disintegration. By a skilled and virtually unique use of the comma, Beckett breaks up his sentences into a series of semiautonomous sense-units, isolating hunks of raw language in such a way that, although the continuity of the thought is not destroyed altogether, each section of the argument that constitutes that continuity stands apart and comes as a surprise, seemingly arbitrary and unexpected, assumable or discardable upon the whim of the moment. Consider the description of Mr. Knott's style of dressing, for instance, in which the comma—the "Beethoven-pause" between blocks of significance—appears more momentous than the phrases that it separates:

> But whatever he put on, in the beginning, for by midnight he was always in his nightshirt, whatever he put on then, on his head, on his body, on his feet, he did not touch again, but kept on all that day, in his room, in his house, in his grounds, until the time came to put on his nightshirt, once again. (P. 222)

There is something vaguely archaic about the ring of these sentences, something tantalizingly reminiscent of the _Areopagitica_ or of the _Anatomy of Melancholy_; but once again, if there is a suggestion of pastiche, it is not in order to bring about a _rapprochement_ with a more ancient style but rather to achieve a further alienation effect: English, not as it once was written but as it _is not_ written. Echoes of John Donne or of Izaac Walton invoked deliberately to undermine the authenticity of twentieth-century narrative prose.

Other devices likewise serve to emphasize the all-prevalence of nonstyle—including that of negativity itself. Time and time again, in _Watt_, faced with the choice of making a statement in positive or in double-negative form, Beckett chooses the latter. Indeed, the challenge of the double-negative waves like the black flag of the anarchists above the doomed linguistic traditionalism of the narrative: "This is not to say that Watt never saw Mr Knott, at this period, for he did, to be sure" (p. 75); "Not that he was always unsuccessful either, for he was not" (p. 84). Or else complex triple, quadruple, or quintuple implied negatives, such as the following:

> For the only way one can speak of nothing is to speak of it as though it were something, just as the only way one can speak of God is to speak of him as though he were a man, which to be sure he was, in a sense, for a time, and as the only way one can speak of man, even our anthropologists have realized that, is to speak of him as though he were a termite. (P. 84).

"Something" here is a *pis-aller* for the ultimate reality of "nothing," which language, even in the ultimate extremes of its negativity, is unable to grasp or to handle.

The variations on an "antistyle" in *Watt* are innumerable, among them the familiar antics of the "Academic Clown."[23] There is, for instance, the borrowing of stylistic tricks and mannerisms from other writers and other situations wholly inappropriate and irrelevant to the thematic material of the argument. Arsène's formal pomposity and reiterated interjections of "Haw!" are borrowed straight from P. G. Wodehouse's Jeeves, with some addition, perhaps, from Dorothy L. Sayers's Bunter and from innumerable other comic or semicomic gentlemens' gentlemen of the period. The naïvely repeated "said Mr. Hackett," "said Goff," "said Tetty" of the opening sequences suggest the deadpan formula of Ivy Compton-Burnett, with something thrown in from the sophisticated ingenuousness of *The House at Pooh Corner*. There are the computerized permutations and combinations of Mary eating onions-and-peppermints, of the Lynch family background to the dog who did or (as the case might be) did not consume the remains of Mr. Knott's supper, or of Mr. Ernest Louit's appearance before the committee responsible for determining his worthiness to receive an award for research. In all of these, step by step, the computer begins, almost literally, to take over from the poet; and the ultimate nonlanguage is that code which electronics can contrive out of oblong holes punched in slips of pasteboard: "Ot bro, lap rulb, krad klub. Ot murd, wol fup, wol fup. Ot niks, sorg sam, sorg sam. Ot lems, lats lems, lats lems. Ot gnut, trat stews, trat stews" (*Watt*, p. 181).

With the computerized automation of Watt's linguistic experiments in part three of the novel, Beckett's search for a nonstyle reaches its climax and its logical conclusion. The "interstices" between languages have become gigantic chasms between language-as-such and the thoughts or concepts that language traditionally is expected to convey. Thought, words, style: the three have become absolutely and irremediably separated from each other; and, because of this separation, we are left with a style *in vacuo*—a style that functions as a nonstyle by having severed all connections with that which it is supposed to represent, while at the same time retaining its unique individuality. "Le pour-soi," wrote Sartre, "est ce qu'il n'est pas." Beckett's English style, in the last stage of its evolution before he turned to French, similarly "is what it is not." It *is* a style; but it *is not*, in that the signifier no longer bears any immediate or positive relationship to the thing signified. A style reveals; a code conceals. In *Watt* Beckett has given a style to a code, and thus has realized the ultimate self-contradition of which literature is capable.

If, as we have argued, the problem that Beckett set himself from the outset was to discover a manner of writing "in the interstices of language"—in the linguistic equivalent of the "Beethoven-pause"—the transition to French would seem in retrospect to have been almost inevitable. Under different circumstances, it might have been Latin, or Esperanto. A foreign language is a code; to learn a foreign language is one of the most computer-like functions of the human mind. By working in French, Beckett avoids the traps he feels to be implicit in establishing a direct or "organic" relationship between the thing signified and the phrase signifying. Instead, the computer *first* translates the concept into the "code" of a foreign

language—that is, into a medium that is not "natural" but artificial—and then, by a second and wholly distinct operation,
works back to the "real" or "natural" language, by translating
from, or deciphering, the code. In other words, from *Molloy*
onward Beckett's prose-poetry in English is, in Watt's phrase,
"language commenting language," and is thus positive and
affirmative within the strict limits that constitute its domain,
rather than language trying, and forever failing, to embrace
reality. The artificiality of the whole procedure is of the essence.
And to remind us of this, here and there Beckett translates with
carefully calculated inadequacy, sometimes even to the point of
clumsiness.

To take one example only. In the exchange between Vladimir
and Estragon, when they attempt to recall the landscapes of the
past, the French runs as follows:

Vladimir. Tout de même, tu ne vas pas me dire que ça [*geste*]
ressemble au Vaucluse! Il y a quand même une
grosse différence.

Estragon. Le Vaucluse! Qui te parle du Vaucluse?

Vladimir. Mais tu as bien été dans le Vaucluse?

Estragon. Mais non, je n'ai jamais été dans le Vaucluse! J'ai
coulé toute ma chaudepisse d'existence ici, je te
dis! Ici! Dans la Merdecluse!24

This becomes in English:

Vladimir. All the same, you can't tell me that this [gesture]
bears any resemblance to . . . [he hesitates] . . . to
the Macon country, for example. You can't deny
there's a big difference.

Estragon. The Macon country! Who's talking to you about the
Macon country?

Vladimir. But you were there yourself, in the Macon country.

Estragon. No, I was never in the Macon country. I've puked
my puke of a life away here, I tell you! Here! In the
Cackon country!25

It grates! "Macon" and "Cackon" neither translate the French wordplay, nor replace it by an English equivalent. As a semi-pun ("Vaucluse"/"Merdecluse" is not exactly subtle, it is meaningless. Surely, one feels, Beckett can do better than that:[26] "It sounds like a bad translation from his own French!" Which is exactly (this is the essence of our argument) what it is meant to sound like.

Thus Beckett's sense of the failure of language is (provisionally) exorcised, and in translating these works of the middle period, he can write some of the greatest prose-poetry in English literature:

> I listen and the voice is of a world collapsing endlessly, a frozen world, under a faint untroubled sky, enough to see by, yes, and frozen too. And I hear it murmur that all wilts and yields, as if loaded down, but here there are no loads, and the ground too, unfit for loads, and the light too, down towards an end it seems can never come. (*Molloy*, P. 40)

To deny that this passage has "style" would be absurd; yet, on analysis, it is a style that nonetheless makes use of those elements of "antistyle" that we have been examining. In their final form, however, and thanks to the procedure by which they have first been required to pass through the "computer-code" of a foreign language, these elements have, as it were, become naturalized. They are no longer negative but positive. They function as words *should* function, that is, as a "comment" on other words; only indirectly and accidentally do they relate to concepts. Only accidentally are they poetry. But for all that, they are stamped with the unique and unforgettable identity of their maker.

1. Samuel Beckett, quoted in John Fletcher, *Samuel Beckett's Art* (London: Chatto and Windus, 1967), p. 29. The poem dates from 1931.

2. *Watt* (Paris: Olympia Press, 1959), p. 220.

3. Niklaus Gessner, *Die Unzulänglichkeit der Sprache: eine Untersuchung über Formzerfall und Beziehungslosigkeit bei Samuel Beckett* (Zürich: Juris-Verlag, 1957), p. 32 n.

4. Samuel Beckett, *Collected Poems in English and French* (New York: Grove Press, 1977), p. 94–97.

5. This illustration is based on three paintings assembled and hung in her office by Emeritus Professor Irene Manton, formerly professor of botany in the University of Leeds, and a knowledgeable collector of modern art.

6. The phrase is taken from Bernard Berenson's memoirs, *Sketch for a Self-Portrait* (1940); but, revealingly, Eleanor Farjeon, describing an identical experience in her autobiography of her childhood, *A Nursery in the Nineties* (1935), refers to it as "being suddenly immersed in It-ness."

7. The failure of the self to penetrate the barrier of words "imposed by Others" is, of course, one of the most important themes of *The Unnamable*.

8. *More Pricks Than Kicks* (1934; rpt, London: Calder and Boyars, 1970), p. 40 ("Ding-Dong").

9. *Malone Dies*, in *Molloy, Malone Dies, The Unnamable* (London: John Calder, 1959), p. 193.

10. "Exercices de Littérature potentielle": see *Dossiers du Collège de 'Pataphysique*, No. 17, dated "22 sable 89 E.P." (= 1962). The idea of a void or "gap" between languages is (*pace* Ludwig Wittgenstein) not without some support from the world of practical experience. I have been assured by a former "direct-interpreter" working with the United Nations (now a reader at the University of Oxford), who has at his immediate command eight European languages, that when he was working under pressure, the concepts expressed by a U.N. delegate in one language would be plunged into a "linguistic void" in his own mind, whence they would reemerge "naked," as it were, to be clad immediately in any of the seven other languages as might be required.

11. See Fletcher, *Samuel Beckett's Art*, especially pp. 24–40; and, more particularly, Lawrence E. Harvey's *Samuel Beckett: Poet and Critic* (Princeton, N.J.: Princeton University Press, 1970), one of the most impressive books of Beckettian exegesis yet written.

12. See below, pp. 46–47.

13. Even Lawrence Harvey (*Samuel Beckett*, p. 134) does not seem to have recognized that "The Fox and Geese" is the archetypal name for an English inn or "public house."

14. From *Enueg I* and *Enueg II*. The italics are mine. The "Parnell" image— that of the "crucified" Irish patriot betrayed by his Judas-people (cf. James Joyce, *A Portrait of the Artist as a Young Man*)—will reappear later, under the image of "Kilmainham." All quotations are from *Collected Poems*, pp. 10–14.

15. See Harvey, *Samuel Beckett*, pp. 80–81.

16. Nor by any means did all English-language poets who were in contact with France at this period accept this idiom: see, for instance, Gertrude Stein or Edith Sitwell.

17. The phrase is taken from John Clive Hall, *A House of Voices* (London: Chatto and Windus, 1973), p. 31.

18. At the symposium at the Ohio State University, no single paper—let alone a full session—was devoted to Beckett's "realism."

19. See Harvey, *Samuel Beckett*, pp. 124–37.

20. *Murphy* (1938; rpt. New York: Grove Press, 1957), p. 14.

21. According to Deirdre Bair, in her tantalizingly incomplete "biography," *Samuel Beckett* (New York: Harcourt Brace Jovanovich, 1978), p. 75, the "Smeraldina" was Beckett's first cousin, daughter of his aunt Frances ("Cissie") Beckett and of the Irish-Jewish William Sinclair. This cousin, Peggy Sinclair, had been brought up largely in Kassel, and was called "Smeraldina-Rima" on account of "her deep green eyes and her passionate love of green clothing." At one period Beckett was in love with her. But one cannot help suspecting that other elements, which Beckett failed to reveal to his biographer, contributed to the portrait.

22. *Play* (London: Faber and Faber, 1964), pp. 10–11.

23. Since these have been analyzed in admirable detail by Hugh Kenner and others, there is no need for me to dwell upon them here. Suffice it to note that they constitute yet another self-parody or "nonstyle."

24. *En attendant Godot* (Paris: Editions de Minuit, 1952), pp. 103–4.

25. *Waiting for Godot* (London: Faber and Faber, 1956), pp. 61–62. The odd fact is that the word "Cackon" (= "caca"; see the "Aca*caca*cademy of An*thropopo*pometry" in Lucky's monologue) would immediately suggest something to a *French* spectator, but not to an English one.

26. Obviously he can—when he wants to. Cf. the transference from French to English in the passage concerning Lousse's parrot in *Molloy* (Paris: Editions de Minuit, 1951), p. 55; *Molloy* (Calder), pp. 37–38.

Rubin Rabinovitz

Unreliable Narrative in *Murphy*

In some of Samuel Beckett's early works, the narrator's commentary is occasionally untrustworthy; in *Murphy* the unreliable narrative becomes an important structural device. Many of the narrator's seemingly plausible statements are in some way misleading or inconsistent. For example, he twice says that Murphy is a "strict non-reader"; but he also reveals that Murphy is familiar with works by Fletcher, Swift, Wordsworth, Dante, Campanella, and Bishop Bouvier, among others.[1] A possible way of resolving this problem is given in a passage where the narrator describes how Murphy was forced to sell some of his possessions:

> He thought of the rocking-chair left behind in Brewery Road, that aid to life in his mind from which he had never before been parted. His books, his pictures, his postcards, his musical scores and instruments, all had been gradually disposed of in that order rather than the chair. (P. 189)

It may be, then, that Murphy gave up reading when he was forced to sell his books; but calling him a strict nonreader is nevertheless somewhat misleading. Moreover, if this explanation resolves one contradiction, it introduces another. Earlier the narrator has assured the reader that Murphy's rocking chair "never left him"; here the narrator includes a reminder that it has been "left behind in Brewery Road."[2]

Another problem involving the rocking chair arises in the opening pages of the novel. The narrator says that Murphy uses seven scarves to bind himself to the chair and then, enumerating them, mentions only six (p. 2). According to some critics (A. Alvarez, for example), this is an inadvertent error.[3] But Beckett is careful about small details. If the error had been an oversight, it would probably have been eliminated when Beckett translated his novel into French. However, the inconsistent enumeration of scarves, the assurances that Murphy is a nonreader, and other misleading statements are retained in the French version. Moreover, many of Beckett's novels have inconsistencies of this sort; John Mood has discovered twenty-eight of them in a single work, *Watt.*[4]

One of the ways Beckett uses unreliable material is illustrated in an exchange between Bim Clinch, the head male nurse at the Magdalen Mental Mercyseat, and Ticklepenny. Bim hires Ticklepenny as an attendant and promises him a salary of five pounds per month. After ten days among the lunatics, Ticklepenny has had enough; he persuades Murphy to take over his job, and asks Bim to pay him for the time he has worked. Bim, who has "a fancy for Ticklepenny not far short of love," agrees to this arrangement (pp. 156–57). But he adds a stipulation: "you will get your one-six-eight," he says, "as soon as your Murphy has given a month's satisfaction and no sooner."[5] Ticklepenny accepts this offer without realizing that after working ten days he is owed a third of five pounds, or one-thirteen-four (one-six-eight is a third of four pounds). The exact value of "Bim's fancy . . . not far short of love" may be difficult to compute, but it is clearly less than six shillings eightpence.

There is another bit of legerdemain in this episode. When Ticklepenny offers Murphy the job, he says nothing about his relationship with Bim. Yet Murphy predicts that he will not be hired if Ticklepenny is involved in "a liaison with some high official, the head male nurse for example."[6] How does Murphy manage to guess the truth so accurately? Either he has become uncharacteristically perceptive or—more likely—the narrator is sharing a joke with the reader. For, despite the premonition about the head male nurse, Murphy (who thinks that the liaison will hurt his chances for employment) still has managed to get things backward.

Many of the inconsistencies in the novel become apparent when one compares related details in widely separated passages. One example involves two appearances of the word "whinge" (to whine or whimper). According to the narrator, "All the puppets in this book whinge sooner or later, except Murphy, who is not a puppet" (p. 122). This suggests—or seems to—that whatever forms of expression will be elicited from Murphy, the whinge is not among them. But some pages earlier the narrator had described how Murphy "threw his voice into an infant's whinge" (p. 37). Nor can the narrator's statement be taken to mean that all the minor characters in the book whinge and are puppet-like, but that Murphy (who also whinges) is not puppet-like. There are other characters, notably Mr. Endon, who never whinge.[7]

Murphy's horoscope introduces a number of other inconsistencies. Some of Suk's predictions, like those about fits and quadrupeds, are accurate; many others are not.[8] Suk indicates that Murphy possesses "great Magical Ability of the Eye, to which the lunatic would easy succumb" (p. 32). When Celia threatens to leave him unless he looks for work, Murphy fixes his gaze on her "with great magical ability"; the result is that Murphy is forced to seek employment (p. 39). Later on, the narrator notes that the M.M.M. is ideally suited for Murphy to take advantage of the "great magical ability of the eye to which the lunatic would easy succumb" (p. 183). Attempting to achieve rapport with Mr. Endon, he stares into his eyes; and again, Murphy is the one who is defeated.[9] Murphy loves to talk, but Suk claims that silence is one of his highest attributes. Like the narrator, Suk has his playful moments: shortly after praising Murphy's silence, he says, "Avoid exhaustion by speech" (p. 32). Celia twice quotes this admonition back to Murphy after he engages in one of his long-winded monologues.[10]

According to the narrator, Suk was told the day and year of Murphy's birth, but not the time (p. 23). Yet the opening words of the horoscope are, "At time of Birth of this Native four degrees of the GOAT was rising . . . " (p. 32). Suk could not have given the position of a zodiacal constellation this accurately without knowing the time of birth to within a few minutes.[11] Again, a repeated word is used to call attention to the inconsistency. The narrator says that Suk would be able to prepare Murphy's horoscope without being told "the precise moment of vagitus" (birth cry); later, the word "vagitus" appears twice in a passage about Murphy's birth (pp. 23, 71). The narrator seems to know when Murphy was born—he describes what occurred in the delivery room; but this knowledge is never shared with the reader. Hence it is impossible to determine whether some of the details in the horoscope are reliable.

There is a way, however, of estimating roughly when Murphy was born, and this points to another inconsistency. The action of the novel takes place in 1935, and Murphy is called young (twice) and a young man (twice on the same page).[12] Assuming that Murphy is at least sixteen but no more than fifty (to take the extreme cases), the year of his birth is between 1885 and 1919. Suk says that when Murphy was born, Neptune was in Taurus and Uranus was in Aquarius.[13] Neptune was in Taurus from 1874 until 1889; Uranus was in Aquarius from 1912 to 1920. Hence one of Suk's statements could be true if Murphy were forty-six or over; the other one, if he were twenty-three or under; but both of the statements cannot be true. In fact there is no time in the nineteenth or twentieth centuries when Neptune and Uranus are in the designated positions simultaneously.[14]

With characteristic evenhandedness, Beckett makes certain that the astronomy in *Murphy* is as unreliable as the astrology. If the comment about the moon promoting magical ability is misleading, so is the statement that is its counterpart, "The moon, by a striking coincidence full and at perigee, was 29,000 miles nearer the earth than it had been for four years" (p. 26). On the night in question (11 September 1935—the date can be calculated from details given in the novel), the moon was in fact full.[15] Perigee, however, was not reached until the next evening; and since the moon is full and at perigee about once a year, the coincidence is not so very striking.[16] On 12 September the

moon was well over 29,000 miles nearer to the earth than it had
been only thirteen days earlier, when it was at apogee. Nor was
it closer to the earth than it had been for four years: when it was
at perigee on 20 April 1932, the lunar distance was less by ten
miles. Indeed, unless someone tampers with its orbit, the moon
never can be "29,000 miles nearer the earth than it had been for
four years"; the difference between the average and minimum
perigee distances is less than 5,000 miles.[17] It is remarkable how
much error the narrator has packed into a single sentence; yet
his information is so plausible, his tone so self-assured, that it
seems almost rude to check on the data.

Another error in astronomy is introduced when the narrator
explains why Murphy can see no stars from the window of his
garret:

> When it was not too cold to open the skylight in the garret, the
> stars seemed always veiled by cloud or fog or mist. The sad truth
> was that the skylight commanded only that most dismal patch of
> night sky, the galactic coal-sack, which would naturally look like a
> dirty night to any observer in Murphy's condition, cold, tired,
> angry, impatient and out of conceit with a system that seemed the
> superfluous cartoon of his own. (Pp. 188–89)

But if Murphy had wanted to see more than the coal-sack, he
only needed to wait a bit and the area framed by the skylight
would have changed: this is one of the many salutory effects of
the earth's diurnal motion. Moreover, if the coal-sack seems
dark in contrast to nearby regions of the Milky Way, it can
hardly be called dismal; and it does contain visible stars.[18] A
more likely explanation for Murphy's inability to see the stars is
given at the end of the quoted passage: he is "out of conceit"
with the celestial system.

According to the narrator, Murphy starts out believing in two
systems: that of the heavenly bodies (astrology) and that of his
own mental processes (pp. 22–23, 75–76). But the narrator notes
"a certain disharmony between the only two canons in which
Murphy can feel the least confidence."[19] Murphy begins to
think of his own system as the superior one: "The more his own
system closed round him, the less he could tolerate its being

subordinated to any other" (pp. 182–83). He becomes more and more convinced that his mind is "a closed system, subject to no principle of change but its own . . . " (p. 109). The stars he had believed in as an influence on his life become the "stars he commanded" and "his stars"; finally Murphy thinks of astrology as "a system that seemed the superfluous cartoon of his own."[20]

Ironically, Murphy's repudiation of astrology is predicted in the epigraph of his horoscope, which is a passage taken from Shakespeare's *Romeo and Juliet*: "Then I defy you, Stars."[21] Murphy, like Romeo, can defy the stars; but neither hero can escape his destiny, which is to die a short time afterward. There is another quotation from *Romeo and Juliet*—again about stars—in *Murphy*: "Take him and cut him out in little stars" (p. 86). This passage is from a speech of Juliet's in which the imminent death of Romeo is foreshadowed:

> Come, gentle night, come, loving, black-brow'd night,
> Give me my Romeo; and, when he shall die,
> Take him and cut him out in little stars,
> And he will make the face of heaven so fine
> That all the world will be in love with night. . . .[22]

The remains of Romeo will be transformed into stars: this idea nicely offsets Murphy's notion that the astral system can be subsumed into his own.

Murphy's separation from the outside world is symbolized by his diminishing ability to see the stars. A related theme occurs in two works that were important influences on *Murphy*: *The Divine Comedy* and *The World as Will and Idea*. In *The Divine Comedy*, Dante loses sight of the stars when he descends into the underworld. Only when he emerges does he see them again; this is described in the last verse of the *Inferno*.[23] There is also a reference to the stars in the last sentence of *The World as Will and Idea*. Describing the insubstantiality of the physical world, Schopenhauer says, "To those in whom the will has turned and has denied itself, this our world, which is so real, with all its suns and milky ways—is nothing."[24] The universe that we believe exists outside ourselves is actually projected from within. In *Proust* Beckett refers to this idea: he says that the outer world is "a projection of the individual's consciousness (an objectivation of the individual's will, Schopenhauer would say). . . ."[25] A similar concept is introduced when Murphy decides that his own system has taken precedence over the celestial system:

> They were *his* stars, he was the prior system. He had been projected, larval and dark, on the sky of that regrettable hour as on a screen, magnified and clarified into his own meaning. But it was *his* meaning.[26]

The struggle for priority between the two systems leads to a new way of understanding the errors and inconsistencies in the novel. If Murphy's is the prior system, there is no need for the narrator's descriptions of celestial phenomena to be in accord with those of the almanac. Indeed, strict conformity to astronomical data would suggest that the system of the novel is subordinate to the system of the outer world. The narrator, however, indicates that the world of the novel is a closed system, and one with priority over other systems.

A related idea emerges in still another passage about the moon. According to the almanac, the moon was visible before dawn on 21 October 1935; and it set long after sunrise.[27] But the narrator, using a balanced sentence, disagrees: "An hour previously the moon had been obliged to set, and the sun could not rise for an hour to come" (pp. 250–51). Symmetry is the controlling factor here, and not the almanac. Once Murphy has repudiated the other system, the narrator no longer feels compelled to follow it. He himself is perhaps the one who "obliged" the moon to set. Soon after this passage he describes the "starless" and "abandoned" sky; presumably it is starless because Murphy has abandoned it.

Other events in the novel do conform to the laws of the external world, but this is part of the narrator's strategy for credible mendacity. Most of the time, fallacious material is introduced sparingly, and is surrounded by easily verified facts. To gain the reader's confidence, the narrator even calls attention to possible errors: "The next day," he says at one point, "was Saturday (if our reckoning is correct) . . . " (p. 149). As might be expected, in this instance the date has been calculated accurately.

When Ticklepenny claims that he once saw Murphy drunk, the narrator finds it necessary to set the record straight: "Now the sad truth was that Murphy never touched it" (p. 86). This, so far as one can tell, is in fact "the sad truth." But this phrase later resurfaces in a less reliable context: "The sad truth was that the skylight commanded only that most dismal patch of night sky, the galactic coal-sack . . . " (p. 188).

One factor that makes the errors hard to discover is that many of them are based on obscure facts. Not too many readers will know that Hippasos was drowned at sea and not (as Neary claims) in a puddle.[28] Another subtle error is introduced in a passage about "Barbara, Baccardi . . . Baroko . . . Bramantip" (p. 16). These are medieval mnemonic terms that represent different types of syllogisms—all of them, that is, except for Baccardi, which has been substituted for a legitimate term, Bocardo.[29] The device resembles an intelligence-test problem where one must discover the item that does not belong in a series. Baccardi also appears in the French version of *Murphy*.[30] Beckett wittily uses the spurious term to allude to a beverage that might provide some respite from the rigors of medieval logic.

A similar sense of playfulness emerges in other unreliable passages where author and reader are involved in a battle of wits. The chess game hints at this idea: Murphy, naturally enough, takes it for granted that the game will be played in the conventional way; but Mr. Endon has introduced new rules. Beckett's readers will probably also begin by assuming that Beckett is following the conventional rules of novel-writing. Discovering that the rules have changed is part of the challenge; but it would be unsporting to introduce the new rules without any warning. Hence Beckett includes errors that are relatively easy to detect, like the faulty enumeration of scarves; these make it easier for readers to discover other unreliable passages.

Many of the recurring passages are similarly used to hint at the pattern of unreliability. The narrator reveals that he has been taking liberties with the dialogue by saying three times that a character's remarks have been "expurgated, accelerated, improved and reduced" (pp. 12, 48, 119). Cleverly, Beckett reveals that the dialogue has not been transcribed verbatim by repeating the disclosure verbatim.

Repetition is often used to underscore ironical passages. Neary's letters to Wylie and Miss Counihan both begin with the same sentence: "I can never forget your loyalty" (p. 199). Neary means, of course, that he will long remember their treachery. The narrator refers four times in as many pages to Murphy's success in achieving rapport with the mental patients (pp. 180–83). This ironically foreshadows Murphy's failure with the only patient he really cares for, Mr. Endon.

Utilizing a technique he introduced in *More Pricks Than Kicks*, Beckett calls attention to unreliable statements by repeating them. The following are among the misleading ideas that are reiterated:

> that Murphy is a strict nonreader (pp. 162, 234);
> that silence is one of Murphy's highest attributes (pp. 32, 39, 164);
> that Murphy possesses great magical ability of the eye (pp. 32, 39, 157, 183);
> that it is a striking coincidence for the moon to be full and at perigee (pp. 26, 121).

Beckett's method involves using a formal device, repetition, to counter the errors in the subject matter. In this way, even when the content flirts with the truth, the style remains faithful to it.

Sometimes—the episode about Ticklepenny's wages is an example—the unreliable narrative contributes to the characterization: one discovers that Bim, in addition to his many other defects as a human being, is miserly and incapable of affection. Other unreliable passages, like those about astronomy and astrology, suggest that it is pointless to argue about which type of knowledge is superior to any other. Every system that attempts to give a faithful and comprehensive view of the outer world will eventually collapse under a weight of enigma or error. The various unreliable passages in the novel all hint at an underlying theme: that the world is not what it seems to be, that it can never be what it seems to be. The unreliable narrative in *Murphy* is in an ultimate sense not at all unreliable; for it depicts, in a truthful way, the illusions and deceptions of the outer world.

1. Samuel Beckett, *Murphy* (1938; rpt. New York: Grove Press, 1957); subsequent references will be to this edition. "A strict non-reader," pp. 162, 234. This discrepancy has been noted by Ruby Cohn; see *Back to Beckett* (Princeton, N.J.: Princeton University Press, 1973), p. 33. References to Fletcher, p. 49; Swift ("Lilliputian wine," etc.), p. 139; Wordsworth, p. 100; Dante ("Antepurgatory," etc.), pp. 77–78; Campanella, p. 17; Bishop Bouvier, p. 72. According to Hannah Copeland, Bouvier's book is an example of the "imaginary works" in *Murphy* (see *Art and Artist in the Works of Samuel Beckett* [The Hague: Mouton, 1975], p. 63). In fact, Jean-Baptiste Bouvier's *Dissertatio in Sextum Decalogi praeceptum et Supplementum ad Tractatus de Matrimoni* was published in Le Mans in 1827, and went through a number of editions.

2. On page 1 the narrator says of the chair, "it never left him"; on page 189 he refers to the chair as "that aid to life in his mind from which [Murphy] had never before been parted." Even so, the original statement is misleading.

3. A. Alvarez calls the passage about the scarves one of the two places he knows of in Beckett's works "where his arithmetic lets him down" (*Samuel Beckett* [New York: Viking Press, 1973], p. 9).

4. John Mood, "'The Personal System'—Samuel Beckett's *Watt*," *PMLA* 86 (March 1971): 255–65. Mood writes, "The mistakes were certainly planned. If there had been one or two, we could write it off as someone's error. Twenty-eight mistakes clearly indicate a deliberate strategy at work, particularly when linked to the many other mistakes pointed out by the text itself" (p. 263).

5. Ticklepenny says he was promised five pounds a month on page 89; he is offered one-six-eight on page 157. The irony in the phrase "a fancy not far short of love" emerges when it is repeated (pp. 156, 157). In the French version of *Murphy*, references to currency are usually converted from sterling to francs (e.g., Murphy's fourpenny lunch); here however, the currency remains unchanged, and the passage is translated with the same figure as in the English version. Beckett preserved the miscalculation, and wanted it to remain subtle: the difficulty of computing in the old British system is what makes Bim's maneuver hard to detect. See *Murphy* (Paris: Les Edition de Minuit, 1965), pp. 69 ("cinq livres par mois"), and 116 ("une livre six shillings et huit pence").

6. Page 92. A phrase related to Murphy's prediction, "Murphy was inclined to think" is repeated on page 92; this calls attention to the passage about the head male nurse.

7. Mr. Endon, who never whinges, may not be a puppet; but on p. 241 he is called a "figurine."

8. The predictions about fits and quadrupeds are on p. 32; Murphy's fit of laughter, "more like one of epilepsy," is described on pp. 139–40; the warning about quadrupeds is justified when the dog Nellie eats Murphy's biscuits, p. 100.

9. According to the statement in the horoscope, the moon's position at the time of Murphy's birth "promotes great Magical Ability of the Eye, to which the lunatic would easy succumb" (p. 32). The reference to the moon may indicate "the lunatic" is really Murphy. Murphy stares into Mr. Endon's eyes on pp. 248–49; and he concedes defeat on p. 250.

10. Celia says, "Avoid exhaustion by speech" on p. 37, repeating a line from the horoscope. Later Celia, "in weary ellipsis of Suk," practices what she preaches and says only, "Avoid exhaustion" when she urges Murphy to remain silent (p. 138).

11. Page 32. Suk is giving the position, in degrees, of the constellation that was rising when Murphy was born (the constellation is "THE GOAT," or Capricorn). Unless Suk invented the figures in the horoscope, he would have needed to know the time of Murphy's birth to within a few minutes: it takes about four minutes for a degree of longitude on the celestial sphere to traverse the horizon.

12. Murphy is twice called a "young man" and twice a "young aspirant" (p. 53). On page 75 the narrator indicates that in a year it will be 1936; and the dates given by the narrator (e.g., he refers to Thursday, 12 September, and to Friday, 11 October, on p. 114) occur in 1935.

13. According to Suk, Neptune is in "the Bull" (Taurus), and "Herschel" (Uranus) is in Aquarius (p. 33). Herschel is an old name for Uranus; and later the two planets are mentioned again (p. 230). The repetition serves as a clue to the unreliability in the horoscope passage.

14. The sidereal period of Neptune is 163.9 years. If Neptune is in Taurus between 1874 and 1889, it would not return to that constellation in the twentieth century; and it would not have been there more than once in the nineteenth century. Information on the zodiacal positions of the planets is taken from Grant Lewi, *Astrology for the Millions,* 4th ed. (New York: Bantam Books, 1978), pp. 268, 259.

15. On page 114 the narrator says that Celia's triumph over Murphy "was gained about the middle of September, Thursday the 12th to be pedantic. . . ." The triumph (which is described on p. 41) comes "in the morning" (p. 29); the narrator says that the moon was full and at perigee on the night before (p. 26). This would be 11 September 1935.

16. The moon was at perigee at about 6 P.M. on 12 September 1935. This and other data about the moon's position are from editions of Joseph Whitaker's *Almanack* (London) for the years 1931–35. According to the astronomer Fred L. Whipple, the moon is full and at perigee about once a year; see *Earth, Moon, and Planets* (Philadelphia: Blakiston Co., 1946), p. 106.

17. The moon's average perigee distance is 225,757 miles, and the smallest perigee distance is 221, 463 miles. The maximum variation in perigee distances would be about twice the difference between these figures, or about 8,500

miles. It should be pointed out that such a figure represents an extreme: monthly variations in perigee distance are far smaller than this. Information about lunar distances is taken from Charles M. Huffer, et al., *An Introduction to Astronomy* (New York: Holt, Rinehart, and Winston, 1967), pp. 145–46.

18. Coal-sacks, also known as dark nebulae, are clouds of dust that obscure the stars beyond them; but some stars, closer to earth than the clouds, still are visible in front of them. The most prominent coal-sack in the northern hemisphere is in the constellation Lynx. For an observer in London (the M.M.M. is near London), only an object at the celestial north pole would seem to remain fixed in the sky. But there is no dark nebula in the immediate vicinity of the celestial pole; and a fairly bright star, Polaris, is located about a degree from the pole.

19. There are other passages that suggest that the diminishing importance of the stars is a sign that Murphy is withdrawing into himself. The second time the narrator says that Murphy has confidence in only two systems (p. 76), he adds: "So much the worse for him, no doubt." The narrator's attitude is like Suk's: both are skeptical about Murphy's theories. Suk advises Murphy to "resort to Harmony" (p. 32); this comment runs parallel to the narrator's observation about the "disharmony" in Murphy's two systems (p. 76).

20. The "stars he commanded," p. 175; "his stars," pp. 76, 85, 93, 183; "superfluous cartoon," p. 189. Murphy's comments about "his stars" can be compared to one about "his own dark" (p. 91). This last phrase suggests that Murphy cannot see the stars from his garret because they are obscured by his own dark.

21. The epigraph (p. 32) is from *Romeo and Juliet*, 5.1.24; the italics are Beckett's.

22. *Romeo and Juliet*, 3.2.21.

23. See Dante, *Inferno*, 3. 23; 16. 83; 34. 139.

24. Arthur Schopenhauer, *The World as Will and Idea*, trans. R. Haldane and J. Kemp (1883; rpt. London: Routlege and Kegan Paul, 1957), 1:532. (The subsequent volumes of this work contain supplements to the first; hence the end of the first volume can be considered the conclusion.) In German, the end of the passage quoted in the text reads, "diese unsere so sehr reale Welt mit allen ihren Sonnen und Milchstrassen—Nichts."

25. Samuel Beckett, *Proust* (1931; rpt. New York: Grove Press, 1957), p. 8. For Schopenhauer's comments on "objectivation of the will," see *The World as Will and Idea*, 1:123 and ff., esp. pp. 140, 219; and 3:48 and ff.

26. Page 183. The italics are Beckett's.

27. The date can be established as follows: on page 235 the narrator says that it is the afternoon of 20 October; the comment about the moon having set refers to the next dawn. Information about sunrise and moonset is taken from Whitaker's *Almanack* (London, 1935), pp. 110, 114. It is possible to detect this inconsistency even without an almanac. The moon in its third quarter rises in the middle of the night and sets in the middle of the day (see Stanley Wyatt, *Principles of Astronomy* [Boston: Allyn and Bacon, 1974], p. 133). The narrator says that there was a full moon on 11 October; hence, eleven days later, on the

night of the 20–21, the moon is just past its third quarter and sets well after sunrise. This corresponds to the information in Whitaker's *Almanack* for 21 October 1935: moonrise, 2:10 A.M.; moonset, 2:36 P.M.; sunrise, 6:34 A.M.

28. Page 47. Beckett's account of the drowning of Hippasos is probably based on a passage in John Burnet's *Greek Philosophy*, Part 1 (London: Macmillan, 1924), pp. 55–56. The wording in Beckett's version of the story resembles Burnet's but Burnet makes it clear that Hippasos was drowned at sea. The joke is preserved in the French version of *Murphy*: Hippasos is drowned in a sewer (*"égout"*), (*Murphy*, p. 40).

29. The distortion is greater than it seems to be because the change of vowels in the Baccardi-Bocardo substitution completely alters the significance of the term. The terms Beckett refers to are the first four in a series of nineteen; each one represents a different type of syllogism. A description of the system can be found in *The Encyclopedia of Philosophy* (New York: Macmillan and the Free Press, 1967), 5:69.

30. *Murphy*, p. 18.

H. Porter Abbott

The Harpooned Notebook:
Malone Dies and the Conventions of
Intercalated Narrative

I wish to focus on how Samuel Beckett's *Malone Dies* carries on one of the traditional modes of the novel: the intercalated or nonretrospective narrative. In what I am calling a mode, I mean to include that abundance of novels in letter or diary form which have been produced from the earliest years of the novel, which are still with us, and which require at least two principal fictions: that the narrative we read is written by at least one of its principal characters and that the time of its writing is contained by the time of the events recorded. *Malone* is the extremest example of the mode I know. So extreme is it that one is tempted to call it a travesty or grotesque satire. My argument is that it is in fact, in its extremity, not satire but a continuation of the mode, carried out in much the same spirit as that of its early practitioners. To tackle this, I must first reduce the field. There is an array of conventions, or *topoi*, that recur in a sort of loose confederation through the history of this mode, many of which can be found, faintly or vividly, in *Malone*. In my argument, I shall focus on three: two central and one peripheral. They are, respectively, the threatened manuscript, the merging of the times of narrative and narration, and the blank entry.

The *topos*, or motif, of the threatened manuscript gives us a good place to start because it bears directly on the crucial documentary character of the mode. It will allow me to expand a bit here at the beginning on the traditional importance, in this mode, of the text as a material object or empirical certainty. In studies of the eighteenth-century novel, this importance has generally been accounted for by its appeal to a conception of reality biased—by science and middle-class attitudes—toward the material and the measurable. Thus an art form came of age disguised as a form of nonart. It pretended not only to tell "true" stories in the words of "real" people (as opposed to professional authors), but also to provide the objective evidence of these stories in the form of letters or diaries that often comprised in themselves the whole of the narration.

But if this emphasis on the physical text had its roots in a bourgeois or vulgarly scientific fixation on the visible and the material, one of its major consistent functions was to give testimony to the invisible and nonmaterial. In a paradox that is perhaps more verbal than real, the text's degree of materiality and visible exactitude constituted its credentials as a testimony of the spirit. In the eighteenth century, this was particularly true of those novels that came out of a Puritan or sentimental frame of mind. When Pamela asks permission to rewrite one of her letters before turning it over to Mr. B., he protests that she must leave it exactly as it is "because," he tells her, "they are your true sentiments at *the time,* and because they were *not* written for my perusal."[1] The letters are an archeological record of precisely how what we cannot see in Pamela—that is, what is really important about Pamela—moved at the time. And as we read them, our invisible natures are moved too. Not to be so moved is to miss their significance—that is, to be hopelessly materialistic.

So what is curious is the combination. The spirit cannot be taken for granted. Correlatively, a story cannot be just a story. A material artifact is required as evidence of a particular spirit. As the time of her certain departure from this world draws near, Clarissa takes great pains to ensure the perpetuation of her letters—the literary evidence of her existence—in their exact form. The urgency of her concern is an odd element in the story of her life, considering her avowed confidence in the universe, how it is constituted, by Whom and to what end. So it is possible that her concern for the texts of her letters in this material world expresses her—and no doubt her author's—submerged uncertainty about the invisible world.

Readers shared Clarissa's anxiety about the physical preservation of the manuscript, and for this reason threats to the existence of the document became standard equipment of the mode I am discussing. Manuscripts have been scorched and water-soaked, rescued from fire, mildewed, eaten by worms, stuffed in boxes, lost, buried, bottled and floated upon the sea. When the diaries of Lermontov's Pechorin are flung upon the ground in anger, one after the other, it goes to the heart. The drama of the survival of the text has become a part of the drama of the tale. Frequently augmenting this drama is the fact that the diarist or letter-writer is dead by the time we read the evidence of his or her life. The text is all that remains. Moreover, a good many of the writers are not only dead as we read but doomed or dying even as they write.[2]

This is the tradition that Malone dies into. In the context of Beckett's literary career, *Malone Dies* comes at that point when Beckett, moving closer and closer to the page, suddenly brought the document itself into focus before plunging on through it into the "Where now? Who now? When now?" of the monologue that follows. At the point of focus, Beckett brings the whole tradition of which I have been speaking into focus at the same time—but seen now, as it were, so close up that it appears a grotesque caricature. Never has there been so wasted a moribund. Rarely has the room in which he writes been so thoroughly an enclosure, so thoroughly an expression of his isolation. And rarely has the document itself been so continually at risk. Its existence depends not on a pen but on a pencil—and one so used that its life is barely that of the writer. Sharpened at both ends, it is reduced by the last pages to a small piece of lead. As for the exercise-book, it gets lost, falls on the floor, at one point is "harpooned" by Malone with his stick.

By such means does Beckett augment the metaphysical anxiety—for so long a part of the mode—that drives reader and writer alike to want to hold fast to the material document. This anxiety is also brilliantly augmented by Beckett's inclusion of a distinct remnant of the novel's middle-class origins: the inventory of his goods and chattels that Malone is so concerned to make. In evoking this annual rite of shopkeepers, here hopelessly botched, Beckett goes beyond satire to the heart of the businessman's very human ailment. You cannot take it with you. Moreover, once he is fully launched on his enterprise, Malone finds that by his definition (those things are his he can lay hold of) "nothing is mine anymore . . . except my exercise-book, my lead and the French pencil, assuming it really exists."[3] Now the French pencil, he cannot lay his hands on. And the lead is doomed. This leaves only one possession, as he has anticipated: "No, nothing of all that is mine. But the exercise-book is mine, I can't explain" (p. 247). Malone's text is his only thing.

In *Malone Dies*, the whole business of possessions and inventories, of the entire material universe, draws to a point. Malone, at the end of this history, resigns himself to the suppressed intuition that led Clarissa to expend so much energy on the fate of her letters. "This exercise-book is my life," he says at last, "this child's exercise-book, it has taken me a long time to resign myself to that" (p. 274). But in resigning himself, Malone at the same time relinquishes both the book and the "life." In coalescing words with things, Beckett puts them on one side of a gulf, on the other side of which Malone maintains his allegiance, however reluctantly, to the wordless and immaterial. In this Malone shows a deeper conviction of the invisible than Clarissa, and a deeper commitment to it, just as his creator exposes the book and its words as a snare and a delusion—not the right vehicle after all. The skewered notebook brings to an end the tradition of meticulous fictional editing that begins with Richardson.

The next element that I wish to discuss is the tendency of nonretrospective art to close the gap between the time of the narrating and the time of the narrated, of *discours* and *histoire*. To put this in other words, the narrative in this mode aspires to the warmest possible relationship to time. Early intimations of this can be seen in Milton's expansion of the conventional epic invocation of the muse to a periodic reunion with time in which he expands on what Malone would call his "present state." This aesthetic merging with time is essentially what Beckett focused on in his valuation of Proust as a romantic. The classical artist, by contrast, "raises himself artificially out of Time in order to give relief to his chronology and causality to his development."[4] From this point of view, the dying Malone, whose time finally runs out, is the ultimate romantic artist; and his exercise-book, the final collapse of art into time.

What is missing in Malone and what is essential to many of his romantic predecessors is a belief that form and time are compatible: moreover, that genuine form (as opposed to artificial, classical form) can be tapped by merging with time. It is a theory that runs parallel to the theory of spontaneous artistic creation and resides in a faith that form is an aspect of the invisible. Goethe's Werther was guided by it in his effusions. Later, Coleridge, drawing on the ideas of Schlegel, called such form "organic" and opposed it to "mechanic" or imposed form. In his Conversation Poems, which are a species of diaristic moments, Coleridge sought to submit himself to this vital forming agency by submitting himself to time. Tennyson sought the same thing in his long poetic diary In Memoriam. As Tennyson points out in the poem itself, it was only through his submission to time that he achieved the form of In Memoriam, a form in the shape of a curve extending from grief to rejoicing.

The difference between Malone and his romantic predecessors is that for Malone form and time are completely at odds. This dissociation, of course, is not new with Malone. During the evolution of intercalated narrative, one can find it implicitly or explicitly in a number of late-nineteenth-century French and Scandinavian diary novels, many of them inspired by the intimate journals of Amiel. The most baldly explicit expression of the dissociation of form and time was developed by Sartre in his diary novel of 1938, Nausea. The difference between Malone and these later representatives of the tradition is that Malone maintains attention on the invisible, both as a mystery and as a kind of presence. Moreover, though one of his terms for the invisible is now "formlessness," he carries over from his romantic precursors their awed regard for it. It is the source of seriousness and gravity. If it is the opposite of Milton's informing Spirit, Malone employs a very Miltonic intensity, echoing the fall of Satan, in expressing his devotion to

> darkness, to nothingness, to earnestness, to home, to him waiting for me always, who needed me and whom I needed, who took me in his arms and told me to stay with him always, who gave me his place and watched over me, who suffered every time I left him, whom I have often made suffer and seldom contented, whom I have never seen. (P. 195)

So, again, as in the case of the threatened manuscript, Beckett maintains our attention on the absent subject by accentuating a traditional element of intercalated narrative. He compounds the collapse of mechanic form by having Malone aspire hopelessly to the condition of the omniscient and omnipotent artist. Malone draws on what remains of the left lobe of his brain to fulfill the requirements of a plan, a plan that, as we know, not only falls in ruins but begins to break down the moment it is formulated. His stories are swamped by his present state; time lies heavy on the notebook. It does so because Malone cannot help but keep faith, more even than his romantic forebears, with the invisible power, shrouded in darkness, that is the source of his vitality—"the nourishing murk," as he calls it, "that is killing me" (p. 193).

The final convention I wish to consider is what could be called the Blank Entry. It is a more infrequent element than the two I have discussed already, one strictly limited to the diary strain of intercalated narrative. In the blank entry, one finds the date, followed by a blank, or a question mark or, at most, some verbal formula for blankness: "Nothing at all to report today." Its close relative is the Boring Entry, which could be any such desultory noncomment as "Ate at 7:00, fell asleep shortly thereafter." They are what can make the reading of real diaries such a low-yield, searingly tedious activity. Duhamel parodied both devices in *Salavin's Journal* when he had Salavin decide to become a saint. Salavin buys a new journal, which he begins with great anticipation:

> On with the new life! Would that I were older by one year, to be able to re-read this journal and weep with joy! I am ready. I'm waiting. I'm off to meet myself.
> January 8—Nothing to report.
> January 9—Nothing to report.
> January 10—Nothing.
> January 11—Nothing that has to do with the situation in any way.
> January 12—Nothing.
> January 13—Nothing. It's snowing, but that's of no importance. (To be struck out if I copy this journal.)
> January 14—Nothing.[5]

And so on for another fourteen entries. In *Nausea* Sartre parodied the same device when he had Roquentin make the entry, "Nothing. Existed,"[6] which was especially coy, since Roquentin had just achieved insights into the linked nature of both Nothingness and Existence.

In fictional diaries, the blank or boring entry is an obvious liability, one that is rarely indulged in with any frequency. Its principal function is one that it shares with a number of those devices that Ian Watt collected under the heading Formal Realism. It is a way of saying, "This is not art" (assuming the logic that if this were art, there would not be this kind of wasted space). It increases the documentary illusion. But the matter is not quite as simple as this because inevitably we cannot help knowing that this *is* art and therefore necessarily concentrated, full of import. So the blank or boring entry is also a way of saying, "Watch out, something must be preparing itself." The ratio of these two opposed functions would appear to depend on just how firmly we believe that, despite the nonretrospective appearance of the document, there is a secret teleology at work. Roquentin's comment about the traditional fat of the retrospective story is apt even for the nonretrospective document: "It was night, the street was deserted."[7] As he says, we do not let these words pass unnoticed. We read them as annunciations of adventure, endowed with meaning by the future that pre-exists them. Nonretrospective structure can at once increase the legitimacy of such dullness as it increases the excitement.

Malone Dies is, in effect, an extension of the principle of the boring entry to the entire novel. It is one of the few books in which the teleological illusion Roquentin writes of, which redeems an entry of its tedium, appears to be convincingly demolished from the start. The only conclusion, a foregone one, is the writer's death, which, in the case of Malone, is basically a matter of being "quite dead at last." It is an arbitrary, radically unclimactic terminus for the words he writes. Its onset is marked by one of the blankest of blank entries:

never anything

there

any more

The only thing blanker is the blankness of the page that one may project from the last word to infinity.

But the actual blankness of the page is, in fact, something that plays a significant role in the body of this text. It pierces the text at points throughout—a whiteness separating blocks of prose. And it figures, if I am right, as the ultimate logical development, not only of the device of the blank entry, but of the mode in which I am locating the book. And it expresses in its blankness the same double quality I have been discussing, for it implies at once nothing and something that exceeds the importance of the text it sets off. There are modern examples one can find of an approach to this extreme.[8] But I can think of few that, in the manner of *Malone Dies*, actually incorporate the total blank as a recurring element in the text—an element that operates, if you will, as a signifier.

"My notes," writes Malone, "have a curious tendency . . . to annihilate all they purport to record" (p. 259). But in the blanks, "the noises begin again . . . those whose turn it is" (p. 206). In one forty-eight–hour blank, he claims that the whole "unutterable" business of Malone and the other was brought to a "solution and conclusion" (p. 222). These blanks are, in effect, the ultimate means of humbling the text. They are where the action is. They signify a presence not completely unlike that for which Derrida took Rousseau to task. In the very violence Beckett exerts against the text, here in the last outpost of the notebook tradition, he preserves not only the idea but the urgency of the text's referential function.

In reviewing these three conventions—the threatened manuscript, the merging of the times of narrating and narrative, and the blank entry—I find that my humanistic perspective on Beckett has acquired a distinctly romantic coloration. I have tried to show how he writes not simply in the mode of intercalated fiction but in the spirit of its early development. In bringing each of these elements to an extreme, Beckett is perhaps the last romantic, asserting his artistic allegiance to what is invisible and mysterious and forever beyond the text.

1. Samuel Richardson, *Pamela*, vol. 1 (London: Dent, 1962), p. 292.

2. Clarissa, Werther, Jacopo Ortiz, Pechorin, Hugo's Condemned Man, Turgenev's Superfluous Man, Poe's author of the "MS. Found in a Bottle," Bernanos' Curé, Mauriac's Louis of *The Nest of Vipers*.

3. Samuel Beckett, *Malone Dies*, in *Three Novels by Samuel Beckett* (New York: Grove Press, 1965), p. 255; subsequent page references will appear in the text.

4. Samuel Beckett, *Proust* (New York: Grove Press, 1957), p. 62.

5. Georges Duhamel, *Salavin*, trans. Gladys Billings (London: Dent, 1936), p. 92.

6. Jean-Paul Sartre, *Nausea*, trans. Lloyd Alexander (New York: New Directions, 1959), p. 140.

7. Ibid., p. 58.

8. I am thinking particularly of such works as Max Frisch's *I'm Not Stiller*, Doris Lessing's *The Golden Notebook*, and Alberto Moravia's *The Lie*, all of them a part of the notebook tradition and all of them, in their individual ways, inviting us to look through the falsehood of words to an invisible and inexpressible internal reality.

Allen Thiher

Wittgenstein, Heidegger, the Unnamable, and Some Thoughts on the Status of Voice in Fiction

I wish to discuss in this paper the relation between modern theories of language and the practice of fiction. Specifically I wish to suggest some homologies between issues raised in Samuel Beckett's *The Unnamable*[1] and theoretical positions found primarily in the work of Wittgenstein and Heidegger, though I shall also make some allusions to the structuralist views of language derived from the work of Ferdinand de Saussure. And more specifically, I wish to ask what is the status of voice in Beckett and how this question is illuminated by considering theoretical or philosophical points of view on the status of voice within a general theory of language. For in a way curiously analogous to fiction, every language theory must ask who speaks and whence the speaker speaks. Modern theory answers these two questions in terms of a series of oppositions that, I would maintain, set the limits for the way we think about the status of voice in a literary text. And in turn, certain key literary texts, such as *The Unnamable*, contest those limits by actually living them as an impossibility.

Much of language theory is concerned with setting the boundaries of the sayable. This creating of boundaries thus sets theory as an irritating other to the literary voice by making of it an arbiter of the boundaries of what might be said therein. This

state of affairs establishes a hostile complicity between literature and philosophy, and in many postmodern works this
complicity gives rise to a kind of *lamento* about the work's desire
for the unsayable.

In this respect, one cannot overestimate the importance that
Wittgenstein's *Tractatus* continues to have for the writer who
faces language as a limit to his voice. In fact, the *Tractatus* remains the *locus classicus* for the notion that the limits of (the)
world are established by language, that the limits of my world
coincide, insofar as I can speak my world, with the limits of my
language. Wittgenstein's first work thus casts many doubts
upon language by suggesting that it is somehow less pure than
such perfect constructs as logic, mathematics—or silence. The
only voice that can meaningfully speak, according to the
Tractatus, is a voice that is certain of a limited number of atom-
istic propositions. Moreover, this meaningful voice can say
nothing about itself, for the speaking voice is excluded from the
world that discourse can represent: "The subject does not belong to the world: rather, it is a limit of the world" (5. 632).
Thus, in a strict sense, the speaking voice can say nothing about
what it is saying. It can only record states of affairs, much like a
hyper-realist catalogue that excludes itself from its listing.

Although Wittgenstein's second period of thought is essentially a critique of the representational view of language that the
Tractatus offers, there is little in his second phase that provides
support for those traditional humanist views of language that
assume an unmediated relationship between self and voice or
voice and discourse. In the *Philosophical Investigations,* voices
arise as forms of participation in the various language games
that, with their innumerable overlappings, make up that entity
we give the name "language." Language games are thus the
multiple public spaces and the rules for their arrangement that
go to make up the world. And if one asks where is the self that
lies behind the speaking voice, the answer seems to be that the
self is only a kind of abbreviation for talking about the multiple
ways in which voices enter into language games. Or, if taken as
a substantial notion, the self can only be viewed as a metaphysical error arising from a misunderstanding about the

nature of language. There is no self to be spoken, no inner locus that is the source of meaning, for the locus of speaking is merely speaking itself.

The writer who turns from Wittgenstein's work to Heidegger's voluminous production may be surprised to find many analogies between the two. In Heidegger's early work, especially in *Being and Time*, he would discover that there is rarely, if ever, such a thing as an individual speaker. For what is taken to be the individual voice is really the voice of *das Man*, the anonymous "they" that speak, through inauthentic speech, the fallen logos of everyday existence. The only authentic voice would appear to be the voice of silence that stands opposed in silent resolve to the "they" that speak a language of publicly determined meanings, a language that has fallen from the plenitude of authentic being. Although Heidegger declares in his later work that language is the house of being, he never really gives up his view that everyday language is a form of fallen logos. But in his second phase, he does summon the poet to become a speaker of authentic language by listening to the call of Being and letting logos speak through him, such as Hölderlin presumedly did. For it is language that speaks, not the Cartesian self that believes it is empowered to use language to mediate its thoughts. It is language that, in speaking, differentiates being against the backdrop of silence. Autonomous saying— Heidegger's *die Sage*—is a showing of being as being itself. Heidegger's claims for language in effect evacuate the self from language, leaving the writer in the difficult position of facing language as either the inauthentic expression of otherness or the grandiose revelation of Being itself.

Heidegger's influence is also instrumental, I think, in the way many have come to interpret the Saussurian distinction between voice and language system. One encounters here an opposition that turns on the difficulty Saussure had in at once vouchsafing the individual's capacity to speak an autonomous *parole*, or speech, and his need to make of the individual speaker a mere repository of the autonomous linguistic system, or *la langue*. Later structuralists have certainly emphasized the second half of the opposition, which coincides with Heidegger's contention that language, not man, speaks. What voice can be said to speak if the speaker is only a storehouse of his culture's linguistic system, of its codes, syntagms, and potential paradigmatic options? Such a question finds an answer of sorts in Derrida's claim that it is therefore language that constitutes the subject, a formulation that aims, I think, to reverse two thousand years' of thought on the subject. And such a view of the autonomy of the linguistic system underlies Foucault's even more resounding and ironic claim that man is dead.

Dead he may be, but this death does not prevent him from speaking, as we see constantly in Beckett's prolonged sonata of the dead. And it seems to me that this elusive Irishman's fiction presents exemplary postmodern responses to the questions and paradoxes that modern language theory brings up. For central to all of Beckett's fiction, and especially to the works written in French and even more particularly to *The Unnamable,* is a constant self-interrogation about the status of the voice that speaks, about its relation to the language it speaks, and about the locus whence it speaks.

Let us recall in this respect how the unnamable comes to be the final speaker in Beckett's trilogy of novels. First Molloy speaks to us about his narration, which is followed by Moran's voice narrating his attempt to join Molloy. Both of these voices seem to be present to the Malone of *Malone Dies* as he, another bedridden speaker, talks about his narration and offers the tale of Macmann. This bloody tale comes to its end with Malone's declaring that he will never say "I" again, although he immediately breaks his vow as he concludes the tale of the homicidal outing from the insane asylum. The refusal to say "I" brings the reader to the voice named the unnamable, who begins his speaking with a question: "Where now? When now? Who now? Unquestioning. I, say I." The original "Dire je" conveys even more forcefully the imperative sense of the voice that must order itself to use the first person pronoun and hence force itself into complicity with the structure of language. And his questions point at the same time to the separation that seems to exist between voice and language. For *The Unnamable* takes the reader into a narrative space that is inhabited by a voice that cannot speak except in nearly contradictory fashion to assert that it is not his language that speaks; thus it is not he who really speaks, though the I-voice would appear to have no choice about using this language if the voice wishes to decry this intolerable situation. For the unnamable finds himself undertaking the impossible quest to get around language, a quest that must perforce fall back onto language, onto stories, pseudo-narrations, other voices and laments, if the quest is to exist at all.

Beckett's reduction of fiction to this kind of self-reflexive rumination obliges us to ask what does it mean to say that voice and language are separated. For the unnamable's plight is perhaps the central one for illuminating the way much of contemporary fiction functions and, moreover, for seeing how theoretical concerns have become the very stuff of this fiction. Or perhaps it would be more precise to say, how literature seeks strategies for overcoming its own unhappy belief in language theory.

The homologies between Beckett's literary performances and the philosophical ones I briefly outlined are many, and they underlie the seemingly paradoxical assertion that voice and language can be separated, that there is indeed a place where, as the unnamable puts it, "language dies that permits of such expressions" (p. 335). *The Unnamable*'s paradox first sends us back to read Heidegger again and to ask if we have found that region of intersection between the realm where authentic language is heard only in silence and the realm of average everydayness where the babble one hears belongs to the anonymous other. For the unnamable, if he dreams of silence, seems to reside precisely in that region where the only language he finds is, by its very ontology, the language of everybody, and hence nobody. His narrative trajectory thus moves toward a paradoxical ending that the other's language prevents from taking place:

All this business of a labour to accomplish, before I can end, of words to say, a truth to recover, in order to say it, before I can end, of an imposed task, once known, long neglected, finally forgotten, to perform, before I can be done with speaking, done with listening, I invented it all, in the hope it would console me, help me to go on, allow me to think of myself as somewhere on a road, moving, between a beginning and an end, gaining ground, losing ground, getting lost, but somehow in the long run making headway. All lies. I have nothing to do, that is to say nothing in particular. I have to speak, whatever that means. Having nothing to say, no words but the words of others, I have to speak. (P. 314)

As pure voice, the unnamable can do nothing, for in Beckett's world to say is to do; and he cannot speak since he has no language, except the language of everyone and no one. The unnamable thus sits chattering, looking across a silent space at Heidegger's authentic man, that hero who remains locked in his quiet resolve. Yet the unnamable's antics let us know that he exists, however paradoxically, and by contrast one might well suspect that quiet authenticity is a figment of a loquacious philosopher's imagination.

For the unnamable is a clown version of the man who would live authentically by speaking his own language. He is a clown who stands in relation to his own discourse much like the philosopher who uttered the axioms of the *Tractatus,* a work of metaphysical nonsense whose goal, according to Wittgenstein, was to annul itself. Yet the unnamable is irremediably caught in a bizarre public space where voices reverberate everywhere, public voices that seem to be a pluralization of *das Man*:

It must not be forgotten, sometimes I forget, that all is a question of voices. I say what I am told to say, in the hope that some day they will weary of talking at me. The trouble is I say it wrong, having no ear, no head, no memory. Now I seem to hear them say it is Worm's voice beginning, I pass on the news, for what it is worth. Do they believe I believe it is I who am speaking? That's theirs too. To make me believe I have an ego all my own, and can speak of it, as they of theirs. Another trap to snap me up among the living. (P. 345)

What the rather schizoid unnamable presumably demands is an ideolect that would be the language of his absolute specificity, for the self that is spoken by public language is a mere convention, a trap designed to ensnare as it transforms one into otherness.

In another sense, Beckett's narrator puts into practice not only the notion that language is a publicly determined repository of usages, but he also has a profound sense that his (or their) language is a social contract. The social bond that language requires is but another form of pluralized otherness and the unnamable refuses that social quality even as he affirms, in common with structural linguistics and the Wittgenstein of language games, the social basis of all language:

> It's of me now that I must speak, even if I have to do it with their language, it will be a start, a step towards silence and the end of madness, the madness of having to speak and not being able to, except of things that don't concern me. . . . Not to be able to open my mouth without proclaiming them, and our fellowship, that's what they imagine they'll have me reduced to. It's a poor trick that consists in ramming a set of words down your gullet on the principle that you can't bring them up without being branded as belonging to their breed. (P. 324)

Wittgenstein often said that to understand how a language game is played, it is often helpful to see how it is learned; for which the unnamable here sets forth the most general pedagogical principle the breed possesses for ensuring that the linguistic system will be, literally, internalized.

Thus the language of the tribe, as Beckett—after Mallarmé—puts it in French, cannot be the language of the voice that is engaged in a curious struggle for sanity. To speak a single word is, as the unnamable would have it, to enter into complicity with the tribe's codified system—or perhaps into complicity with the tribe's way of theorizing about its linguistic system. To speak is to force the voice to enter into an alterity that can be only a form of alienation. And even to say "I"—that "putain de la première personne"—is to accept the linguistic token that designates all voices. To say "I" is to accept something of a hoax fostered by the tribe's system of pronouns: for can "I" be "I" if every voice is "I"? Structural linguistics may point out that such a pronoun functions as a shifter, but this will bring little semantic succor to the speaker who feels that precisely such a semantic feature makes a mystification of the whole notion of personal identity.

In this novel, Worm does not speak, nor, declares the narrator, does he, and Mahood is aphonic. With this voiceless cast, who can, then, speak in this text, except perhaps language itself? And on the other side of language there might be— farcical hypothesis—a self possessing a voice unmediated by language, the pure self of Wittgenstein's *Tractatus* or Heidegger's unalienated man. Except, of course, that this view of the separation of language and self is a schizo-comedy that takes desperate delight in its own impossibility. In this sense, Beckett's work ushers in the era of the schizo-text that is perhaps the postmodern text *par excellence*. Beckett's work gives full expression to the voice alienated from itself, the voice for which the first and the third person pronoun are a matter of indifference. The speaker lives the "I" as an "it," for the voice is present to itself only as otherness:

> My voice. The voice. I hardly hear it any more. I'm going silent. Hearing this voice no more, that's what I call going silent. That is to say I'll hear it still, if I listen hard. I'll listen hard. Listening hard, that's what I call going silent. I'll hear it still, broken, faint, unintelligible, if I listen hard. Hearing it still, without hearing what it says, that's what I call going silent. Then it will flare up, like a kindling fire, a dying fire. Mahood explained that to me, and I'll emerge from silence. Hearing too little to be able to speak, that's my silence. (P. 393)

And thus the notion that one might listen to one's voice as the voice of someone else brings us to the paradox that one might speak silence.

For Beckett's narrators speak clamorously about silence. Like Wittgenstein's metaphysician narrator of the *Tractatus*, Beckett's narrators spend enormous amounts of logical energy saying the unsayable and talking about the unspeakable. And as in the case of Heidegger's vision of authenticity, one has the feeling that silence would be a kind of utopia where the voice, divested of the tribe's language, would have direct access to itself. In silence speaking and listening, I and it, would no longer be separated. The voice would be a pure self in which, as Derrida might have it, consciousness would be fully present to itself as a plenitude unmediated by the alienating otherness of the tribe's linguistic system. Yet Beckett's is a self-reflexive comic vision, and his noisy praise of silence mirrors Wittgenstein's dream of purity and Heidegger's claims for authenticity as in a distorting mirror:

> . . . with regard to me, nice time we're going to have now, with regard to me, that it has not yet been our good fortune to establish with any degree of accuracy what I am, where I am, whether I am words among words, or silence in the midst of silence, to recall only two of the hypotheses launched in this connexion, though silence to tell the truth does not appear to have been very conspicuous up to now, but appearances may sometimes be deceptive. . . . (Pp. 388–89)

Appearances may be deceptive; yet in spite of all one's worst intentions, it does appear that the mere saying "I" fosters the illusion that a self has been created, that a character is present, that a voice speaks. The tribe's linguistic system has many powers, and Beckett's narrators are constantly playing with variations on the idea that mere naming suffices to grant existence or to offer being. Heidegger's poet may have the task of authentic naming and thus confer being against the backdrop of silence; but Beckett's unnamable narrator clearly wants to resist the power of language to hustle him into existence. To say "I"—how can this confer being when it offers existence to every "I" and thus to the pluralized no one.

In Beckett's work and in many other contemporary texts, we find at work a comic equivocation about the nature of language. For, on the one hand, these texts declare that merely to name cannot of course confer existence, and that to accept the deceitful appearances of mere pronouns is to give consent to a fraud fostered by language. But, on the other hand, it is precisely the nature of literary language, or a feature of the ontology of fiction, that to name is to confer existence. Heidegger can, in his later writings, play with one side of this equivocation, and

Beckett, as if in response to these extraordinary claims for poetry, can play with the other side. And of course both are right, for to name in literature is to confer being—merely fictive being, yet being nonetheless.

In another respect, however, Beckett's equivocation with regard to fictive and nonfictive language functions as critical irony. By allowing his narrators to act as if they were dealing with nonfictive language, Beckett allows them to undertake an ironic critique of errors that can only exist as illusions in the realm of nonfictive language. The schizo-text comically blurs the line of demarcation between fictive and nonfictive text in order to live out the madness that our various philosophical systems would ascribe to our daily lives. The schizo suspension of logic allows the unnamable to live his narrative project as an experiential critique of language theory, much as Wittgenstein flirted with madness in order to create such antimetaphysical fictions as the following:

> One may say of the bearer of a name that he does not exist; and of course that is not an activity, although one may compare it with one and say: he must be there all the same, if he does not exist. (And this has certainly already been written some time by a philosopher.)[2]

Seen in this light, the claim of Beckett's characters not to exist is at least as comprehensible as the claim that to say "I" might confer existence.

To conclude, I should like to note then how Beckett's work, offering the "unnamable" as the name of our narrator, preludes with a great contradiction to the proliferation of postmodern works whose voices know not whence they speak or speak from that equivocal space called the text. Many of these works would go further than Wittgenstein or the unnamable in denying that language can reach any private sphere, that there could be such a thing as a private language, or that there could be a self that might exist beyond the voice that is created by language. Yet few of these works have Beckett's richness, perhaps because they fail to allow for the view that there might be a not-I, a self to be translated by what is other than the self of language, alienated in the tribe's fallen discourse. The unnamable also stands as a contradictory protest against, as well as ironic affirmation of, the idea that character and self may only be functions of language. After all, who can be happy with the belief that his voice grants him a self merely because rules of grammar have been hypostatized into metaphysical entities? Beckett's unnamable thus speaks with a voice that opens up most of the space of postmodern narration: voice is a comic automaton spoken by language, often the fallen language of public delirium that we have come to call pop. And, of course, these notions about voice and language tell us much about what has happened in contemporary fiction to what once was called character. Characters around 1900, as Queneau shows in his *Flight of Icarus (Le Vol d'Icare)*, had such ontological substance that they could be stolen or could abandon the novel in which they were to appear. No such fears haunt the writer for whom a character is simply a repository of the tribe's language and need act only as a nominal function.

1. *Three Novels by Samuel Beckett* (New York: Grove Press, 1965). All quotations are from this edition. Page references appear in parentheses in the text.

2. *Zettel*, ed. G. E. M. Anscombe and G. H. von Wright; trans. G. E. M. Anscombe (Berkeley: University of California Press, 1970), no. 61.

Kristin Morrison

Neglected Biblical Allusions in Beckett's Plays: "Mother Pegg" Once More

Certain biblical allusions in Samuel Beckett's plays seem to have gone unnoticed. For example, the name "Mother Pegg" with its possible translation as "nail" and subsequent connection with crucifixion is faithfully repeated by most commentators on *Endgame*, but the much more immediate biblical allusion in that passage is ignored. What I want to do here, briefly, is to point out a few neglected references and indicate what their presence contributes to the play; and also to point out something about Beckett's manner of alluding to the Bible that may account for the fact that some of his references seem to remain unidentified.

There are, of course, biblical allusions in Beckett's plays that are unmistakable: Vladimir's story about the two thieves is an obvious example. But the references I am talking about are less obvious for two reasons: first, they do not usually comprise an entire dramatic unit (the way Vladimir's foray into a typical problem of nineteenth-century Higher Criticism does); second, they are usually so brief in their presentation that the reader/listener must be attuned to the slightest echo. The allusions I am talking about hinge only upon a salient word or two. For example, in *That Time* consider the phrase "the passers pausing to gape." There is not much to confirm this as a biblical allusion;

yet we *know* that it is because Beckett has said so. And, also, anyone steeped in biblical stories would probably be reminded of the Crucifixion when hearing these words and not simply of a spectacular construction site or an interesting mugging on the upper West Side. This kind of biblical allusion depends upon verbal echo and good specialized memory: words and images heard so often and so clearly associated with their topic that they supersede all other uses and associations. The combination of "gape" and "passers" does it for this reference. In rehearsal notes for the German première of *That Time*, Walter Asmus records Beckett's remark that this phrase *is* from the Bible and records as well Klaus Herm's identification of the passage, "'Yes, from St Luke's Gospel'" and Beckett's interesting response, "'I looked it up, but I didn't find it, aha, Luke. . . .'"[1] Beckett is riding on the kind of memory I just described: the single word or two triggering an entire biblical allusion. He does not need to find the passage in order to use it; his audience does not need scholarship to recognize the words or feel their effect. What is operating here is not erudition but, rather, simple deep-in-the-bones knowledge of biblical story and the specific King James words and images that convey it.[2]

The process of synthetic memory behind this phrase "the passers pausing to gape" is particularly interesting and revealing. The allusion is as much to Mark and Matthew as it is to Luke. All three gospel writers record Jesus' being stared at and reviled as he hung on the cross: "And the people stood beholding" (Luke 23:35), "And they that passed by railed on him, wagging their heads" (Mark 15:29), "And they that passed by reviled him, wagging their heads" (Matthew 27:39). Luke's version contains a word that suggests the "gape" of Beckett's allusion; and Matthew and Mark provide the "passers." Furthermore, all three gospel writers are themselves alluding to Psalm 22, which is associated with the Crucifixion both in the New Testament and in the liturgy for Good Friday; that description of the suffering savior contains the phrases "They gaped upon me" and "They look and stare upon me." Thus all these passages contain Beckett's *image* of the "passers pausing to gape" but no one of them contains all his actual words, which seem to come from a composite memory of these various related biblical passages.

Beckett himself has stated, "Christianity is a mythology with which I am perfectly familiar, so naturally I use it."[3] And Vivian Mercier has described his own and Beckett's experiences with the study of Scripture and religion at Portora Royal, founded by the same King James I whose Authorized Version of the Bible so frequently appears in Beckett's work.[4] The record of Beckett's use of biblical allusion is charted throughout various studies by virtually every major Beckett scholar.[5] If some few references have remained without commentary, it may be that they have seemed to a given critic too obvious to mention; but it may also be that their very brevity, as well as their perfect "fit" into context, has caused them to pass unnoticed.

This seems to be the case with the Mother Pegg passage from *Endgame*. Hamm and Clov have been talking about the wasted state of the world; Hamm has protested that he does not know what has happened or whether it matters, and Clov challenges Hamm's feigned innocence by this accusation:

> When old Mother Pegg asked you for oil for her lamp, and you told her to get out to hell, you knew what was happening then, no?
> *Pause.*
> You know what she died of, Mother Pegg? Of Darkness.[6]

This passage with its emphasis on oil for an empty lamp and its fatal outer darkness contains clear reference to the New Testament parable about the wise and foolish virgins, a story about salvation and damnation, ultimate life and death:

> Then shall the kingdom of heaven be likened unto ten virgins, which took their lamps, and went forth to meet the bridegroom. And five of them were wise, and five were foolish. They that were foolish took their lamps, and took no oil with them: but the wise took oil in their vessels with their lamps. While the bridegroom tarried, they all slumbered and slept. And at midnight there was a cry made, Behold the bridegroom cometh; go ye out to meet him. Then all those virgins arose, and trimmed their lamps. And the foolish said unto the wise, Give us of your oil; for our lamps are gone out. But the wise answered, saying, Not so; lest there be not

enough for us and you: but go ye rather to them that sell, and buy for yourselves. And while they went to buy, the bridegroom came; and they that were ready went in with him to the marriage: and the door was shut. Afterward came also the other virgins, saying, Lord. Lord, open to us. But he answered and said, Verily I say unto you, I know you not. Watch therefore; for ye know neither the day nor the hour wherein the Son of man cometh. (Matthew 25:1–13).

There is an allied parable, also about a marriage feast (Matthew 22:1–14), that develops this imagery further, ending with a description of the damnation of one who is not properly prepared: "Then said the king to the servants, Bind him hand and foot, and take him away, and cast him into outer darkness; there shall be weeping and gnashing of teeth. For many are called, but few are chosen." Oil, lamp, hell, darkness: these are the words in Beckett's passage that trigger the allusion.[7] Kingdom of heaven, wedding feast, light in the darkness, the savior who comes unexpectedly: these are the words of hope and promise, the encouragement and the warning the parables contain. They express in little the whole Christian message of salvation, here used for ironic contrast, to intensify the sense of hopelessness in *Endgame*. Hamm is the god who damns by withholding, or by being unable to provide, the means that make life possible, whether it be bread in the wilderness (which he had earlier denied to the multitudes) or light in the darkness (which the lamp and the oil represent). That Clov's accusation rankles is illustrated by the fact that a few moments later the phrase "Of darkness!" interrupts Hamm's speculations about his own demise. It is important, I think, not to hear this phrase simply as a rather standard literary archetype in which "darkness" stands for death and other such negatives but rather to recognize the quite specific biblical allusion it carries.[8] It may be that Mother Pegg's name is supposed to suggest crucifixion. But that particular allusion seems much less germane to the details of the play than does the set of parables I have just cited. Yes, *any* suffering can analogously be called a crucifixion; but *Endgame* is rich in specific references to food, to bread, to inner place and outer wilderness, to light and darkness, to salvation and loss—to what are the central images of these particular parables. The allusion itself does not change or add anything to the sense of misery and hopelessness that the play has previously established; it simply intensifies what is already there. The authorial memory that *found* those images—lamp, oil, darkness—relies on other memories to recognize them, perhaps not consciously, at the moment, but enough so that the play is drenched once more with a feeling of fatal loss, a loss not peculiar to this peculiar scene, but one for which there is a long history, a loss that the old stories of our culture have recounted again and again. The biblical allusion lurking in this particular passage universalizes it by quietly reminding the audience of words they have heard before.

This allusion in *Endgame* seems to me to be quite clear. There is another but more obscure use of the parable of the wise and foolish virgins in *Waiting for Godot*.[9] One of the critical lines in that parable is the statement, "Behold, the bridegroom cometh, go ye out to meet him." These words seem to be echoed in Vladimir's triumphant announcement, "It's Godot! We're saved! Let's go and meet him!"[10] Like the attendant virgins of ancient ceremony, these two derelicts have waited for someone who they are sure has a special claim on them, and in waiting have proved themselves worthy. "What are we doing here, *that* is the question. And we are blessed in this, that we happen to know the answer. Yes, in this immense confusion one thing alone is clear. We are waiting for Godot to come—" (p. 51+). In the parable, of course, the bridegroom *does* finally arrive and take those who are ready into the wedding feast (an image of salvation and blessing). But in this play, Vladimir is wrong; they are not saved, as he says, or blessed (that is to say, Godot does not arrive); and Estragon is right, they are "in hell" (p. 47+). Once again the parable has served as ironic contrast to the dramatic scene: the received wisdom of Vladimir's world is untrue. He may regulate *his* behavior and set *his* expectations according to the old stories, but the old stories do not observe their part of the bargain; he may keep *his* appointment, but the bridegroom does not. In the parable, of course, the bridegroom tarries, arriving finally at midnight; and it is precisely this detail of the story that traps Vladimir, the never knowing if he has waited long enough: perhaps Godot *will* come, tomorrow "without fail" (p. 58+). Vladimir is not, of course, consciously referring to this parable when he exclaims, "We're saved! Let's go and meet him!"; but its ethic resides in him, as his echo of its words suggests. And the audience, however vaguely recognizing the reference, feels once more a grimly comic moment of blighted hope. "Your only hope left is to disappear," Vladimir had said (p. 47+). Nonetheless, he and Estragon continue to wait, ambivalently hoping for a salvation, a deliverance, even though the various stories of salvation in this play mock any real hope they might have.[11]

At this point, I must emphasize that I am *not* suggesting a Christian interpretation of Beckett's plays (in fact, I think a Christian slant rather badly distorts them). Nor am I suggesting that Beckett is mining his plays with Christian symbols. Nor do I imply anything about his personal beliefs. None of that. I am merely interested in verbal echoes of biblical passages, passages so well known that their distinctive phrases and images are securely fixed in the memory of any ordinary church-goer or careful Bible-reader; phrases that Beckett uses easily, not with the rather deliberate erudition of a Joyce or an Eliot, but comfortably, as part of the natural flow of the dramatic scene. Almost always these allusions are ironic, but not in a way that twists a scene away from its surface meaning; their irony simply reinforces an irony already present.

And as I search to describe what I *mean* by an easy, integral use of biblical allusion, I find myself thinking about the lucidity that Beckett's critics have noted in his prose style. Despite the erudition that lurks there, the sentences themselves are immediately available. The metaphorical coordination of the language is subtle; the connections among words and allusions (their buried images and associations) are solidly forged but not intrusive, not even, in fact, noticed unless we double back to examine what has made a graceful passage so very felicitous. The same felicity that characterizes Beckett's prose style generally also governs his use of many biblical allusions. They merge perfectly and unobtrusively with his larger purpose, present often only as subtle verbal echoes, whispered reinforcements of moods, themes, ironies already established. They blow through the plays like "the wind in the reeds"—a subtle yet significant presence.[12]

1. *Journal of Beckett Studies*, No. 2 (1977), p. 93.

2. It is interesting in this regard to note Alan Schneider's comment not about the cause of some of Beckett's words but about their effect: "Beckett's plays stay in the bones. . . . His words strike to the very marrow. . . ." ("Waiting for Beckett: A Personal Chronicle," in *Twentieth Century Interpretations of "Endgame,"* ed. Bell Gale Chevigny [Englewood Cliffs, N.J.: Prentice Hall, 1969], p. 21).

3. Colin Duckworth, *Angels of Darkness* (London: Allen and Unwin, 1972), p. 18.

4. "Samuel Beckett, Bible Reader," *Commonweal*, 105 (28 April 1978): 266–68.

5. For purposes of this discussion, see in particular Ruby Cohn's chapters on *Endgame* in *Samuel Beckett: The Comic Gamut* (New Brunswick, N.J.: Rutgers University Press, 1962) and *Just Play* (Princeton, N.J.: Princeton University Press, 1980).

6. *Endgame* (New York: Grove Press, 1958), p. 75.

7. Revisions in early versions of *Endgame* also help sharpen the biblical associations of the Mother Pegg passage. In the typescript of *Endgame* in the Special Collections at the Ohio State University Library, Beckett has changed the sentence "When old Mother Pegg asked you for oil for her lamp and you sent her packing" by crossing out the phrase "sent her packing" and writing in "told her to go hell" [*sic*], thus making even more explicit the biblical reference.

8. Although it is true, as Richard M. Goldman maintains, that the various critical interpretations of *Endgame* fall short of the play (as indeed they do with any complex piece of literature), it is also true that relevant information can help illumine the play. His question "Who was Mother Pegg? Can one *die* of darkness—in its physical or even metaphorical sense?" becomes decidedly less rhetorical in the light of the biblical allusion Clov's accusation contains. See "*Endgame* and Its Scorekeepers," in Chevigny, p. 37.

9. Josephine Jacobsen and W. Mueller, in *The Testament of Samuel Beckett* (New York: Hill and Wang, 1964), have identified a passage in *The Unnamable* that also contains "oblique references to the twenty-fifth chapter of the Gospel according to Saint Matthew" (pp. 127 f.); they do not, however, identify the presence of this same passage in *Endgame* or *Waiting for Godot*. Though this particular identification in *The Unnamable* is accurate, Jacobsen and Mueller tend throughout their book to overstate the religious elements in Beckett's work, moving beyond clear textual references and going so far as to compare Beckett with St. Francis and Thomas à Kempis (see pp. 49 f.).

10. *Waiting for Godot* (New York: Grove Press, 1954), p. 47+. This edition is numbered consecutively only on the verso side of each leaf; pages with numbers will be cited here by their designated number; the next, facing page will be given that same number and the designation "+."

11. There are three biblical references to salvation in this play: the easily identified account of the two thieves and the parable of the sheep and the goats, along with this more obscure allusion to the attendant virgins. All have an ironic function.

12. This phrase suggests yet another neglected biblical reference. In *Waiting for Godot*, Vladimir's false alarm concerning Godot's arrival is met with Estragon's "Pah! The wind in the reeds" (p. 13+). The line has enough meaning on its own to make sense to any member of the audience; but those familiar with the Bible will immediately remember that the same image is used to refer to the Messianic herald who goes unheeded: "Jesus began to say unto the multitudes concerning John, What went ye out into the wilderness to see? A reed shaken with the wind?" (Matthew 11:7). Thus the line has an overlay of ironic meaning. Literally, the phrase in context means, "there is nothing"; but through its biblical reference, the line suggests that once there was something or someone who went unrecognized; thus those who waited but did not detect him were not saved. The irony of this line in this particular play does not come from any suggestion that there really *is* salvation for Vladimir and Estragon if only they could see it, but quite the contrary, that there truly is "nothing"; all the many references to hope and salvation that occur in the play—whether as metaphors and idioms readily available, stories to be told, quotations to be identified—reveal the extent to which Vladimir and Estragon have been misled by their culture. They carry around with them shards of belief, snatches of biblical phraseology, fragments of philosophy and theology (as does Lucky in his monologue) that only tantalize them with desiring the impossible. Estragon is closer to their real situation when he remarks, "There's no lack of void" (p. 42+). In their desert, no savior appears.

Yasunari Takahashi

Qu'est-ce qui arrive? Some Structural Comparisons of Beckett's Plays and Noh

"Beckett and Noh" may sound a farfetched subject, for unlike Yeats or Claudel or Brecht, Samuel Beckett is, on his own evidence, quite unfamiliar with Noh; much less has he ever tried to imitate or steal the riches of this ancient theater form of the East. The absence of actual influence, however, would be all the more significant if it could be shown that the two theater forms, with a vast temporal and spatial distance between them, do share some fundamental characteristics.

"Nothing happens, nobody comes," complains Estragon. This would remind any "Japanalogist" of Claudel's famous dictum: "Le drame, c'est quelque chose qui arrive, le Nô, c'est quelqu'un qui arrive."[1] One is almost tempted to suspect that Beckett is here making a conscious allusion to the insight of the French playwright-diplomat. But the allusion, if conscious, should be surprising for its wry obliqueness. For if one can claim that *Waiting for Godot* is a negation of the European notion of drama wherein some action *must* take place, one can also claim that the play is at the same time a negation of the essential dramaturgy of Noh insofar as Claudel is right in the second half of his dictum and insofar as Estragon is right in the second half of his complaint.

Or maybe *negation* is not exactly the word. For something does happen, or indeed many things do happen, on this place dubiously called "The Board" (the stage): businesses with hats and shoes, gestural mimicries, dances, games, quarrels, even an attempt at suicide. But none of them are "real" dramatic actions: they are all "pseudo-actions" performed simply to kill time, all "non-events" tending toward no logically climactic moment. Similarly, someone does come if you count Pozzo or Lucky or the boy. But they are obviously not that "someone" who, by "arriving," is supposed to make Noh what it is, any more than they are Godot himself.

Here some remarks on the origin and the structure of Noh would be in order. Noh is closely connected with the ancient Japanese belief in the unpacified spirit of the dead. The unquenched passion of love, grief, or hatred endows the dead with a sort of immortality, and the ghost is compelled from time to time to emerge out of the Buddhist purgatory in a corporeal form that was his or hers in life and visit the world of the living in order to gain a partial relief from present torments by telling someone the story of his or her agony, somewhat in the manner of Coleridge's Ancient Mariner. In the typical structure of a so-called Fukushiki Mugen-Noh (dream-noh in two parts), the Shite (protagonist) first appears as an ordinary village woman and then, after an exit, reappears as a veritable ghost to enact her life story before the eye of the Waki (secondary character), a traveling priest, who finally manages to pacify her agonized soul by the power of his prayer. Noh in this light could be regarded as theatrical transformation of a ritual of exorcism of the demonic power of the dead.

But in a slightly different though related light, the protagonist of Noh could also be taken for a specimen of what Japanese anthropologists call "mare-bito," literally, a "guest," but a special kind of sacred guest. This "epiphanic" stranger was entertained by the villagers with sumptuous hospitality in the hope that he would turn himself into a benevolent spirit and sanctify the village with his holy blessing. One might think of the *Oresteia*, in which the Erynies (the Furies) are transformed into the Eumenides (the Kindly Ones), who the Athenians hoped would bless the city of Athens. Of course, Zeami's theater is conceived in a scale that is anything but Aeschylean;

it is far less epic and totally apolitical, far more refined in its private lyricism—so much so that you could almost call it a "minimalist" art. Nonetheless, it is important to see in Noh a form of "holy theater" whose ultimate aim lies in making an epiphany possible, that is, in preparing a space, a kind of "void," so that this empty space may be filled in by the arrival of a strange guest, a sacred spirit in a human form, a god incarnate.

What is to be stressed in this connection is the importance of the Waki, for it is he who actually does the preparing for the epiphany. Much more than a simple traveler, he is a priest possessed with a shamanic power to perceive (or indeed evoke) a supernatural presence (one notices here a curious reversal: he, a stranger from elsewhere, meets an indigenous spirit, a ghostly inhabitant of the place). He is a medium requisite for the supernatural hero to take flesh momentarily. It is even possible to argue that the central action of a Noh play, the "coming" of the Shite in the second part, really takes place in a dream of the Waki, which is why it is called a "dream-noh." In any case, the audience finds itself at one with the Waki in an atmosphere taut with tension, waits for the apparition, watches the Shite dance out his or her undying fire of passion, and finally experiences a certain catharsis, be it Aristotelian or not, of fear and pity.

Now some of the structural peculiarities of *Waiting for Godot* would seem to be illuminated by the light shed by the above observations on Noh. Didi and Gogo are seen to be not so much the real protagonists (Shites) as the secondary players (Wakis) who wait for the Shite to arrive. Of course they are far from resembling the serious-looking priest of Noh; they are much more like the comedians of Kyogen, a genre of farce usually performed as an interlude between two pieces of Noh plays. As for Pozzo, his arrival in the first act gives the Wakis an illusion that he might be the awaited Shite, which, however, is quickly proved to be false. And although his reappearance in the second act, much transformed and probably revealing his true identity, does remind us of the Shite in the second part of Noh, he is after all a "pseudo-Shite," a miserable caricature of the true Shite, who is supposedly none other than Godot. Thus Didi and Gogo have to go on waiting for a true epiphany, and Godot's failure or refusal to come must leave the space, the stage, empty and unblessed with the visit of a ghostly guest. No transformation of reality, no communion of the sacred and the profane, takes place. No catharsis is allowed to the audience.

It may indeed be doubted if the coming of Godot, should it take place, would be of any help to Didi and Gogo, for the fact that his name itself sounds like a parody of God might imply that all they can hope for is an endless sequence of "pseudo-epiphanies" of "pseudo-Gods." One almost wonders if that is not precisely the state of modern man as envisioned by Beckett and if that is not precisely the state of Western theater as embodied in the structure of *Godot*. I would submit that both situations are made poignantly conspicuous by the very absence of those elements that constitute the vision and the dramaturgy of Noh. Perhaps it is not so frivolous as it may seem to call *Godot* a kind of "anti-Mugen-Noh."

Another aspect in which *Godot* sharply contrasts itself with Mugen-Noh is its attitude toward the past. The Shite in Noh is an apparition from the past, often a very distant time; he or she is dead, but the past is not; the presence of the Shite, which is as it were the time past made flesh and voice, is even more potently present than that of any human being alive. In contrast, everything in *Godot* is here and now (though "here" and "now" in this play are admittedly ambiguous enough in comparison with the unitary time-space scheme of a realistic play). The "dark backward and abysm of time" whose memory might torment the characters is deliberately dismissed; there is an almost hysterical revulsion against the "remembrance of things past" whenever the characters are faced with questions concerning the past. All this, of course, may be a paradoxical testimony to their obsession with time, and it is true that Didi and Gogo listen to the voices of the dead in the air, but there is no such encounter of the living and the dead, of the time present and the time past, as we find in Noh.

After *Godot* it seems as if Beckett keeps approaching with

ever increasing seriousness an austere theater that, both in its skeletal bareness of structure and in its thematic obsession with past and memory, reveals a special affinity with Zeami's creation. *Endgame* is a play concerned with eschatology, the imminent end of a game that is Western civilization itself. But in spite of (or perhaps exactly because of) that, we witness the characters being haunted by poisonous memories. Out of the dialogue between Hamm and Clov emerges their deep love-hate relationship nurtured since their first contact when Clov was a child. We even see the time past literally present in Hamm's parents, still alive in the ash cans that obviously are parodies of graves. However, this play is probably too fiercely dramatic in content and too complex in form to make us feel its latent affinities with Mugen-Noh, and we have to wait for *Krapp's Last Tape* to meet a really suitable example.

The play presents Krapp on the stage as the protagonist (Shite), but in this seeming monodrama, he is also playing the role of Waki, at least during those spaces of time in which he is straining his ears to listen to his own taped voices. And it is these voices that take the role of Shite during those moments. It goes without saying that there is a world of difference between the disembodied voices, on the one hand, that, coming out of a modern machine, with mechanical repetition narrate the stories of past passions (or "pseudo-passions"), and on the other hand, the overwhelming physical presence of the Shite in Noh, who both narrates and beautifully "dances out" his old but still-too-real passion, just as the half-crazy forgetful old man listening to his own voices is difficult to identify with the sane and intelligent priest who both watches and listens to the "other" character. And Krapp is of course utterly incapable of exorcising or pacifying his former self. Nevertheless, we find in *Krapp* the first unmistakable emergence in Beckett's canon of an essentially Noh-like structure: the voice (Shite) arriving out of an alien time-space dimension versus the character (Waki) listening to that voice.

The purest example of this structural principle is *Not I*. Here we have, on the one hand, a Shite reduced to a bare outline of a "Mouth" of a woman, emerging out of the darkness and recounting what she pretends to be another woman's life, though it is only too clear that it is her own life that she is narrating and that her babbling is an inadequate but compulsive attempt at reliving her earthly life. And we have, on the other hand, a typical Waki, whom Beckett calls "Auditor," vaguely priest-like with his hooded figure, facing "Mouth" diagonally across the stage (as in Noh), listening intently like a confessor to her voice, and apparently trying ineffectually to absolve the tormented soul.

But we must remember that *Not I* is a rare exception in its clear-cut separation of the two roles. All the other plays by Beckett show a more ambiguous "doubling" of Shite and Waki, or (to put it the other way round) "splitting" of ego and alter-ego. Krapp cannot be a Waki pure and simple because both the voice and the life it narrates are his own. Or take *Eh Joe*. One might think that Joe, the ostensible hero who remains silent throughout this television play, gets relegated to the role of Waki when the Beckettian Shite appears as a female voice. But one is reminded by the voice itself where it comes from: "You know that penny farthing hell you call your mind. . . . That's where you think this is coming from, don't you?" In Noh the Shite makes his or her entrance from the "Kagami-no-ma" (the looking-glass room), which is not simply a greenroom but symbolically represents an "other world," a purgatory, the depths of Jungian collective unconscious. Joe's "mind" does look as if it were a Beckettian version of Kagami-no-ma, but one must admit that this "penny farthing hell" is, if anything, more Freudian and personal than it is Jungian and archetypal (it is a superb joke that Joe's mind is materialized as a television set out of which issues a voice). The fact that the voice, albeit not his own, comes from his own mind and recounts his own life should deter us from claiming him to be a pure Waki.

Rather it is our impression that Joe, with his face close-up and frozen in a tense expression, resembles what in Noh is known as "Hita-men" (Shite in a maskless role), and the muteness with which he listens to the voice could be compared to that particular style of Noh action called "I-guse," whereby the Shite sits utterly still and dumb while the chorus ("Ji-utai") chants long passages that are sometimes a description of his misfortune and sometimes of his interior monologues. It should be noticed that the chorus in Noh has the astonishing freedom to enter inside the protagonist's mind and voice his own thoughts, hence the splitting of speech and act, as in I-guse, which the Western audience of Noh often finds very irrational and confusing.

So I would suggest, at the risk of making my argument rather too complicated, that what we find in *Eh Joe* is the tripartite structure of Noh (Shite, Waki, and chorus) telescoped into a double structure. Joe listening to the woman's voice is at the same time the Waki listening to the Shite and the Shite listening to the chorus. Conversely, the voice is the Shite emerging out of "elsewhere" into the presence of the Waki at the same time that it is the chorus narrating to the Shite his own life story.

It will not be difficult to detect a similar device not only in earlier plays like *Krapp* but also in most recent plays. *That Time* is an amalgam of *Krapp* and *Eh Joe*, for here is an old man sitting in the dark just listening to his own voices from three different periods of his life. He is a helpless passive Waki victimized by the aggressive, ghostly voices, but he is also a Shite caught in his anguished efforts to come to terms with his own past as narrated by those voices. *Rockaby* likewise splits the woman's physical presence in a rocking chair and her recorded voice. What is new about this play (for Beckett never repeats himself) is that the voice uses a third-person pronoun: " . . . till in the end / the day came / in the end came / close of a long day / when she said / to herself / whom else / time she stopped." This produces an effect quite different from the first person used in *Krapp*, the second person in *Eh Joe* and *That Time*, or even from the third person in *Not I*, which, as I have pointed out, has a different dramatic structure. One of the most curious moments in the play occurs when the woman joins the voice, speaking in unison: "time she stopped." Although one is reminded of Krapp joining in the laughter of the taped voice, the closest parallel one can think of will probably be the impression one gets when the Shite in Noh joins the chorus to recite a third-person narrative describing him.

Ohio Impromptu is unique in having two characters on stage, Listener and Reader. Except for the fact, however, that the voice of *Rockaby* is here incarnated as Reader, the fundamental structure remains unchanged; for it is suggested that Listener and Reader are, despite their separate identities, those halves of a split self that we are by now familiar with (see Beckett's direction that they be "as alike in appearance as possible"). And what Reader reads from the book is clearly a story of Listener's life, forcing upon him (Listener) a cruel realization of his life as a failure.

Beckett started writing plays at the point in the history of the Western theater where all the realistic conventions of drama, including the assumption that the theater has nothing to do with the sacred, broke down, and it seems to be that, in his ruthless effort to strip the theater of everything that is not absolutely necessary, he has arrived somewhere close to where Zeami started six hundred years ago. In both Zeami's and Beckett's theater, nothing happens (everything has already happened), but someone does come out of an unknown "sacred" country that Beckett in one of his latest plays, *Ohio Impromptu*, calls the "profounds of mind." That "someone" is at once "the other" and one's deepest self; that "country" is at once "unknown" and half-remembered. Of course, Beckett, under a malediction undreamed of by Zeami, has had to delve down into the depths of modern self-consciousness where it threatens to turn into solipsism, autism, and schizophrenia ("that way lies madness"). It is a triumph of Beckett's art that he has successfully incorporated the very structure of the split soul of the modern man. Zeami's ideal of theater consisted in "transmitting a *hana* [i.e., flower] from mind to mind." Although in Beckett's "theater of mind" what is transmitted from mind to mind is something too bleak to be called "flower," we are grateful to him for creating a theater that is as deeply concerned as Zeami's with the agonies of a soul that badly needs pacifying.

---

1. Paul Claudel, "Nô," in *Oeuvres en prose* (Paris: Gallimard, 1966), "Bibliothèque de la Pléiade," p. 1167.

Frederik N. Smith

Fiction as Composing Process: *How It Is*

Twenty years ago, shortly after the publication of *Comment c'est*, Hugh Kenner remarked that the novel "looks like a draft of itself, as *Endgame* feels like a rehearsal of itself; packets of language, set apart by spaces, like notes for paragraphs never to be composed, jotted down as some eternal voice dictates."[1] Others have observed that *How It Is* resembles a "rough draft" or "manuscript."[2] These descriptions are apt. The subject of the book is the composing process itself. The novel demonstrates how the romanticized joys of authorship border in fact on a schizophrenic tug-of-war within oneself, where every flash of inspiration is countered by a terrible realization that what one has just thought may be somehow inaccurate, ill-conceived, or spoken in a voice not one's own.

Writing is for Samuel Beckett an excruciatingly arduous task, and he typically uses the personal challenges of this task as the raw material for his fiction.[3] His first published story, "Assumption," is about the struggles of a hypersensitive young author who is suffering from writer's block. But it is in the trilogy that Beckett's preoccupation with the process of storytelling begins to subsume the story itself. The degree of his sensitivity to the mechanics of writing is demonstrated in this one astounding sentence from *Malone Dies*: "I hear the noise of my little finger as it glides over the paper and then that so different of the pencil following after."[4] It would have seemed that there was no place to go from here. But in *How It Is* (the immediacy of the title perhaps suggests the shift in focus), Beckett retreats from the page, or rather goes behind it, attempting to catch the flux of the writing process at the moment it is occurring. Here we read: "ballpoint at the ready on the alert for the least never long idle if nothing I invent must keep busy otherwise death."[5] Of course Beckett is fictionalizing here as well. But whereas in *Malone Dies* the emphasis is on the writing situation (pencil, exercise-book, room, lighting, and so on), in *How It Is* the emphasis is only secondarily on the requisite situation, and primarily on the mental and imaginative operations of the writer himself as he composes. Beckett's remarkable sensitivity to the sound of the pencil moving across the paper in *Malone Dies* is matched in *How It Is* by an even more incredible sensitivity to his own process of turning the stuff of memory and imagination into words.

Don Quixote, Tristram Shandy, Tom Jones, Pale Fire, Lost in the Funhouse, Project for a Revolution in New York, and *Malone Dies* are all works of fiction about the problem of writing fiction. In this respect, *How It Is* belongs to the same genre. It differs from these other novels, however, in that it dramatizes the problem at a more primal stage. It is in a sense an *Ur*-novel. It is a published text that looks not so much like notes or manuscript or draft, but rather like something *prior to* the completion of a draft. It purports to document the process of writing a novel as it is occurring within the artist himself, to be a record of that series of miraculous moments when invention is busy transforming memories into words on the page. In particular, the many references to dark and light and the halting, laborious journeying through a primeval mud suggest a Genesis situation in which something—in this case a literary work—is being shaped out of the mud of one's own experience. The odd "stanzas" of the novel quite literally imitate the stumbling attempts to get started. And each stanza is composed of a series of phrases that draw attention to themselves as fragments of half-conceived, broken-off sentences. The pun in the original French title is revealing: this is truly how it is to begin.

How It Is dramatizes the dilemma within every writer between the chaos of the artist's inspiration and the need to give form to that inspiration. "The problem," says Peter Elbow, "is that editing goes on *at the same time* as producing. The editor is, as it were, constantly looking over the shoulder of the producer and constantly fiddling with what he's doing while he's in the middle of trying to do it."⁶ Beckett shows us more clearly than any other writer—and in this novel more clearly than in any of his other novels—the lonely struggle of all writing, which is characterized by an ongoing competition (I am aware of this as I conceive and revise this very sentence) played out inside the writer's own skull, inside his "little chamber all bone-white" (p. 134). "I'm the brain," says Beckett at one point, "of the two sounds distant still" (p. 89). The novel is in a sense a transcription of the struggle for dominance between the right hemisphere's immediacy, its ability to work by way of images, and the left hemisphere's logicality, its desire to organize and correct.⁷

The innumerable allusions in *How It Is* to various stages of the writing process hint at a step-by-step procedure of writing. These allusions can be used to construct a schema that would account for the phases Beckett himself may go through in the difficult process of contriving a novel out of his own real-life images torturously disentangled from the past:

"Vast tracts of time"
↓
Memories
↓
Internal composition
Inspiration vs. revision
↓
External composition
Drafting and redrafting
↓
Published text

The endlessly repeated phrase "vast tracts of time" suggests not only the frightening white page but also the faraway time and space that have made up one's life but are lost altogether, or perhaps lodged as mere fragments in one's memory: "dear scraps recorded somewhere" (p. 25). Some form of the phrase "bits and scraps" is used nearly fifty times, and seems to signify the bits and scraps of one's memory as well as the composing process itself, which is the process of attempting to turn these fragments into "my life present formulation."[8] These fragments are recoverable only as "images" or "scenes" (both words are repeated frequently) that fade in and fade out like the scenes of a film ("brief black and there we are again") or the staging of a scene of a play ("ABOVE the light goes on little scenes"). Sometimes these bits and scraps can be captured in jottings taken down in a notebook ("reread our notes"), and then through a process everywhere challenged by physical obstacles ("here something illegible in the folds") or mental lapses ("at evening with his face to the huge sun or his back I forget") transformed slowly, painfully into a work of fiction.[9] The whole process is an inching forward out of obscurity into a precarious and perhaps specious semicoherence: "prior to the script the refinements difficult to describe just the broad lines on stop that family beyond my strength he floundered I floundered but little by little little by little" (p. 61).[10] These words are an appropriate description of the building up of *How It Is* itself, which would seem to contain numerous vivid images and recollections of Beckett's own childhood and youth.[11] Of course we can never be sure—and this is as it should be—where autobiography leaves off and fiction begins.

Invention in the novel is pitted against revision or the need to edit. One pole of the composing process is imagination or inspiration, described by Beckett as "these sudden blazes in the head" that the writer experiences as a sort of "spectacle" (p. 35). So too the indispensable sack, wherein the traveler keeps his provisions, suggests the scraps stored in the writer's memory.[12] The other pole of the process is revision, or the writer's need to prune, to delete, or to make stern judgments on the products of his imagination. This second self is referred to when Beckett the creator wonders whether this other "might not with profit revise us by means for example of a pronouncement" (p. 140). He is "the scribe sitting aloof" (p. 44) and the "me bending over me" (p. 133). The competition between these two poles of the composing process is analogous to the ongoing struggle for authority in the relationships between the narrator and Pim, Krim and Kram, and the more generalized "victim" and "tormentor." The endlessness of this repeated contest would seem to suggest that the best composition occurs when neither imagination nor revision gets the upper hand. Creativity is more than raw inspiration. But so too it is a great deal more than correctness and tripartite organization and finding a way to have done.

Beckett's text bears a striking resemblance to some of Janet Emig's experiments with "oral composition."[13] Emig was able to capture something of the dynamics of composition by bringing together her students' produced texts with tape recordings of their oral comments on those texts *as they were writing them.*

> It was all yellow and everything as you walk into this (ten-second pause) you know. It was yellow and orange. Could I hyphenate yellow and orange if I want? (writing) . . . It will make the construction better. *I walked into a warm-looking yellow-and-orange dress shop on East Randolph.*[14]

Minus the punctuation and capitalization, this passage would look (and sound, if read aloud) a great deal like one of Beckett's stanzas in *How It Is*:

> one day we'll set off again together and I saw us the curtains parted an instant something wrong there and I saw us darkly all this before the little tune oh long before helping each other on dropping with one accord and lying biding in each other's arms the time to set off again (P. 57)

Although Beckett says at one point in the book that his process is "unbroken no paragraphs no commas not a second for reflection" (p. 70), there is, clearly, time for momentary reflection, and the reflection becomes part of the text itself. Emig suggests that a pause in the composition of a text is a moment of rest, a time for reconsideration before moving ahead;

Beckett's breaks in his text suggest the same sort of temporary slacking of creative energy.[15] The passage from *How It Is* is clearly as "oral" as the passage from Emig. Only Beckett is not so kind as to italicize for us those words—if any at all—that have actually reached the page.

Furthermore, Emig makes the point that there is a recursive tendency to all writing, a journeying forward into the unknown, then a doubling back, then a journeying forward again. This tendency is apparent in both of the above passages, which reflect a hesitant, repetitive groping toward a description rather than being themselves finished descriptions. What we have in both cases is a sort of dialogue with the self, an unvocalized attempt at a particular phrasing followed by an unvocalized doubt as to the aptness of the proposed phrasing, and then a new formulation of the description. We watch as a statement is being worked toward, yet perhaps never fully realized. We are shown the struggle between alternate formulations: Is the shop "yellow" or "yellow and orange"? Are the speaker and Pim "lying" or "biding" in each other's arms? And note the shift in tense in each passage. Both at least theoretically have as their subject a past happening, but both also try to deal with a present verbal formulation of that past, and at the same time attempt (in the first instance) to point to a future possible formulation, or (in the second instance) to project a verbal formulation of a possible future happening.[16] The handling of time is certainly one of the most difficult challenges in any writing, and Beckett's valiant efforts to break his narrative into a neat "before Pim with Pim after Pim" is everywhere undermined by the text's blurring of tense. The time of the story proper gets confused with the time of the telling of the story. "All my fault lack of attention want of memory," admits Beckett, "the various times mixed up in my head all the various times before during after vast tracts of time" (p. 107).

How It Is is filled with reachings back into time and forward into the text, but these sudden bursts of inspiration are continually interrupted by Beckett's desire to approve or disapprove what he has just thought to himself. Runs of more than several words are rare: "this voice ten words fifteen words long silence ten words fifteen words long silence long solitude" (p. 126). The subjective, personal voice of inspiration is repeatedly broken off by the objective, impersonal commentary of the reviser. Phrases such as the following occur throughout: "something wrong there" (which appears twenty-four times in the novel), "need then to emend what has just been said," "nothing to emend there," "not an iota to be changed in this description," "not right," "correct," "a mistake," "drivel drivel," "no point skip," "all hangs together," "no objection," and "a little less of to be present past future and conditional." Even phrases such as "the sack we're talking of the sack" would seem to be the author's objective self calling him back to the subject (and the writing task) literally at hand. As in all composing, these dogmatic interjections have at least the potential effect of crushing the tender shoots of authorial inspiration; and the response of Beckett's reader must be much the same, for one's attention is thus repeatedly yanked away from the immediate subject and redirected toward a choice between a hypothetically better or worse verbal formulation of that subject.

The drama of this struggle between inspiration and revision is literally found on every page of *How It Is*. An alternate word or phrase is repeatedly substituted for another without the deletion of the initial formulation: "I'll describe it it will be described" (p. 27), "midnight no two in the morning" (p. 44), "I am right I was right" (p. 55), "happy no unhappy" (p. 97), "a cry nay a sigh" (p. 143).[17] These substitutions and the inclusion of internal reactions to words that have just happened in the mind account for much of the peculiarity of the style of this novel: "happiness one hesitates to use those awful syllables" (p. 25); "a fine image fine I mean in movement and colour" (p. 27); and "tormenter or victim these words too strong" (p. 115). Gradually, in the course of the novel, this pre-textual debate between imagination and revision becomes ever sharper. The interior composing process is by definition a divided one, and at times the supposed author is trapped between two equally demanding urges: the phrase "I hear yes then no" occurs repeatedly. And as the vivid images of part one begin to fade, "yes" and "no" appear more often. There is an increasingly frustrating split within the author's own head. His desperate attempts to make his story neat and certain only feed his anxiety, and in the final pages of the book the composing process has diminished to a schizophrenic shouting match between the inspirational "YES" and the editorial "NO."

Often whole stanzas are based on a reproduction of the process of an as-yet-unformulated thought as it lurches through the mind. And Beckett will not oversimplify this process:

> as I hear it and murmur in the mud that I hoist myself if I may say so a little forward to feel the skull it's bald no delete the face it's preferable mass of hairs all white to the feel that clinches it he's a little old man we're two little old men something wrong there (P. 54)

Of course the absence of punctuation and the minimalization of grammatical connectives enable us to track the evolution of this thought without being reminded that what we are reading is in fact *written* discourse. So too the lack of punctuation permits the running-together of the supposed speaker's description of a present-tense movement, the speaker's interior weighing of the validity of his sensations, and the supposed author's questioning of his own process on writing about both of these. Thus the description "I hoist myself a little forward to feel the skull" is interrupted both by the *speaker's* interior reactions ("it's bald" and "that clinches it he's a little old man") and by the *author's* interior reactions ("no delete," "it's preferable," and "something wrong there"). But Beckett deliberately wants to blur these two different sorts of comments on the described actions in order to fuse the process of the story with the process of telling the story. Indeed, he suggests they are one and the same. Hoisting a little forward in the primeval mud is equivalent to formulating a murmur out of the inchoate mass of one's memory. The staggering, uncertain movement of Beckett's syntax reproduces both. And something is dreadfully wrong in either case.

Beckett in *How It Is* probes yet further into the nature of the composing process. Part of the ongoing struggle between an author's sudden blazes of inspiration and his need to give form to that inspiration is the problem of *voice* in writing. Discovering the voice of his own inspiration is one difficulty for the author; but perhaps more difficult is the delicate job of transcribing his inner voice into words which manage to express the sound of that inspiration. Thus "voice" can mean either inspiration (for the writer) or the rhetorical form which captures this inspiration convincingly (for the reader)—Beckett uses the word in both senses. And references to voice increase as he works his way through *How It Is*, suggesting that this dual problem becomes gradually more important. Implicit in the novel are the following very real questions: Is voice an individualized characteristic of an author's writing or somehow programmed into him by "the voice of us all"? Does an author have one or many voices? And more particularly, is it possible for voice to rise above what Elbow calls "the habit of compulsive, premature editing," which can interfere with the writer's attempts to get his own consciousness onto the page?[18]

Although not every writer is as self-conscious about this matter as Beckett is, the presence of voice in a text is of critical importance to all writers and all readers. It marks the difference between what Richard Lanham calls the "monotone haste that swallows prose like castor oil" and prose that takes on a life, that has a rhythm and an identifiable tone, that creates a more or less distinct impression of someone speaking.[19] Of course, voice in written discourse is nothing more than the arrangement of words in such a way as to give the *effect* of such a presence, and Beckett understands this: "my voice so many words strung together" (p. 95). But words and phrases can be strung together like beads on a string, in which case there is no voice but only words; or words and phrases can be placed in such positions that they do in fact give the impression of someone speaking. And *How It Is* is a text that reads for the most part "almost mechanically at least where words involved" (p. 64). The majority of the book is composed in a phrase-plus-phrase-plus-phrase fashion that sounds as if it were written not by an author but by a computer. Sporadically, however, such voice-less prose gives way to a momentary colloquialism that *must* have been spoken by a human being. Beckett's novel is in effect a demonstration of the irrepressibility of his own authorial voice.

A good example of the mechanical laying down of words is the following stanza, which itself seems to allude to the labor of composition.

> intent on these horizons I do not feel my fatigue it is manifest none the less passage more laborious from one side to the other one semi-side prolongation of intermediate procumbency multiplica-tion of mute imprecations (P. 41)

The lack of punctuation, the verbal and phrasal disconnected-ness, and the piling up of academic polysyllables never permit this prose to rise above an uninflected monotone.[20] There is no voice here. And most of the novel sounds like this. But once in a while, such voiceless prose is interrupted or overcome by a decidedly human phraseology that carries with it an undeniable rhythm and tone: "the word we're talking of words I have some still" (p. 26); "I always say when a man's name is Pim he hasn't the right" (p. 59); "the Boms sir you don't know the Boms sir" (p. 60); "Krim says his number's up so is mine" (p. 81); and "that wasn't how it was no not at all" (p. 144). The dependence in these excerpts on monosyllables, personal pronouns, and contractions moves the prose into a greater informality and allows a human inflection to emerge in spite of the absence of punctuation. Indeed, Beckett demonstrates that such conven-tional signals are helpful but not absolutely necessary in creat-ing voice in written discourse.

Not infrequently Beckett within a single stanza allows his computerized style to give way, unexpectedly, to the sound of a real human voice. The following is an example. And note that the passage itself is at least in part *about* voice.

> blue the eyes I see them old stone perhaps our new daylight lamps it's possible I agree and in the head the dark and friend I agree but this voice the voice of all what voice I hear none and who all damn it I'm the thirteenth generation (P. 83)

Beckett's eyes are in fact blue, and he would seem here to be looking—or imagining that he is looking—at himself. But the personalized subject opens with a voiceless multiplication of phrases that by this point in the text has become the norm, typically introduces perceptual options by way of a "perhaps" and an "it's possible," and then seems to permit a response to itself in the form of an "I agree" and a "friend I agree." But who is this friend? And who is doing the agreeing? And in this bifurcated context, the reference to the "voice of all" seems oddly wrong, for we would seem to be already in the presence of at least two voices.[21] Suddenly, however, as if demanding to be heard, as if reasserting itself over both the voiceless text and the confusion of voices above, there booms an angry "damn it I'm the thirteenth generation." Is this the superior Krim? Is this the unnamed speaker emerging momentarily from all his words? Is this Beckett parodying himself? In any case, we listen as a voiceless text begins first to fragment into a schizophrenic conflict with itself, and is then overcome by an unmistakably singular voice—not of some generalized "all" but of an individual defending his inherited right to his presence in the book. And his right to his own voice. Not surprisingly, *How It Is* concludes with a final assertion of the importance of voice: "only me in any case," admits Beckett, and "my voice yes mine yes not another's no mine alone yes" (p. 146). The author's personal voice has in a sense survived the struggle to create.

Beckett's novel is thus a brave attempt to bring onto the page the creative process, a process that remains most mysterious. He has of course fictionalized this process. *How It Is* is a novel and not necessarily a documentary of his own creative process. The repeated objections that there is "something wrong there" are fictionalized objections to something Beckett has himself written quite self-consciously. So too the search for a voice is a drama Beckett has intentionally built into his novel. Nevertheless, a glance at the original manuscript and first and second typescripts of *How It Is* would suggest that in the process of writing about the composing process, Beckett was in fact *doing* the same kind of things he has used as the stuff of his fiction.[22]

One of the most interesting aspects of the material behind the final version of *How It Is* is the fact that Beckett worked increasingly hard to give his novel the look of unfinishedness, or, more accurately, the look of something scarcely begun. The first scrap of *Comment c'est*—a two-and-a-half-page fragment entitled "L'Image"—was published in November 1959, and the solid mass of text lends its pages at least the superficial appearance of traditional fiction.[23] But five months later, in a manuscript dated May 1960, Beckett abandons capitalization and punctuation altogether; and only a few months after this, in the first several pages of the English version, published in the *Evergreen Review* (Beckett was at this time writing in French and English simultaneously), the text is broken into stanzas for the first time.[24] Although it is not my purpose to trace the evolution of Beckett's English text, it is worth noting that the idea of a novel that pretends to be only a fragmented, internal record of the beginning of a novel was something that seems to have come to Beckett as he was in fact struggling to begin. In March 1960, in the very early stages of this new and difficult composition, when sending John Calder a piece of it in English, he referred to the enclosed material as a "work in regress."[25] That is how it was. Quite literally, Beckett's progression forward into this new novel was turning out to be a regression backward into the composing process.

Indeed, his efforts to prevent the text of *How It Is* from assuming the appearance of a conventionally printed text continued right down to the final stages of publication. The French *Comment c'est* had included many stanzas that look like stolid, rectangular units of type, their last lines running all the way to the right-hand margin; Beckett clearly wanted to avoid this effect of finality and certainty in the English version of his novel. On one page of the galley proofs for the Grove Press edition, he wrote a note to his printers: "If this comes at foot of page it will have to be changed, on principle that last line of page must always be incomplete or carried forward by hyphen to following page." But the convention-minded typesetters persisted, and on one sheet of the London page proofs, Beckett wrote with understandable impatience, "As indicated on galley proofs, there must never be a full line at foot of page," and went on to show the printers exactly how he wanted the line set, indicating that the "same mistake" occurred on eight other pages. In retrospect these typographical quibbles seem quite humorous, but for Beckett at the time the need to publish a text that would appear more fragmented, even less finished, than the original French version must have become almost an obsession. His sense of his novel had evolved, and he wanted his current notion of it to be reflected in the published English text. Ultimately, Beckett had his way. In numerous places in both the New York and London editions, it is clear that the type-setters have added space to a line so as to avoid having the last line of a stanza end at the right margin. And the author must have taken exquisite delight in discovering that on page 22 the final word of the stanza, "bottom," had to be hyphenated so as to bring its second syllable to the *top* of page 23, where "tom" stands alone.

In a nice phrase—"the fragility of euphoria" (p. 38)—Beckett captures the idea behind *How It Is*.[26] Writing—like living—is a tentative, precarious, and certainly most difficult task. Moreover, the precariousness of any attempt to transform a thought or image into words is intimately connected with the precariousness of one's own being. The pangs of composition are the pangs of existence. Even the comparatively vivid images of part one are qualified by such phrases as "if I may believe the colours" (p. 29), "that must have lasted a good moment" (p. 31), and "I wait for us perhaps to come back" (p. 32). One's past is fleeting at best. One's future is hypothetical. In truth only the present exists for the writer as writer and the writer as human being. At the beginning of part three, Beckett mentions "the humming-bird known as the passing moment" (p. 103). The moment. The voice. The text. That is *all* there is.

1. *Samuel Beckett: A Critical Study*, new ed. (1961; Berkeley: University of Caifornia Press, 1968), p. 190.

2. Michael Robinson, *The Long Sonata of the Dead: A Study of Samuel Beckett* (London: Rupert Hart-Davis, 1969), p. 213; and James Knowlson and John Pilling, *Frescoes of the Skull: The Later Prose and Drama of Samuel Beckett* (1979; rpt. New York: Grove Press, 1980), p. 78.

3. The entire corpus testifies to the difficulty of composition for Beckett. See also Richard L. Admussen, *The Samuel Beckett Manuscripts: A Study* (Boston: G. K. Hall, 1979), pp. 11–12.

4. In *Three Novels by Samuel Beckett* (New York: Grove Press, 1965), p. 208.

5. *How It Is* (New York: Grove Press, 1964), p. 81. Subsequent references to the novel will be to this edition and will be included within the text.

6. *Writing without Teachers* (Oxford: Oxford University Press, 1973), p. 5.

7. As background, see the interesting article by W. Ross Winterowd, "Brain, Rhetoric, and Style," in *Linguistics, Stylistics, and the Teaching of Composition*, ed. Donald McQuade (Akron: L & S Books, 1979), pp. 151–81.

8. This phrase appears frequently; see "my composition" (p. 52), "script" (pp. 61 and 69), "monologue" (p. 79), "recordings" (p. 107), "scriptions" (p. 112), and "narrations" (p. 139).

9. Beckett even jokes about the exercise-books of various colors that he typically uses for his actual composing: "blue yellow and red respectively simple once you've thought of it" (p. 82). See also Admussen, p. 10.

10. On his first typescript, Beckett changed "prior to the writing" to "prior to the script." Similarly, on page 69 he changed "graphy" to "script." See note 22 below.

11. See G. C. Barnard's discussion of the image of Beckett as a child praying at his mother's knee (p. 15)—clearly taken from an old photograph—in *Samuel Beckett: A New Approach* (London: V. M. Dent & Sons, 1970), p. 70. There are numerous such images in part one.

12. Cf. Beowulf's "word-hoard." But elsewhere Beckett suggests that the sack is a womb, a lover, or the speaker's own body.

13. *The Composing Processes of Twelfth Graders* (Urbana, Ill.: National Council of Teachers of English, 1971), pp. 40–42.

14. Ibid., p. 59.

15. Ibid., pp. 66–67. Cf. the many references in *How It Is* to "silence" and also to "long pause" (p. 72) and "without pause" (p. 136).

16. Cf. Jean-Paul Sartre, *Being and Nothingness*, trans. Hazel E. Barnes (New York: Philosophical Library, 1956), p. 36.

17. Beckett had experimented with this approach to writing as early as *Watt* (1953; New York: Grove Press, 1959), p. 40: "The fit is perfect. And he knows this. No. Let us be calm. He feels it."

18. *Writing without Teachers*, p. 6.

19. *Style: An Anti-Textbook* (New Haven, Conn.: Yale University Press, 1974), p. 100. And here I echo Susan Gibson, *Voice Audience Content: A Writer's Reader* (New York, Longman, 1979), p. 2.

20. Beckett's novel is filled with such academic rarities: "instanter," "frequentation," "capillarity," "scissiparous," "introrse," "dextrogyre," "thenar," "subprefecture," "malar," "infinitudes," etc.

21. Indeed, the reader himself might say "I hear none" or ask "who all."

22. The manuscript of *How It Is*, plus the first corrected typescript, the second corrected typescript, the author's corrected galley proofs and page

proofs are all housed in the Special Collections at the Ohio State University Library in Columbus, Ohio.

23. The piece appeared in *X: A Quarterly Review* 1 (November 1959): 35–37. See Ruby Cohn's discussion of "L'Image" in *Back to Beckett* (Princeton, N.J.: Princeton University Press, 1973), pp. 227–29.

24. *Evergreen Review* 4 (September–October 1960): 58–65. And see Admussen, p. 34.

25. Beckett adds: "The best that can be said for it is that it is not definitive." This letter is dated 17 March 1960, and is now at the Humanities Research Center, the University of Texas at Austin.

26. Cf. *Watt*, p. 73: "This fragility of the outer meaning. . . ."

Judith E. Dearlove

"Syntax Upended in Opposite Corners": Alterations in Beckett's Linguistic Theories

Throughout his career, Samuel Beckett's style, mood, and attitudes toward art change. These changes are related to, and grow out of, a series of changes that occur in Beckett's semantic and syntactic principles. Linguistically, Beckett moves from a celebration of syntax at the expense of semantic content, through both identification and later dissociation of the two, to a period of reconciliation in which he accepts the solace of form as being itself an adequate semantic comment.

Beckett's early linguistic attitudes are suggested by the Verticalist manifesto he signed in 1932 advocating use of language as "a mantic instrument . . . which does not hesitate to adopt a revolutionary attitude toward word and syntax, going even so far as to invent a hermetic language, if necessary."[1] According to the Verticalists, the artist is free to—perhaps even obligated to—fashion new syntactic orders and hence new patterns of meaning. This Verticalist conception of language that informs the prose of Beckett's earliest works is perhaps most clearly displayed in "Text,"[2] a published extract of the unpublished *Dream of Fair to Middling Women*. Basically, the piece portrays an exchange between a "lust-be-lepered" lover and the woman he unsuccessfully importunes to be his "bonny bony doublebed cony." The real interest, however, lies not in the situation but in the language that compounds aural devices into one long (approximately 180-word) sentence. Within the first two dozen words alone, there is a remarkable accumulation of alliteration, assonance, consonance, and internal rhyme: "Come come and cull my bonny bony doublebed cony swiftly my springal and my thin Kerry twingle-twangler comfort my days of roses days of beauty. . . ." Sound replaces meaning as the interpersonal relationship is subsumed under a verbal one. We are more interested in the way words tumble about each other's meanings than we are in the lover's frustrated efforts to tumble about with his cony. The piece celebrates not humanistic concerns but rather the power of the artist who forces his words to operate on all levels of meaning simultaneously, who makes each word refer both forward and backward in a flowing prose. For example, in a dazzling display of metaphysical transitions, Beckett transforms the woman into a hunted rabbit, to nibbled-up lettuce, to a plant covered by an insect's secretion, and back to a woman. The very density of images, in which human, animal, and vegetable allusions interconnect and overlap, testifies to an underlying belief in the possibility of order, in the reality of the external, and in the capacity of language to project and display that order and that reality. Such beliefs affirm an order antithetical to the uncertainty, fluidity, and chaos that Beckett postulates, forcing him to find new linguistic models for his art.

For the major portion of his career, Beckett pursues the linguistic theory he ascribes to Proust and Joyce, that form is a spatial configuration of meaning: "for Proust the quality of language is more important than any system of ethics or aesthetics. Indeed he makes no attempt to dissociate form from content. The one is a concretion of the other, the revelation of a world."[3] An idea resides in its shape, and style reflects more accurately than any content a speaker's vision of the universe. It is as if Beckett could not argue strongly enough for the identity of form and content, for he insists on underlining his points in discussing Joyce: "Here form *is* content, content *is* form. . . . His writing is not *about* something; *it is that something itself.*"[4] The identification of form and content encourages Beckett to emphasize the structure of his own works and the shapes of his ideas: "I am interested in the shape of ideas even if I do not believe in them. . . . It is the shape that matters."[5]

Beckett's purported interest in the shape rather than the validity of ideas finds its best formal expression in the trilogy where form and content are made to *seem* identical and indivisible as the narrator creates himself, and incidentally the text we read, through the very act of narration: ". . . I'm in words, made of words, others' words."[6] Despite all assertions, however, the narrator/narrated is as irretrievably split as are form and content. On the one hand, the narrator is the formless, fluid speaker who rejects all that is alien to the nonverbal core of himself. On the other hand, he resides in the fixed shapes and external orders of his spoken words. He exists, as the Unnamable observes, in the interstice between internal and external:

> . . . I'm in the middle, I'm the partition, I've two surfaces and no thickness, perhaps that's what I feel, myself vibrating, I'm the tympanum, on the one hand the mind, on the other the world, I don't belong to either. . . . (*The Unnamable*, p. 383)

In "Shades of Syntax," Hugh Kenner examines the linguistic implications of Beckett's efforts to conflate form and context, observing that it is "a typical Beckett strategy, to equate syntax with logic, lull us with their coincidence, then trap us with the consequence."[7] Kenner argues that, unlike a Joycean "interior monologue" in which the mind "exerts no effort to control its own contents," Beckett presents us in a work like *How It Is* with a narrator "struggling to utter sentences, which means to control his thoughts, which means to grasp and comprehend the reality in which he partakes. Each block of type is a unit of his effort; we can gauge his progress by keeping track of the syntactic order he achieves" (pp. 30–31). The "overall symmetry" of *How It Is* creates the illusion that the narrator has achieved order and control. But the control is syntactic not semantic; the narrator has ordered his words to attain a symmetrical form, but he has understood little: "his effort . . . is overwhelmed . . . by all the grim data he has not managed to clarify nor explain" (p. 31).

In the 1960s, instead of continuing to ignore the tensions between semantics and syntactics, Beckett reverses his linguistic theory and emphasizes their disparity. Instead of identifying form and content, he counterpoints them. In a 1961 interview with Tom Driver, Beckett acknowledges that form does not have to *be* content: "The form and the chaos remain separate. The latter is not reduced to the former. That is why the form itself becomes a preoccupation, because it exists as a problem separate from the material it accommodates."[8] The shape of a work of art can be separate from the idea it accommodates. Structure may, in fact, work in opposition to chaos as it does in the *Residua*, where Beckett creates structures that mathematically and scientifically describe fantastic objects, people, and images. Paradoxically, the very artifice of these carefully constructed structures points toward their underlying structural meaninglessness, whereas the arbitrariness beneath their order gestures toward a more fundamental absence of order. "Lessness," for example, presents a randomly arranged collection of words, images, and sentences. In order to read the work, the reader must reverse Beckett's creative process and break the piece down into sentences and phrases, regroup the components, and analyze the resulting families of sentences. The piece thus exists between composition and decomposition.

In his residual works, Beckett successfully accomplishes what his Verticalist pieces failed to do: he uses language and literature to capture the essence of the void by implication and exclusion: he expresses the chaos by avoiding it. Beneath the form lies the fluidity, uncertainty, and "mess" that Beckett seeks to accommodate. In the words Beckett used to distinguish himself from Kafka: ". . . Kafka's form is classic, it goes on like a steamroller—almost serene. It seems to be threatened the whole time—but the consternation is in the form. In my work there is consternation behind the form, not in the form."[9]

The new mood of the most recent fictions marks yet another stage in Beckett's linguistic explorations. Instead of striving to portray the "consternation behind the form," "Sounds," "Still

3," and *Company* return to the solace of form. Serenity is possible because the pieces are indifferent to the distinctions between internal and external realms that troubled earlier narrators. The figure in "Sounds" listens equally for the noise of the lightest leaf or for the sighs of his own breath. His postures intimate both Belacquaesque hermeticism, as he sits with his head in his hands, and exterior connections, as he stands embracing a tree. Even his speech patterns mix once mutually exclusive worlds. The wind is described in terms of the self and its mutterings: the wind makes "no more sound than a ghost or mutter [of] old words once got by heart. . . ."[10] It is no longer necessary to denounce associations or to seek absolute answers. Peace comes as the agonized questions that informed earlier quests fade away: "No not yet not listening again in vain quite yet while the dim questions fade where been how long how it was" (p. 156). Imperatives, interjections, permutations, and interruptions disappear. Direct contradiction is replaced by alternative possibilities. Repetitions become less insistent, the phrases longer, the rhythms more sustained. As commas and periods become less frequent, the prose becomes more fluid and tranquil. The syntax and lexicon become simpler and more conventional. The recent pieces dispense with a learned vocabulary including terms such as *commissure, cacodemons, deasil;* they eliminate word games such as the ones the narrator of "All Strange Away" plays with "Emma/Emmo" and "haven/ heaven" (p. 9); and they avoid the unconventionally ordered syntax of: "And finally for the moment and then that face the tailaway so common in untrained speakers leaving sometimes in some doubt such things as which Diogenes and what fancy her only" ("All Strange Away," p. 5). We are proffered instead the comfort of the familiar and the solace of conventional linguistic forms.[11]

Although the most recent pieces are without urgency, they are not without energy. "Sounds" and "Still 3," for example, are serene but not static. Just enough imagination persists to keep the narration going. Almost inaudible sounds recur just frequently enough to keep the silence from being absolute. Barely perceptible images appear just often enough to forestall the growing darkness. Instead of an impasse, the pieces project a tranquil diminishing. Instead of falling into exhausted silence, the pieces drift softly to rest. As in Valéry's "The Spinner," which ends at the same moment its drowsy spinner nods into sleep, Beckett's pieces tranquilly blend into the spreading calm:

> Leave it so then this stillest night till now of all quite still head in hand as shown listening trying listening for a sound or dreamt away try dreamt away where no such thing no more than ghosts make nothing to listen for no such thing as a sound. ("Sounds," p. 156)

There are no more sounds or images to disturb the peace, and an impotent speaker has been reconciled to an ambiguous universe.

Reconciliation leads not to an exhausted silence but to images of serenity. Urgency, not artistry, disappears. Beckett no longer seeks the linguistically impossible: his art does not have to *be* the chaos. It is enough if he can return to conventions without reasserting their assumptions. A sense of sufficiency predominates, enabling Beckett to create from the solace of traditional linguistic forms new shapes to accommodate the uncertain and fluid human condition. To alter a phrase from "All Strange Away," syntax need no longer be upended in opposite corners.

1. "Poetry Is Vertical," quoted by Sighle Kennedy, *Murphy's Bed* (Lewisburg, Pa.: Bucknell University Press, 1971), p. 304.

2. Samuel Beckett, "Text," *New Review* 2 (April 1932): 57. This piece, which is an extract from the unpublished *Dream of Fair to Middling Women* (1932), has been reprinted by Ruby Cohn in *Samuel Beckett: The Comic Gamut* (New Brunswick, N.J.: Rutgers University Press, 1962), p. 308.

3. Samuel Beckett, *Proust* (New York: Grove Press, 1957), p. 67.

4. Samuel Beckett, "Dante . . . Bruno. Vico . . Joyce," in *Our Exagmination Round His Factification for Incamination of Work in Progress* (Paris: Shakespeare and Co., 1929), p. 14.

5. Samuel Beckett quoted by Harold Hobson, "Samuel Beckett: Dramatist of the Year," *International Theatre Annual* 1 (1956): 153.

6. Samuel Beckett, *The Unnamable*, in *Three Novels by Samuel Beckett* (New York: Grove Press, 1965), p. 386.

7. Hugh Kenner, "Shades of Syntax," in *Samuel Beckett: A Collection of Criticism*, ed. Ruby Cohn (New York: McGraw-Hill, 1975), p. 29.

8. Samuel Beckett quoted by Tom F. Driver, "Beckett by the Madeleine," *Columbia University Forum* 4 (Summer 1961): 23

9. Samuel Beckett quoted by Israel Shenker, "Moody Man of Letters: A Portrait of Samuel Beckett, Author of the Puzzling *Waiting for Godot*," *New York Times*, 6 May 1956, Section 2, p. 1.

10. Samuel Beckett, "Sounds," in the Appendix to John Pilling, "The Significance of Beckett's *Still*," *Essays in Criticism* 28 (April 1978): 156.

11. Contrast, for example, the following passages from "All Strange Away" and "Sounds":

Light out, strike one to light, light on, light all the same, candlelight in light, blow out, light out, so on. No candle, no matches, no need, never were. ("All Strange Away," *Journal of Beckett Studies*, No. 3 [Summer 1978])

Sounds then even stillest night here where none come some time past mostly no want no not no want but never none of any kind even stillest night seldom an hour another hour but some sound of some kind here where none come none pass even the nightbirds some time past in such numbers once such numbers. Or if none hour after hour no sound of any kind then he having been dreamt away let himself be dreamt away to where none at any time away from here where none come none pass to where no sound at any time no sound to listen for none of any kind. ("Sounds," p. 155)

S. E. Gontarski

Film and Formal Integrity

Far from working directly on celluloid, as some experimental filmmakers do, Samuel Beckett labored over his filmscript for *Film*, and many of his most interesting and revealing struggles with material and medium took place before the script was completed. Beckett's revisions for its composition reveal not only characteristic aesthetic preoccupations but also the particular difficulties Beckett had with film. In the composition of *Film*, we see a word man groping with an unfamiliar medium.

A full biography of the composition of *Film* is not now possible because textual evidence is not as complete as for other works. Beckett's primary creative effort is recorded in a gold, soft-covered, seventy-leaf notebook (22 cm × 17 cm exterior measurement), now on deposit at the University of Reading's Beckett Archive, which contains two full holograph versions of *Film*.[1] The first, called both "Notes for Film" and "'Percipi' Notes," dated Ussy, 5 April 1963 (that is, 5.4.63), consists of sixteen pages (Beckett's pagination) and was completed at Ussy on 9 April 1963. The subtitle Beckett began with is an accurate description of the work: "For Eye and Him [revised to "One"] who do not wish [revised to "would not"] be seen" (p. 2). The version on the title page suggests that he has a very clear idea of the nature of this work from the beginning: "For one striving to see one striving not to be seen." This earliest version is followed on pages 17–19 by a series of holograph notes and by a second version, called "Outline Sent to Grove," undated at the start, which continues on pages 20–36, and was completed in Ussy on 22 May 1963. The second draft is also followed by "notes," pages 36–47. (The remaining twenty-three leaves are blank except for the last, where, in June of 1963, Beckett began his translation of *Texts for Nothing.*) The earliest typescript, dated May 1963 and on deposit at Washington University, St. Louis, is six leaves long.[2] The notes in this version are again separate, in holograph, written on six graph-paper leaves, foliated 7–12. Finally, the Reading Beckett Archive owns a forty-leaf "Shooting Script," with 20 July 1964 noted as the shooting date. Moreover, the primary textual material is augmented by a transcript of a production conference, and a series of fourteen comments (thirteen numbered, one not) that Beckett made after seeing a rough cut of his film.

The earliest notes available suggest that Beckett apparently began the composition of his film uncharacteristically, with a clearly established theme that remained unaltered throughout (though simplified, of necessity, in shooting), the Berkeleyan philosophical principle "esse est percipi" (that is, being is being perceived): "Eye: Those who look at Eye [on] street stairs turn horrified away." Beckett calls this early draft "'percipi' notes" (p. 2) and refers, further, to "H [Him] perceiving perceived by E" (p. 1). Beckett's major creative problems here were to develop and to shape visual images not in order to embrace Berkeley's idealism but rather to explore the essential human consequences that follow from the philosophical proposition; or, in Beckett's words, "No truth value attaches to above, regarded as of merely structural and dramatic convenience."[3] This comment stands as a fundamental component in Beckettian aesthetics. Beckett's art is often more concerned with formal relationships than with something we might call theme. In his production conference, Beckett explained the formal importance of the opening (lost in shooting): "I want to fortify the analogy between the inspection of the street and the inspection of the room in the complete series by having the elements involved inspected in the same order. If it's 1-3-5-2-7-6 . . . we give numbers to the elements in the room—exactly in the same order—by E in the street and by O in the room. . . . It's a kind of integrity, formal integrity."[4]

Despite the film's abstract theme and Beckett's concern with formal balance, his early creative concerns are with realistic detail, with fixing his work in a precise time and place, with setting O in a particular place, in a particular year, at a particular time of day. In the early pages of his notebook, Beckett explores a series of possibilities. The time is changed from 1914 to 1929. The time of day is at first "midday or early afternoon," then, temporarily, "evening." But this is rejected: "Not evening, to remove possibility of his putting off light in room. Midday. Street animated by midday break. Or early morning and people on the way to work. Not Winter in this case." Even O's age is specifically set at "50"; yet he is also said to have been "25 in 1914." Beckett's mathematics may be a bit off; if O was born in 1889, he should be 40 in 1929, but arithmetic is less in question here than the fact that in Beckett's early stages of composition, matters of time and place are important to him. As the work develops, however, these realistic underpinnings are mostly eliminated as Beckett moved characteristically toward higher levels of abstraction. And in his production conference, Beckett consistently stressed the near abstract nature of the whole film: "it's on an absolute street . . . absolute exterior, absolute . . . transition . . . abstract almost." "The principle of the room," Beckett continues, "is to seek the minimum . . . a formal minimum. Even the table that carries the . . . bowl . . . just a support . . . a kind of abstract support."

In addition to the setting's being more concrete in the early versions of *Film*, Beckett is very concerned with logical motivation for O's behavior, and in fact the plot is generally more realistic than the final one. Such realistic preoccupation, evident in this early notebook for *Film*, seems almost the fulfillment of Beckett's 1936 comment to V. I. Pudovkin that he wanted to "revive the *naturalistic*, two-dimensional silent film" (italics mine).[5] In the final film, however, O's reasons for avoiding perception, his desire to negate being, his reasons for going to the room—that is, much of what might pass for plot in the film—are absent. Yet in the holograph versions, motivation is clear, and in composition this information is transferred to the "Notes." Only there do we learn that O has gone to his mother's room, to which he has not been for some time, to care for her pets while she is in the hospital. Such information is potentially very revealing, even autobiographical, yet Beckett denigrates it: "This has no bearing on the film and need not be elucidated" (p. 59). Yet in his production conference, Beckett returns to these realistic underpinnings by way of "explaining" the film. "One might suppose," he tells the crew, "that his mother has gone to hospital." With this information, of course, the film makes more logical sense, is considerably more conventional, and is even potentially autobiographical. It provides a psychological reason for O's escaping being, responding to fears and uncertainties surrounding his mother's illness or impending death (she, after all, must be quite old). As such the film is another study of the possible responses to loss and precedes by only three months Beckett's discarded monologue of an orphaned girl in "Kilcool."[6] In fact, with the knowledge that the room is his mother's, we can see another variation on the theme of a mother's death that we find in *Krapp's Last Tape* and *Footfalls*. Beckett finally cut most suggestions of the film's realistic, psychological, logical level. In the notebook version, for instance, O carries "a suitcase," which might suggest a lengthy stay, not the final "briefcase." As late as the typescript, Beckett had O compare the apartment number against a slip of paper from his pocket, and further, he entertained the possibility that the picture on the wall would be one of O. Almost nothing in the final film hints at this realistic level. Why O is in this room would remain an enigma without Beckett's published notes. But in the production conference, Beckett frequently refers to the realistic subtext of his film. One reason he posits for O's bumping into the couple is that he is "wondering has he got the right house . . . looking up the street."

Although Beckett was firm about the absence of dialogue from the start, the film was originally intended to contain more sound than the final, single "ssh." The opening scene was to include at least realistic sound: "No cars. One cab drawn by cantering nag, (hooves) driver standing brandishing whip. Bicycles" (p. 3).[7] After O's incident with the couple, we were to hear, "Sound of his panting" (p. 6). The opening scene was lost in filming to the strobe effect, but the panting was cut by design, and with the cuts more of the realistic level of the film was eliminated. Beckett was clearly interested in emphasizing the unreal, stylized, comic qualities of the film. He wanted to stress the "unreal quality" of the room. Of O's walk Beckett says, "He storms along in comic foundered precipitancy" (*Film*, p. 12). And in a notebook entry, Beckett reminds himself, "O as comic physically as possible. Short fat in preference to tall thin (because of chair)" (p. 17). Of the film generally, Beckett notes, "Climate of film comic and unreal" (*Film*, p. 12). The emphasis on the comic and unreal is designed to counter the realistic nature of the medium and the potentially melodramatic plot. He even entertained the possibility that the dog and cat routine should be an animated cartoon but rejected that idea quickly on formal grounds, "then others necessary, two more at least." In a set of written comments (also on deposit at the Beckett Archive of the University of Reading) that Beckett made after seeing an early version of the film, he expressed disappointment about the dog and cat scene: "Because I don't feel the animal gag at all funny, I find it too long. *Mais libre à vous.*" This statement is the clearest we have that Beckett seems to have been unsuccessful, to have lost some control over the project.

The most revealing portions of the notebook versions demonstrate Beckett's struggling with his medium, trying to subjugate it to theme. Most of his problems were technical. E's point of view, Beckett notes, should not be compromised, so that E and O never share the same field of vision, and the perceptions of E and O are mutually exclusive. As Beckett notes to himself, H (that is, O) "perceives only when he feels himself not seen, i.e., when E directly or nearly directly behind him. . . . When he feels himself seen, or beginning to be seen, he closes his eyes" (p. 1). This technical limitation understandably upset Buster Keaton because his face then would almost never be on film. O could never turn 90° and perceive an object, since in that relationship with E, O would close his eyes and cease perception. This sort of convention, of course, imposes an extraordinary limitation on movement in the film. It is theme limiting the possibilities of medium.

A second problem that Beckett had to contend with resulted from his major cinematic innovation; he had to distinguish in quality the perception of E and O. O's perception had originally been restricted to the room, but in filming, Beckett (or someone on the crew) decided to prepare for the images of different quality that were to appear in the room sequence. This question of different perceptions, Beckett notes, "poses a problem of images which I cannot solve without technical help" (*Film*, p. 12). He rejects, however, any attempt to express the images simultaneously, as by "composite images, double frame, super-imposition, etc." (*Film*, p. 58). Once again technique remains in the service of theme as Beckett rejects any physical image suggesting unity and any technical sophistication of the medium. The solution is clumsy, as O's perception is a bit fuzzy, shot through a gauze filter, a solution originally entertained in his notebook (p. 9).

The most interesting thematic use of medium that Beckett contemplated was ultimately rejected, probably because it would have altered the climactic tone. In the final image, the investment, Beckett wanted to suggest that E and O are mirror images of each other. E then would be "alter O" (p. 9). The penultimate image would be O, patch over right eye, frowning, followed by E, patch over left eye, smiling. Photographically, we would have had a print and its negative, the smile even a reversal of the frown. But the final image would have been Keaton's smiling face, and the bit of playfulness with the medium would have disrupted the final tonal balance. Beckett cut the sequence with the final comment, "impossible."

That bit of mirror-image playfulness would also have de-tracted from the ending ironies. For one, we see that we may be most conscious of self-perception, or rather it may, like Proust-ian memory, come crashing into our consciousness, when our defenses are weakest, as in dreams, but it is always with us. The lack of self-perception is merely an illusion, for we see O even when he believes he is not being perceived; *we* and the camera perceive him even when he is "safely" within what Beckett calls the "angle of immunity." And here again we have Beckett exploiting his medium, using the camera as a relentless, omnipresent perceiver. Much of the artistic struggle with *Film*

was technical from the first. As late as the production conference, Beckett suggested that his principal problem was to find
technical equivalents to the two visions: "we're trying to find a
technical equivalent . . . a visual, technical, cinematic equivalent for visual appetite and visual distaste . . . a reluctant . . . a
disgusted vision [O's] and a ferociously . . . voracious one
[E's]."

Despite Beckett's technical achievements with *Film*, the work
never coalesces. Beckett seems, at almost every stage of the
creative process, to have been engaged in a battle with his
medium. The immediate rapport between artist and machine
evident in the composition of *Krapp's Last Tape*, for example, is
missing in *Film*. Despite his attempts, the final product appears
to have been something different from what Beckett wanted,
more realistic, less comic. He tried to maintain an atmosphere
of unreality, to move the work toward higher levels of abstraction, to dramatize a fundamentally internal conflict, to balance
or counteract the pathetic level of the film with comedy, but the
final atmosphere of the film remains realistic, the conflict more
external than internal, and much of its comedy falls flat. Admittedly, some of Beckett's original vision was lost in translating
script to film, including some of the formal symmetry that has
been such an aesthetic preoccupation in the later work. But the
replacement of the early street sequences with the opening eye
seems to have been fortuitous. It moved the film further along
toward the desired unreality and abstraction and was themati-
cally consistent with the emphasis on perception. Further, the
opening eye provided the initial disruption of audience expec-
tation that Beckett is so fond of, especially in plays like *Not I* and
That Time, which feature body parts as the primary stage image,
and as such the eyeball anticipates those later plays. But the
image may finally lack subtlety and integration. It may disrupt
initially, but assaults only temporarily. Our sense of security is
quickly restored once we view the street scenes. And the eyeball simply does not dominate the work as do the mouth of *Not
I* or the floating head of *That Time*. In the manuscripts of *Film*,
we can see clearly what Beckett would like to do, in what direction he was trying to shape the play; but in the final work, we
can also see much of that intention unrealized. Perhaps the

work began with too rigid a design. Unlike *Film* most of Beckett's works take their shape through the act of composition. *Film* seems to be one of Beckett's least existential works, since essence exists well before being. What we are left with in *Film* is a string of unsolved problems. Beckett does not solve these problems for another two years, some nine months after the actual shooting of *Film*, when he turns to television drama, restricts himself to the room, uses the camera as a slowly advancing, penetrating force, and can dramatize the interior struggle, the voices in the skull as effectively as he does in *Eh Joe*. But Beckett does not fully achieve the sort of "formal minimum" he mentioned at the production conference until *Ghost Trio* and . . . *but the clouds*. . . .

1. University of Reading MS. 1227/7/6/1. See also *The Samuel Beckett Collection: A Catalogue* (Reading, England: The Library, University of Reading, 1978), p. 43.

2. See Richard L. Admussen, *The Samuel Beckett Manuscripts: A Study* (Boston: G. K. Hall, 1979), p. 48. Admussen notes, "one or more drafts are missing between A and B," that is, between the notebook at Reading and the typescript at Washington.

3. *Film* (New York: Grove Press, 1969), p. 11.

4. A tape of this production conference, which included Alan Schneider (director), Boris Kaufman (cinematographer), Barney Rossett (producer), and Samuel Beckett, is on deposit at Syracuse University. This is probably the poolside conference Schneider refers to in "On Directing *Film*." Quotations used with the permission of Samuel Beckett. My thanks to Martha Fehsenfeld for her transcript.

5. Deirdre Bair, *Samuel Beckett: A Biography* (New York: Harcourt Brace Jovanovich, 1978), pp. 204–5.

6. See my essay, "Beckett's Voice Crying in the Wilderness, from 'Kilcool' to *Not I*," *Papers of the Bibliographical Society of America* 74 (1980): 27–47.

7. *Film* was reshot in 1979 by David R. Clark for the British Film Institute. Max Wall played O. This version, while interesting in its own right, runs counter to the direction Beckett was trying to move his work in the manuscripts and in the filming. Clark shot his *Film* in color, added music (Schubert's "Der Doppelgänger"), reintroduced sounds Beckett specifically cut from his script, and added vaudeville routines (O gets his foot stuck in a bundle of rope early in the film and, in the room, keeps kicking his briefcase away as he bends to retrieve it). Clark's version of *Film* is not necessarily worse or better than Schneider's, but it is considerably different from the film Beckett was trying to make. See "*Film* Refilmed," *The Beckett Circle* 1 (Fall 1978).

Hersh Zeifman

Come and Go: A Criticule

As the curtain rises on Samuel Beckett's 1965 play *Come and Go*, the soft light from above dimly illuminates three motionless figures. Flo, Vi, and Ru—friends since childhood—are sitting side by side on a narrow bench-like seat; apart from the fact that each is wearing a differently colored full-length coat, the three figures are as alike as possible. Each woman in turn briefly exits, swallowed up by the surrounding darkness, allowing the two remaining to whisper some unheard, but obviously horrifying , secret about the one who has departed. When the three are once again reunited after their momentary exits, they clasp hands in a kind of chain, and Flo intones the play's closing words: "I can feel the rings." Since they have just been reminiscing about love and "what came after," Flo's comment would appear to refer to their wedding rings. Normally one would have expected this final comment to have come from Vi—partly because, given Beckett's concern with repetition and formal patterning, she was the first to speak, and partly because, as at the beginning, she is sitting in the center, theatrically the most focused position. The fact that it comes from Flo, then, strengthens the wedding ring hypothesis; of the three, she is the only one holding two left hands, and thus the only one who could possibly be in direct contact with all three wedding rings. Yet Beckett clearly states in his notes to the play: "Hands made up to be as visible as possible. No rings apparent."[1]

Come and Go is so brief a play (even by Beckett's recent minimalist standards) that, in the time it takes an audience to
wonder, like the bewildered Mr. Shower or Cooker of *Happy
Days*, "What does it mean? . . . What's it meant to mean?"² the
curtain has already fallen. And yet, despite its brevity, the central images of *Come and Go* continue to haunt us long after the
play is over. Who are the three women? What is it that they
whisper? What are the nonexistent rings Flo refers to? And why
are we so deeply affected by this enigmatic, strangely moving
"dramaticule" that takes only a few minutes to perform?

Part of the answer to this last question—and thus indirectly
to the previous ones—lies in the fact that, for all its deceptive
verbal spareness, *Come and Go* is dense with literary echoes and
mythic resonances. A subtle thread of allusions winds its way
through the play—specifically, allusions to Shakespeare.
Beckett has always been a great admirer of Shakespeare.
Deirdre Bair informs us that, as a child, Beckett kept a small
bust of Shakespeare on a bookshelf in his room;³ as an adult, he
honored Shakespeare's memory in a more meaningful way,
incorporating numerous Shakespearean quotations into his
writing. From his first published play *Waiting for Godot*, in
which Lucky refers to "the divine Miranda" (p. 28B) of *The
Tempest*,⁴ to one of his most recent, *A Piece of Monologue*, in
which the speaker evokes *The Merchant of Venice* through his
description of the rain "dropping gentle on the place beneath,"⁵ Beckett's drama has consistently made use of Shakespearean allusions. *Come and Go* is no exception. The play is a
series of "threes": three women; three brief movements; a
three-word title; a roughly three-minute performance time;⁶
and, appropriately enough, three Shakespearean echoes to tie
the play's images together and to help answer some of our
puzzling questions.

The first of these echoes, as almost every critic of *Come and Go*
has noted, is the first full line of dialogue in the play—Vi's
"When did we three last meet?"—in which we hear, too insist-
ently for mere coincidence, the opening line of *Macbeth*: "When
shall we three meet again?" (1.1.1). The three women of *Come
and Go* are thus immediately associated with *Macbeth*'s three
witches—"the weird sisters":

> The Weird Sisters, hand in hand,
> Posters of the sea and land,
> Thus do go about, about;
> Thrice to thine, and thrice to mine,
> And thrice again, to make up nine.
> (1.3.32–36)

"Weird" is derived from the Old English *wyrd*, meaning "fate"; Holinshed's *Chronicles*, Shakespeare's source for *Macbeth*, makes the etymological link explicit by referring to the witches as "the goddesses of destiny."[7] Like their Shakespearean counterparts, then, Beckett's threesome—hand in hand, each going about, about—evokes an image of fate—or, rather, the Fates, another trio of sisters, spinning out the web of their life and pondering their destiny.

The first Shakespearean echo thus suggests the theme of the play: *Come and Go* is, on one level at least, about human destiny. And because we are so firmly rooted, from the very outset, in a Shakespearean ambience, we are more prepared to catch the play's subtle second echo: the significance of the characters' names. In an earlier manuscript version of *Come and Go*—or, more precisely, in a tentative first sketch of a dramatic situation that would later evolve into *Come and Go*—Beckett referred to his three women simply as A, B, and C. The dialogue begins with a conversation between A and B, during the course of which they mention C's sister. Beckett apparently could not come up with the right name for the sister, and, instead of merely burrowing further into the alphabet, he gave her the title "Mrs" followed by a dash. In a later draft of the scene, a version he entitled "Good Heavens," the women were still being identified by letter, but Beckett had now chosen a specific name for the sister—Mrs. Flower. In yet a later draft—this one much fuller, and mercifully in typescript—the reference to the sister is dropped, but Beckett kept the "flower" concept of her name and transferred it to his three women, whom he calls Viola (a flower similar to a violet or pansy), Poppy, and Rose.[8]

When Beckett finally came to write what we now know as *Come and Go*, he retained relatively little of his previous rough sketches. But he did retain, I suggest, the "flower" names for his characters—names that sum up their fate: "As for man, his days are as grass: as a flower of the field, so he flourisheth. For the wind passeth over it, and it is gone; and the place thereof shall know it no more" (Psalms 103:15–16). Beckett has evoked this psalm frequently in his writings, but in *Come and Go* he strengthens and particularizes the image—first, by personifying the flower in actual characters; and second, by selecting not just any flower names but very deliberate ones. In *Hamlet* the mad Ophelia, mourning the death of Polonius, offers *flowers* to the characters assembled on stage, alluding specifically to *rue* and *violets*, both of which are implicitly linked with death:

> There's rue for you; and here's some for me. We may call it herb of grace a Sundays. . . . There's a daisy. I would give you some violets, but they wither'd all when my father died. (4.5.177–82)

Flo(wer), Ru(e), and Vi(olet)—Beckett's three women bear the cryptic traces of Ophelia's death-flowers; the secret they share is embodied in their very names. Thus the words they dare not speak aloud compose a threnody, whispered intimations of mortality: each of them is suffering from the same terminal disease, the inevitability of death. In "Good Heavens," Beckett had made the point explicit:

A   Mrs Flower told me C was condemned.
      She whispers in B's ear.
B   (*appalled*) Good heavens!
A   The worst kind. (*Pause.*) Three months.
      (*Pause.*) At the outside.
B   Does she know?
A   Not a suspicion. She thinks it is heartburn.[9]

In *Come and Go*, however, Beckett wisely opted for a more oblique approach. The horror of the characters' whispered secret does not need to be spelled out; it is more palpably, powerfully evoked in being left unspoken.

By naming his women Flo, Ru, and Vi, Beckett thus associates them, through an allusion to *Hamlet*, with both natural

phenomena (flowers) and death. A similar association underlies Flo's image of "rings," except that the natural phenomena
are now different ones. For the characters in *Come and Go*, time
is running out. Only yesterday, it seems, they were young
girls, sitting together "in the playground at Miss Wade's. On
the log." Now they have become like the log itself, the age of
which is determined by the number of rings etched in its wood.
"I can feel the rings," comments Flo, her veined hands clasping
the others'. On one level, this is a brooding reference to their
lost youth, to the rings of the log she recalls in her mind. On
another, it is an image of the pain and hellishness of their life,
for the rings suggest both the movement of *Macbeth*'s weird
sisters circling their "hell-broth" ("Round about the cauldron
go" [4.1.4]), and the circles of hell in Dante's *Inferno*. And on
still another level, the most profound level, it is a haunting,
implicit acknowledgement of the characters' inescapable common destiny: the "rings" of inevitable aging culminating in
their death. (Compare Beckett's description of the Elsner sisters
in *Molloy*: "Two old hands, veined, ringed, seek each other,
clasp" [p. 163].)

And what do we do while awaiting this destiny? As the
play's title suggests, we come and go—shuffling aimlessly back
and forth, marking time with the sound of our footfalls, moving
somewhere but getting nowhere. It is an image Beckett has
used repeatedly in his work. Malone, for example, comments:
"Yes, I leave my happiness and go back to the race of men too,
they come and go, often with burdens" (p. 23). Similarly,
Camier remarks "I sense vague shadowy shapes, . . . they
come and go with muffled cries."[10] In *Endgame* we find the
following exchange:

Hamm: How are your legs?
Clov: Bad.
Hamm: But you can walk?
Clov: I come . . . and go. (Pp. 35–36)

And Watt, attempting to emphasize the distinct "other-
worldliness" of his employer, Mr. Knott, describes him significantly as "one who neither comes nor goes . . ." (p. 57).

In the play *Come and Go*, however, Beckett uses the image somewhat differently. It is now not simply something to do while awaiting our destiny but rather an evocation of that destiny itself, an evocation of death. Our third Shakespearean echo is from *King Lear*: "Men must endure / Their *going* hence, even as their *coming* hither" (5.2.9–10; my emphasis). When each of the women in turn leaves the light and disappears into the darkness, we see acted out in that symbolic movement what is simultaneously being whispered about her. The verbal death verdict is thus translated into visual terms—a "going hence." Come and go—birth and death. For Beckett it is this entire birth-death cycle that is ultimately shown to be meaningless. When the three women clasp hands at the end, the unbroken chain they form becomes an ironic emblem of eternity.[11] The monstrous treadmill never ceases: eternity is one endlessly repeated cycle, a coming into life followed by a going into nothingness.

Between the coming and the going, amid the coming and the going, there is nevertheless always time for pain and suffering. No wonder, then, that the three women of *Come and Go* are basically interchangeable. Each may have a slightly different "color"—the shade of her coat,[12] the shade of her flower-name—but, as in physics, the apparent color-spectrum is in reality merely a single color, variously refracted. Their individuality has narrowly constricted bounds: each is free to speak her *"appalled"* "Oh!" in a slightly different tone and inflection;[13] each is free to suffer and die in her own way. (Ophelia: "O, you must wear your rue with a difference" [4.5.179–80].) Like all Beckett's characters, they are victims of a heartless metaphysical ruse difficult to endure, an infinitely cruel divine hoax—specters from an abandoned work.

The final English-language text of *Come and Go* contains 127 words, most of them monosyllables, many of them repetitions; interestingly enough, the word most frequently repeated is "not." In an attempt to dramatize nothingness, Beckett has pared the play of all superfluities, has shed layer after excess layer until what remains is only the barest minimum of dramatic form. As Hugh Kenner has commented, "Beckett has very nearly made a play out of silence."[14] Very nearly, but not quite. The words are few, but they have powerful reverberations. Kenner notes elsewhere that the title of the play evokes T. S. Eliot: "In the room the women come and go / Talking of Michelangelo."[15] The allusion is doubtless there, but if I had to choose a line from Eliot's poetry that best relates to *Come and Go*, I think I might be tempted to choose instead "Those are pearls that were his eyes"—Eliot's allusion in *The Waste Land* to *The Tempest*.[16] For in the play's reverberations, what I hear most hauntingly are the traces of three Shakespearean quotations. *Come and Go* is skeletal drama of a very remarkable kind: a five-act Shakespearean tragedy played in three minutes by three ghosts playing with three echoes—Beckett's art of allusion at its most delicate and its most cunning.

1. All references to *Come and Go* are to the "final," most complete text of the play, published in *Modern Drama* 19 (September 1976): 257–60. See Breon Mitchell's accompanying article, "Art in Microcosm: The Manuscript Stages of Beckett's *Come and Go*," pp. 245–54.

2. Samuel Beckett, *Happy Days* (New York: Grove Press, 1961; rpt. 1970), p. 43. Unless otherwise stated, page references to Beckett's works are from the sixteen-volume *Collected Works of Samuel Beckett* (New York: Grove Press, 1970), and will henceforth be cited in the body of my text.

3. Deirdre Bair, *Samuel Beckett: A Biography* (New York and London: Harcourt Brace Jovanovich, 1978), p. 20.

4. There are a number of allusions to Shakespeare in *Godot*. For an informative discussion of Beckett and Shakespeare, see Ruby Cohn, *Modern Shakespeare Offshoots* (Princeton, N.J.: Princeton University Press, 1976), pp. 375–88.

5. Samuel Beckett, *A Piece of Monologue*, *Kenyon Review* 1 (Summer 1979), p. 2; Shakespeare, *The Merchant of Venice*, 4.1.180–1. All references to Shakespeare are from Peter Alexander's edition of *Shakespeare: The Complete Works* (London: Collins, 1951), and will henceforth be cited in the body of my text.

6. Ruby Cohn has noted that, in Beckett's own production of his French translation of the play, *Va et vient*, at the Odéon, Paris, 1966, he "slowed the playing time from three to seven minutes, so that each gesture seemed wrested from stillness" (Ruby Cohn, *Just Play: Beckett's Theater* [Princeton, N.J.: Princeton University Press, 1980], p. 235).

7. Richard Hosley, ed., *Shakespeare's Holinshed* (New York: G. P. Putnam's Sons, 1968), p. 17.

8. I am grateful to the librarians at Reading University for allowing me to consult these manuscripts, which are in their Samuel Beckett Collection.

Note, by the way, that Richard L. Admussen, in *The Samuel Beckett Manuscripts: A Study* (London: George Prior Publishers; Boston: G. K. Hall & Co., 1979), p. 29, lists these manuscripts incorrectly. What Admussen labels draft A ("Good Heavens") is, in fact, two separate drafts, and thus should be labeled A and A_1; A_1, the manuscript entitled "Good Heavens," is an emendation of the earlier, untitled manuscript A.

9. Ibid. "Heartburn" is an emendation; Beckett originally wrote "acidity," but then struck it out and wrote in "heartburn."

10. Samuel Beckett, *Mercier and Camier* (New York: Grove Press, 1975), p. 19.

11. See James Knowlson, "Good Heavens," *Gambit*, vol. 7, no. 28 (1976), p. 102.

12. In Beckett's own production of *Va et vient*, even this minute color differentiation was muted: the coats were three shades of gray (see Ruby Cohn, *Just Play*, p. 235).

13. Beckett's French translation of the play makes the point more subtly by replacing the "Oh!" with three slightly different words meaning much the same thing: "Miséricorde!"; "Malheur!"; "Misère!" (Samuel Beckett, *Va et vient*, in *Comédie et actes divers* [Paris: Minuit, 1966], pp. 40–41).

14. Hugh Kenner, *Samuel Beckett: A Critical Study* (Berkeley: University of California Press, 1968), p. 225.

15. Hugh Kenner, *A Reader's Guide to Samuel Beckett* (London: Thames and Hudson, 1973), p. 174; T. S. Eliot, *The Love Song of J. Alfred Prufrock*.

16. T. S. Eliot, *The Waste Land*, II. *A Game of Chess*, 1. 125. Cf. *The Tempest*, 1.2.399.

Antoni Libera

The Lost Ones: A Myth of
Human History and Destiny

The Lost Ones,[1] like other works by Samuel Beckett, reflects two
separate but parallel realities, one objective and one subjective,
but the latter is only another way of perceiving the former. In
other words, while the narration of *The Lost Ones* is a description and a source of information, apparently objective, it is at
the same time an interpretation and a commentary. Someone—
whom we shall call the observer—finds himself in an unrealis-
tic, seemingly underground universe ruled by its own internal
time so that we cannot determine how long he has been there.
His observations enable him to establish a synthetic image of
this strange world. After explaining to himself the life and laws
of this universe, he reports them on the basis of his own infer-
ences. The text of *The Lost Ones* is the result, and it resembles a
report or a treatise. It is at once an account and a speculation.
Analyzing it, one has to distinguish information from interpretation, fact from hypothesis, and to bring to the fore those
questions that the observer avoids.

The universe is described as a cylinder some sixteen meters in
diameter (fifty meters circumference) and sixteen high, made of
an unknown, rubber-like substance, which produces no sound
when hit and which somehow emits light and heat. In the
upper half of the wall, all the way round, there are twenty
niches, disposed in four irregular quincunxes. Many of them

are connected by tunnels hollowed in the wall, but some are blind. The niches and tunnels are something of a mystery. We never know whether they were made by the inhabitants of the cylinder or are natural features. Their irregular patterns as well as the fact that some are blind make the observer believe that they were probably drilled or dug by the cylinder dwellers: some "completed" by meeting other tunnels, one simply abandoned, "as though at a certain stage discouragement had prevailed" (p. 12). The observer, however, never speculates about the discouragement. In fact, he avoids a series of significant questions. He does tell us that the wall is so hard that even scratching a mark into it seems impossible and that the only tools available to the cylinder's inhabitants are their hands and the rungs of the ladders. But he doesn't speculate about how the niches might have been dug or what happened to the excavated substance? These are the sorts of questions the observer should be asking himself. He does, for example, explain a similar phenomenon, the missing rungs, which "are in the hands of a happy few. . ." (p. 10). But how could the bodies arrange the niches so harmoniously, since, we learn, they plant their ladders randomly, without looking at the walls? Moreover, according to the observer, no one in the cylinder can appreciate this harmony. The origin of the niches and tunnels finally remains a mystery.

But there are aspects of the cylinder that we know with some certainty. It contains fifteen ladders that are part of the environment. The interior of the cylinder fluctuates with light and heat, which oscillate origin-less but regularly from wall, floor, ceiling, and even tunnels. The light increases and decreases four times per second, and the temperature changes from five to twenty-five degrees and back in eight seconds. From time to time suddenly and unexpectedly, both vibrations cease. This period never lasts more than ten seconds, in which time all activity in the cylinder stands still.

The cylinder is the abode of two hundred and five naked bodies of either sex and all ages. They differ in their motion and in the types of activities they perform and are divided into four groups: those who are in motion, those who pause sometimes, those who lead a sedentary life, and those who remain perfectly still. We learn that the first group contains twice as many members as the second, the second three times as many as the third, the third four times as many as the fourth, and the fourth group consists of 5 members. Thus one can easily calculate that 20 of the cylinder dwellers sit (4×5), 60 pause (3×20), and 120 are in motion (2×60). Four of the five still bodies ("the vanquished," as the observer calls them) sit with their backs against the wall in the position that "wrung from Dante one of his rare wan smiles." It is the position of Belacqua (a version of whom we saw in Beckett's early short stories) in Dante's Purgatory. Seeing him, Dante smiled and described his posture as follows: "one of them, who seemed to me weary, was sitting and clasping his knees, holding his face low down between them." Beckett echoes the image with the description of "the first among the vanquished": "She squats against the wall with her head between her knees and her legs in her arms. The left hand clasps the right shinbone and the right the left forearm. . . . The left foot is crossed on the right" (pp. 56–57).

The bodies in motion either circle around the arena, wait their turn to climb the ladders, look for an appropriate queue or an appropriate place to plant the ladder, stand in line or on the ladder, climb it, sit in the niches, or crawl in the tunnels. All these activities, and the order of performing them, are subject to certain rules, which the observer attempts to reconstruct. However, he is only partly successful. The helpless questions he asks prove that certain things remain unexplained.

All activities seem to have one purpose: finding a way out of the cylinder. But is there evidence that this is indeed the motive pushing the bodies to act? The various movements and actions may be merely a disorderly bustle. One has to admit finally that in the description of the life in the cylinder there is no proof that the action is purposive. Besides, a purely behavioristic description cannot in itself constitute a proof, since behaviorism does not explain intentions. All that we know about these motives comes from the observer.

He says, "From time immemorial rumour has it or better still the notion is abroad that there exists a way out" (pp. 17–18).

Those words are followed by a characterization of two fundamental beliefs shared by the inhabitants of the cylinder concerning the type and location of the exit: "One school swears by
a secret passage branching from one of the tunnels and leading
in the words of the poet to nature's sanctuaries. The other
dreams of a trapdoor hidden in the hub of the ceiling, giving
access to a flue at the end of which the sun and other stars
would still be shining" (p. 18). But how does the observer know
about all this? We assume he does know because he gives the
information so categorically. Whenever he does *not* know or
only suspects something, he never fails to make that clear. He
states repeatedly that there are things he does not know—what
is beyond the cylinder, for instance ("nothing but mystery")—
and he does not find the ultimate explanation to many phenomena. There are no grounds, therefore, to believe that in this
case his abilities are out of the ordinary. His intelligence and
cognitive possibilities seem to be average. So how can he know
the content of their beliefs? Granting that he does not possess
supernatural powers, the only source of information is speech
or writing, but the bodies in the cylinder do not use language
(this is why the phrase "rumour has it" has been replaced by
"the notion is abroad").

In such circumstances the observer's knowledge comes from
introspection. We shall discuss shortly how this knowledge is
possible, what it means, and what results from it. It is worth
noticing now, however, that it casts a new light on the observer. It means that in a way he belongs to the cylindrical
universe and that he is neither an outsider nor a stranger.
Moreover, he seems to be connected or even tied to it. "The fact
remains," he notes, ". . . that of these two persuasions the
former is declining in favor of the latter but in a manner so
desultory and slow and of course with so little effect on the
comportment of either sect that to perceive it one must be in the
secret of the gods" (p. 19). And earlier, ". . . Here all should
die but with so gradual and . . . so fluctuant a death as to escape the notice even of a visitor" (p. 18). The observer is then
not a visitor, but is in a privileged position, "in the secret of the
gods."

The description of these beliefs, however, does not explain why the bodies look for the exit. It is not clear whether they want to leave their abode in order to find out what lies beyond its limits or simply to learn whether or not there is an exit. The members of the first group want only to satisfy their curiosity, since they believe that the mythical trapdoor in the ceiling would lead to a long chimney that itself would be impossible to climb. The others are closer to having the desire to leave the cylinder. However, considering the ambiguity of the expression "nature's sanctuaries" (p. 18), one does not know what they really expect on leaving their abode. It seems, however, that both beliefs indicate a longing for a world of nature as we understand it. For the first group, it is symbolized by the phrase "the sun and other stars" (p. 18), for the second by the abstract notion of "a sanctuary."

Let us now return to the observer's hypothesis. He believes that the process he discerns is the principle of life in the cylinder. The fact that the bodies are divided according to motion and that the immobile ones formerly moved like the others leads him to conclude that the quest is not perpetual and invariable, but is diminishing and one day will cease completely. This deduction, "the notion" as he calls it, enables him to create a general theory of life in the cylinder. In the very beginning, all the inhabitants were in motion: "all roamed without respite" (p. 34); but finally, after a long period of constant bustle, the first body ("the woman vanquished") gave up. What was the reason? Was it due to the lack of force or rather to a lack of belief in the existence of the exit? We have no direct answer. However, the fact that the observer names the still bodies "the vanquished ones" and their attitude "abandonment" (p. 31) suggests that it was the second case, a failure of belief. He also stresses that the perfectly still cannot be considered as blind, that is, as people unable to continue to search. Significantly he attributes such a mistake to a "thinking being coldly intent on all these data and evidences" (p. 39), who seems to ignore the cylinder's fundamental secrets. These observations are further proof that the observer is not a mysterious stranger but a native.

After "the woman vanquished" (p. 56) came others, and the slow process—in which the bodies, one by one, grew motionless—was begun. The process suggests deterioration; the body begins to stop; then it assumes the sedentary position, and finally stops moving altogether. Sometimes the transition is more violent. In most cases, however, the change from one stage to another is neither abrupt nor irreversible. The body that assumed a sedentary position can continue its search just as before, until finally, having exhausted this need, it becomes immobile. Before it becomes perfectly still, however, it resumes the sedentary position and tries to search with its eyes. In order to describe the pace of this evolution, the observer uses the following simile: "Even so a great heap of sand sheltered from the wind lessened by three grains every second year and every following year increased by two . . ." (p. 32). But no one comes back to the state of perpetual motion. Those who paused will never circle incessantly again. This is perhaps the grain by which the metaphorical heap diminishes every second year.

The gradual abandonment of the quest leads inevitably to complete cessation. Considering that each body requires a different amount of time to go through the whole cycle, the body that will remain will be the one that requires most. The observer suspects that after waking from lethargy the most persistent body will begin its last search. By this time, the others will have renounced it long ago. After performing some movements (it is difficult to predict which), it will finally approach "the woman vanquished" and look into her eyes, where it will see nothing but "calm wastes." Then it will leave her and squat somewhere, becoming immobile forever. At the same time, the light will fade and the temperature will drop to zero. The supposition is astonishing, since it assumes that the light and heat depend somehow on the bodies and their quest. But according to the laws of the cylinder, the relationship should be reversed; motion should depend on energy fluctuation. But the future is finally beyond the observer, except for a creative (fictional) possibility: "Then light and climate will be changed in a way impossible to foretell. But the former may be imagined extinguished as purposeless and the latter fixed not far from freezing point" (p. 15). It is also worth noticing the observer's attitude to the notion of the exit. His description of life in the cylinder and his vision of the end make us believe that there are two possibilities: he is convinced either that there is no exit or that there is no possibility of finding it, at least in the time allowed to the most persistent body. However, we never learn the observer's direct opinion on this question. Whether an exit exists or not, and, if it does, where it is located, are questions never settled. He says only that the abode is "vast enough for flight to be in vain." The force of this statement is pragmatic. It neither explains the reason for this futility nor provides information. It only shows the observer's ignorance on this matter. We can assume that if he did have something in mind, he would put it forward. Once more we are led to believe that he belongs to the world of the cylinder.

Now that we have characterized the life in the cylinder and learned how it is seen and understood by the observer, we may try to determine the meaning of this world. What do the cylinder and its inhabitants represent? Who is the observer? And finally, how are we to understand the interpretation that he calls "the notion"? We have already suggested that the observer belongs to the world of the cylinder and, at the same time, uses human language and is familiar with Western culture (he knows Dante, for example). He symbolizes, therefore, a form of humanity in its weird abode, and the cylinder may be interpreted as the human world, or more precisely, its allegorical image. The two hundred naked bodies inhabiting the cylinder would be the humans living on earth, and their situation and behavior would represent the human condition and activity. Life in the cylinder is a model of human history. The anonymous observer, who is not one of the bodies, but knows at least as much about the cylinder as its inhabitants do and, moreover, can draw conclusions and speculate, is the personification of the human mind, which, in spite of being tied down to the earth, can, nonetheless, grasp it and learn the truth about it. He is the spirit of humanity—its power of self-analysis, its self-knowledge—which, though restricted by the boundaries within which man is confined, goes far beyond the individual consciousness. It is the sum of human experience and therefore a common property. This is why the result of its speculation, the observer's report (the text of *The Lost Ones*), is not written in the first person. His attempt, which we are shown, to gain both descriptive and interpretative knowledge constitutes not an individual observation but a myth, the myth of the history and destiny of humanity. His "notion" is a theory of history, and the final vision, an apocalyptic prophecy.

But what then is the significance of the myth? How does it help us interpret man and his life on earth? The gradually ceasing search for the exit, which is the essence of the bodies' lives, has a double meaning. It shows that the inhabitants of the cylinder long for a world different from the one they know. The need to leave their abode indicates that they are not "comfortable" there (there is not enough space, and it is at the same time too hot and too cold). This feeling is not, however, eternal and after some time dies down. Hence adaptation to these conditions *is* possible. The abandonment of the search means that the bodies have grown accustomed to the situation and no longer seek change. Adaptation, however, means closing one's eyes and ceasing to see, that is, not accepting the surrounding reality. This total renunciation leads to a final disappearance of the whole environment. After the last body becomes motionless, everything will turn into darkness, which in a way will annihilate the cylindrical world. It seems that the cylinder is not a cage into which the bodies were crammed but a lighted space created by the bodies themselves. The cylinder is just a glow that assumes an illusory shape in the middle of the neutral and boundless darkness. The cylinder is not, therefore, a necessary condition of the existence of the bodies but rather their function, or, still better, merely their way of being. The fact that this way of life restricts and compels the inhabitants of the cylinder and provokes them to run away, or alter their situation, means that its foundation—that is, the essence of being—is corrupt, false, and unfulfilling. Since the source of the erroneousness is the mere fact of existence, the only way of eliminating it is complete annihilation. This will not be attained immediately, but slowly, due to the gradually growing, albeit at first absent, awareness of the dependence. It is a process of purging, and this is the essence of the bodies' life.

What will happen when this process reaches its end? Or rather, putting aside the destruction of a given form of being, what is this end? The answer is to be found in the position the bodies finally assume, the position of the vanquished ones. At this point, let us notice that this very position is assumed by the two bodies in the white rotunda in *Imagination Dead Imagine*; there it suggests the fetal stage of life. Hence one can view the liberation from one form of life as a return to the starting point or to an even earlier phase. The two bodies in the white rotunda, however, and the two hundred bodies in the dark cylinder are something completely different. So the liberation is not quite a return to the original starting point, but rather the approach to the beginning of a new one. It is like a return to a point situated in the same place but on a different circle of a spiral.

Beckett gives us no hint of the future. What is going to happen next? One can only guess. If we assume that in Beckett's late prose the human body symbolizes the potentiality inherent in the world of being something like man, and the eyes, by opening, the means by which that potentiality is realized, then the general vision of existence suggested by Beckett would be as follows: the world as substance wants to find a form for itself. It does this by lighting up its darkness with the light it can produce. However, the world as substance does not know what this form should be. In other words, it does not know how to go about illuminating itself, and by what light. This is why the comportment of the world resembles a persistent process of experimentation.

Originally it assumed the form of a rotunda, as in *Imagination Dead Imagine*. But the form was not satisfactory. The memorable words, "there is better elsewhere," express this. "Elsewhere" means here "differently," a different way of self-illumination. So the world "opens" itself anew and becomes the reality of the cylinder. But this again proves unacceptable. From this perspective it longs for a "natural" reality, with the sun and other stars. But there is no possibility of passing from the cylinder to that reality. There can only be a new "opening," a new self-illumination. This is why, the moment the world assumed the form of the cylinder, the light began to fade, which in practice meant a gradual abandonment of the quest. When the light disappears completely, the world comes back to the starting point and everything may begin again. What will be the result of the new attempt? What reality will the eyes see when they open once more in another way? Perhaps they will see that much-desired reality with the sun and other stars. Thus instead of the cylinder there will be the boundless firmament and the bodies will find themselves on the earth as true human beings. Will this be a successful and final attempt? *Is* it a successful and final attempt? *Is* the world satisfied with this world? To judge from our experience as human beings, it is not. If it were, the work entitled *The Lost Ones* could never have been created.

The dialectic of the world manifests itself not only in the ontological sphere but also on lower levels of cognition. The fluctuating substance of life that during millions of years appeared in various shapes, only to be subsequently rejected, assumed finally the human shape. Each of those forms—a protozoon, an alga, a Neanderthal man—was concentrated only on itself. Everything it did was meant to prolong the life of the species, to ensure its survival. In fact, however, this always resulted in the abandonment of that form and its attributes, and the passage to a different stage. Such was also the case with our predecessor, the Neanderthal man. He, gathering all the force he could muster, fought to withstand nature, to struggle for existence, to propagate his own kind, such as it was—hairy, a little stooped, and seemed with the very breath of his being intent on preserving his species, his Neanderthal world. And yet so intent, he destroys it with every step, with every act of propagation; so intent, he removes himself from it, razes it, thrusts it into oblivion. Instead of preserving his essence, he dissipates, annihilates it; instead of remaining himself, he becomes man.

Man's behavior is similar. He gradually exhausts all the possibilities of his existence. He becomes, for instance, the man of antiquity: he creates religions and laws that he retains for some time and then rejects in order to become a Christian. He is successively the man of the Middle Ages, the man of the Renaissance, the man of the Enlightenment. Each of these stages or forms of humanity is different, each has a different foundation, each represents a different kind of quest; each gives a different cognitive perspective and reveals a different vision of the world. For some this is a progression. For Beckett it is a regression. It is the elimination of various paths leading back to some starting point. The history of the world is in fact the history of "depopulation." It is the history of man's freeing himself from himself. Such a conviction is expressed in the very first sentence of *The Lost Ones*: "Abode where lost bodies roam each searching for its lost one" (p. 7)—in the French version, "son dépeupleur." The entire text seems to support this thesis. The mysterious word *dépeupleur*, which appears only in the sentence quoted above, may finally refer to the way of getting out of oneself, a search for a radical way of enabling one to stop being oneself. The bodies search for an exit, but in fact each searches for its lost one. They want to leave their abode, but in fact they relinquish the search, which is the essence of their life. People build and expand man's kingdom on earth, but in fact they are leading to the exhaustion of their possibilities and attributes. They want to be more human and leave behind the world of animals, but in fact they begin to turn into a species that has nothing in common with man.

Does this myth utter a truth? There can be no final answer to this question. However, as opposed to other myths created by man, it does not pretend to be ultimate and unshaken, nor does it require blind faith. On the contrary, it seems to stress its own relativity. The constant refrain-like repetition, "if this notion is maintained," suggests the observer's skepticism toward his own ideas, which is quite understandable; for if he maintains the inconstancy and relativity of everything, he cannot exclude himself from this rule, and must question his own "notions."

Finally, it is also worth considering that the vision of man's history presented in *The Lost Ones* has much in common with the conceptions of Giambattista Vico. It might even be said that *The Lost Ones* is a poetic representation of his famous argument that all human actions lead to goals different from the original motivating force of those actions, namely, to the realization of the goals of divine Providence. And in this case, divine Providence is the will to change from one form of existence to another.

1. Samuel Beckett, *The Lost Ones* (New York: Grove Press, 1972). All references are to this edition.

Enoch Brater

The *Company* Beckett Keeps: The Shape of Memory and One Fablist's Decay of Lying

Every work by Samuel Beckett is likely to strike its reader as the discovery of some rich archaeological find. The Beckett specialist, moreover, Joyce's ideal reader suffering an ideal insomnia, can hardly wait to get his hands on each piece in order to track down that "stiff interexclusiveness" of those tempting relationships to earlier materials. And so it is with *Company*: here Beckett again locates his work within the familiar network he has made so authentically his own. As readers of these texts, we too have a stake in charting the limits of such an exclusive territory. Yet the investment of our energy is a bit more problematical: almost before we have had a chance to appreciate the work on its own terms, we begin to situate it in the canon through a process Beckett long ago disparaged as "literary bookkeeping."[1] The dilemma, of course, is by now inevitable. Beckett sets the trap, and we enjoy falling for the bait, especially when the bait is, as in the present instance, a kind of caviar to the general. But there is always a "danger in the neatness of identifications": it makes us inadvertently undermine the integrity and originality of *Company* at the same time that it encourages us to elevate its status as yet another victory in the battle this writer's words continue to wage with form. The point of this essay will be, then, twofold: to demonstrate how *Company* draws on the allusive texture of Beckett's formidable literary past and to show how he now transforms it into something we may not have seen in precisely these same terms before.

In *Company* the specific allusions to Beckett's works are legion. Let us pause for a moment to reflect on the following *catalogue raisonné*, which is, it must be pointed out in advance, by no means complete. We might begin with *Endgame*, where Hamm is one of the first to complain of something dripping in his head. "Perhaps it's a little vein," he speculates. *Endgame* as source material is particularly promising for, like *Company*, it features Zeno's "grain by grain in the mind"[2] as well as a possible encounter with a dead rat. "What an addition to company that would be!" (p. 16), we read here, "A rat long dead" (p. 27). "If I don't kill that rat he'll die," Clov, we recall, had long ago lamented. Or, to keep our genres straight, we might prefer to begin with *Malone Dies*, which offers us the additional satisfaction of a narrator, hero, and novelist *manqué* who, like this one, "on his back in the dark" (p. 7), suffers a similar decay of lying—and in both senses of the word. But what precisely does any text signify when it speaks of a protagonist "loosely as lying" (p. 55)? "Which in other words," *Company* continues, "of all the innumerable ways of lying is likely to prove in the long run the most endearing?" (p. 55). The pun on "lying" will come up again, for this "fable" will resume "where the act of lying cut it short" (p. 62). Beckett, however, constructs his narrative truth from just such a pregnant series of lyings-in. Positions, once physical, now turn to Watt's "semantic succour": "From time to time with unexpected grace you lie" (p. 61). A little language is, once again, a dangerously animated thing.

Malone Dies provides the proper atmosphere for a variety of other items: it uses the same anti-novelistic strategies of inventing names for characters along the way and then quickly dismissing or replacing them, it wonders aloud about its own narrative authority (is the figure under a sheet clothed or naked?), and it suggests a number of possible topics that might be taken up in the interests of the narrative. *Malone Dies* also delivers a prominent feature to *Company* in the shape of memory, for it shares with it the same cutting retort a mother makes to a young boy when he asks her if the sky is not in reality much less distant than it appears to be. Let us look at the different shapes Beckett has the same "memory" assume as it passes from one literary permutation to the next:

> One day we were walking along the road, up a hill of extraordinary steepness, near home I imagine, my memory is full of steep hills, I get them confused. I said, The sky is further away than you think, is it not, mama? It was without malice, I was simply thinking of all the leagues that separated me from it. She replied, to me her son, It is precisely as far away as it appears to be. She was right. But at the time I was aghast. I can still see the spot, opposite Tyler's gate.[3]

> You make ground in silence hand in hand through the warm still summer air. It is late afternoon and after some hundred paces the sun appears above the crest of the rise. Looking up at the blue sky and then at your mother's face you break the silence asking her if it is not in reality much more distant than it appears. The sky that is. The blue sky. Receiving no answer you mentally reframe your question and some hundred paces later look up at her face again and ask her if it does not appear much less distant than in reality it is. For some reason you could never fathom this question must have angered her exceedingly. For she shook off your little hand and made you a cutting retort you have never forgotten. (*Company*, pp. 10–11)

Although in *Company* Beckett carefully suppresses the autobiographical details of one of the first "loopings of the loop" at the Leopardstown racecourse near his boyhood home in Foxrock, a suburb of Dublin, the memory, distilled this time, lingers on—and not only for its author. In using a scene he has used before, Beckett makes us share in his novelistic history: our memory in this instance is carefully focused all the way back to *Malone Dies*. Beckett has taken a detail from his own life and elevated it into fiction, a fiction he counts upon us to remember. Seen in this context, the haunting lines of *Company* begin to refer to us and to our own situation as Beckett's reader: "Yes I remember" (pp. 16 and passim).

Despite all these close approximations—and there will be others—one must be careful not to overemphasize the similarities uniting *Malone Dies* and *Company*, for the latter text will be just as liberal in its borrowings from other Beckett works. The window looking west and the "some movement however small" (p. 20) remind us of *Still*, as does the highly specialized vocabulary of "withershins" (pp. 38, 50), which, contrary to "deasil" in the earlier work, means to move in a direction contrary to the apparent course of the sun, that is, counterclockwise and therefore unlucky. The computation of distance traveled is right out of *Enough*, though here we read about another character "with bowed head on the verge of the ditch" (pp. 14–15) who converts "into yards" (p. 15) (the ditch in this case coming from *Molloy* or *Waiting for Godot*). The voice "now from one quarter and now from another" (p. 15) re-creates the staging of *That Time*, and a voice avoiding the first person singular brings us back to *Not I*, as does Croker's Acres, a real place near Beckett's childhood home. *Not I* also brings to *Company* its Listener, called in this case the "hearer," and yields as well the special emptiness of "No trace of love" (p. 47) and the disturbing imprecision of not knowing whether one is "standing or sitting or lying" (p. 26), though in this instance "kneeling" is omitted from the battery of possible posturings. The "God save you little master" (p. 17) in the vignette of the old beggar woman resurrects the whole bloody business of a savior from *Waiting for Godot*, a work that will be referred to again when, like Estragon, a female character assaulting the voice's memory murmurs appealingly, "Listen to the leaves" (p. 48). The speculation on crawling is from *How It Is*; the "comfort" of mathematics makes us think of Dan Rooney ("Not count! One of the few satisfactions in life?"); an unwanted pregnancy and a painful delivery resemble the uneasy situation in *First Love*; "conjuring of something out of nothing" (p. 53) recycles Watt's lexical predicament; the "All you had seen was cloud" (p. 25) reshapes the central metaphor in ". . . *but the clouds* . . ."; the "dissolve" (p. 42) to a father sitting on a bench in a summerhouse uses a technical option of Beckett's "comic and unreal" *Film*, as does "of course the eye. Filling the whole field. The hood slowly down. Or up if down to begin. The globe. All pupil. Staring up. Hooded. Bared. Hooded again. Bared again" (pp. 20–21); the "footfalls" (p. 14 and passim) and the "unnamable" (p. 32) bring to light the play and the novel of the same names, and with this in view, a "Devised deviser devising *it all* for company" (p. 46; emphasis mine) especially resembles the May who so addictively revolves "it all" as she paces back and forth before us on stage; the "Be again" (p. 20) repeats a futile command of *Krapp's Last Tape*, a work that shares with this one a "lamp left lit above you" (p. 59); a "tiny cycle" (p. 17) brings to mind those misshapen vehicles we have seen before in pastures similarly "strewn" with uneaten sheeps' "red placentae" (p. 35); the absurd position of "Head resting mainly on occipital bump aforesaid. Legs joined at attention. Feet splayed ninety degrees. Hands invisibly manacled crossed on pubis" (p. 57) sounds like a further development of the physiognomic irregularity we have met before in *Imagination Dead Imagine*; "Hodgkin's disease or if you prefer Percival Pott's" (p. 61) is medical terminology as technical as the "Bright's disease, Grave's disease, strangury and fits" specified in *Murphy*, where "conation" is also an option; the "Palest blue against the pale sky" (p. 25) asks us to reconsider two prominent images from the ruins of *Lessness*, a piece inevitably referred to in the repeated appearance of such "lessness" words as "moonless," "starless" (p. 54), "cloudless" (p. 25 and passim), "bootless" (p. 55), and, finally, "comfortless" (p. 55); "the unthinkable last of all" (p. 24) repeats a moment of closure from *The Lost Ones*, which also brings to *Company* a French "esquisse" (p. 45) in place of its own "aperçu" and makes us consider a similar geometry of space that replaces cones, cylinders, and quincunxes with oblongs, rhomboids, and a rather spectacular "rustic hexahedron" (p. 38); and "Better a sick heart than none" (p. 26) messes up the same biblical quotation that Winnie mangles in *Happy Days*, though in this case "Better a sick heart than none." An M and a W put in cameo appearances in this prose tract, and we should be relieved to see that Belacqua Shuah, Dante's ever-present Florentine lute-maker, is also here. At long last, a text bids him a tender and generous farewell for, having waited so long in Beckett's fiction to be purged, he is "now perhaps singing praises with some section of the blest at last" (p. 60). "Yes," we say again as we read this text, "I remember."

The mention of Dante's "first quarter-smile" (p. 60) might make us think that at least some of the allusions in *Company* point back to a literary tradition that is not entirely of Beckett's own making. Yet in this citation, the emphasis is not so much on Dante as it is on Beckett's earlier use of him, that special Dante appropriated all the way back in *More Pricks Than Kicks* and the figure of Belacqua who walks through Beckett's fiction all the way up to *The Lost Ones* and *Company*. Beckett has taken a small piece of *The Divine Comedy* and therefore made it an integral part of his own intimate repertory. He has done the same with his gleanings from the Bible. "Better a sick heart than none" is Beckett, not the book of Psalms, and the memory is of Winnie rather than of David. Shakespeare will be similarly colonized: "labour lost" is the same kind of residual allusion to the Bard that skirts the surface of such earlier works as *Footfalls*, *That Time*, *Come and Go*, and *Happy Days*, to mention only a few of the most notable.[4] The "half blind" (p. 16), "the shadowy light" (pp. 18–19), the "dark" that "lightens" (p. 19), and the "Died on to dawn and never died" (the last phrase by way of *A Piece of Monologue*) similarly resurrect Milton and more particularly Beckett's earlier use of him in such works as *Happy Days*, where an intrepid Winnie opens act two with a direct quotation from *Paradise Lost*: "Hail, holy light." Beckett, of course, can be counted on to elevate Joyce and his own indebtedness to this modern master to such distinguished company: "Bloom of adulthood. Imagine a whiff of that" (p. 38). Dante, Shakespeare, the Bible, Milton, Joyce: the company Beckett keeps is rarely uncertain. External allusions in this work are primarily there to remind us of the same literary patterns Beckett has urged us to consider before as he weaves the web of his own private mythology.

The shape of fictional memory in *Company* will also extend to the characteristic intrusion of learned vocabulary that we associate with so many other enterprises, the "hog's setae" of *Happy Days*, the "Schimmel" of *From an Abandoned Work*, the "ramdam" of *All That Fall*, the "tremolo" of *The Lost Ones*, the "passing rack" of *Footfalls*, or the "viduity" of *Krapp's Last Tape*, which the seedy hero actually looks up for us in a dictionary. In

Company the hermetic language is extended, this time embracing such a motley of items as transportation, the French language, and human anatomy. Let us begin with the "De Dion Bouton" (p. 14), the automobile manufactured in Paris circa 1904 and conveniently parked in this story in the family's coach house. The text will make a sly reference to this same vehicle later on when, in the subsequent vignette that takes place in the summerhouse, the characters sit "vis-à-vis" (p. 39). The De Dion Bouton was one of the few automobiles that allowed for this possibility. It featured a four-passenger model called, in fact, the "Vis-à-Vis": seats faced one another and the steering mechanism was placed in the center. "Vis-à-vis" neatly links recherché automotive history with recondite language study. Here Beckett has some fun with the French pronunciation of "Haitch," the name this text momentarily considers for its "hearer," yet another English word, like the "he," the "him," and the "hope" of the same paragraph, which also begins with an "Haitch." The French language, of course, considers two phonemes for "h," the *h-muet* and the *h-aspiré*: "Let the hearer be named H. Aspirate. Haitch. You Haitch are on your back in the dark. And let him know his name. No longer any question of his overhearing" (p. 31). "H" is therefore no name at all for the simple reason that it is so difficult to pronounce for a French speaker: "Then let him not be named H. Let him be again as he was. The hearer. Unnamable. You" (p. 32). The fictional language for the human anatomy in *Company* will prove as esoteric and in at least one instance similarly tricky. "All the way from calcaneum to bump of philogenitiveness" (p. 51) is a mistake in the published text that should read, according to Beckett, "All the way from calcaneum to bump of philoprogenitiveness."[5] Like Krapp we are sent scurrying to the dictionary: philoprogenitiveness means tending to produce offspring, prolific; of, relating to, or characterized by love of offspring. This makes for a properly improper pun; the bump is phallic and also takes us back to Hamm's "accursed progenitor."

Before entirely abandoning the arrant pedantry of what this text calls "readier reference" (p. 42)—which for the purpose of the argument will force us to omit the "i" in the Beckett tradition and thereby take for *reader reference*—let us notice some of those narcissistic rhetorical flourishes that have become characteristic specialties in the Beckett iconography. The whole motif, in fact, of appealing so slyly to the reader has been a pose taken up before. *Murphy* makes a novelistic pact with its reader by directly addressing him as the "gentle skimmer," and May in *Footfalls* calls our attention to an old Mrs. Winter, "whom the reader will remember," though unfortunately no such reader, "strange or otherwise," has been able to track her down, much to our dismay and frustration. Several other linguistic patterns will accompany us back to still other voices in narrative situations we have already confronted. "Up to a point" (p. 12 and passim), for example, reenergizes a critical moment of sexual innuendo in *Enough,* and "nought anew" (p. 15 and passim) recycles the "nothing new" (by way of Ecclesiastes) on which the sun shone, having no alternative, all the way back in *Murphy*. The use of a simple word like "home" will also prove similarly self-referential. In *Malone Dies* we read, "The man has not yet come home. Home," which *Company* renders as "And never once overstepped a radius of one from home. Home!" *Not I* also picks up on the same rhetoric of meaning: ". . . one evening on the way home . . . home! . . . a little mound in Croker's Acres . . . ," as does *Ill Seen Ill Said,* where the linguistic phenomenon takes place three times:

> At this rate it will be black night before she reaches home. Home!
>
> How find her way home? Home! Even as the homing bird.
>
> Alone night fallen she makes her home. Home!

In each case the elementary repetition of a single word makes a simple sentence wax lyrical in its yearning for a lost security forever out of reach. But foremost among all these syntactical echoes is the word-sentence "Imagine" (p. 7 and passim), which was, of course, used so effectively in *Imagination Dead Imagine* and again in *All Strange Away*. Consider "Imagine" and one comes to see straightaway the difficulties inherent in any of these prose undertakings. As a single word, capitalized and followed by a period, the reader first takes it as a verb. The subject, however, falls far from the verb and lands, characteristically, somewhere in the void. Grammatically, the subject is supposed to be understood, but it is also supposed to be suppressed, a pronoun the person and number of which we expect will be conventionally clarified in the context of what follows. Yet *Company* will use convention to confound and expand beyond any easy presuppositions. "Imagine," then, functions simultaneously as an imperative, an invocation, and a casual observation addressing both the narrative voice and the reader. Once invited in this way to utilize his own creative faculties in conjunction with this text, the gentle and unsuspecting "skimmer" embarks on a subtle adventure that implicates everything and everyone, past allusions as well as present readings, as the title *Company* so disingenuously suggests.

But the allusions that really make the difference in *Company* are not the specific self-references this particular text makes sometimes subtly, sometimes aggressively, to so many of the earlier works. What matters here is the evocation of a new pattern of memory that refers to the earlier works not so much nominally as it does stylistically. For *Company* offers us two distinct rhythms, one for mind and quite another for heart. Both provide us with uncertain "company":

> Yet a certain activity of mind however slight is a necessary adjunct of company. That is why the voice does not say, You are on your back in the dark and have no mental activity of any kind. The voice alone is company but not enough. (P. 9)

This particular voice, however, is woefully "reason-ridden" (p. 33); it makes for some good company, "but not enough." The highly cerebral reflections on the nature of the voice, its origin, its person, and its number, soon turn in another direction. A vignette suddenly intrudes, providing, one suspects, more welcome "company" in the shape of remembrances of things past. Memory, as in *Krapp's Last Tape*, adds a significant and powerful dimension to *Company*, one that will be employed with tantalizing restraint. The appearance of these digressions from the current dire situation, as suddenly represented by the voice in the dark, gives the piece far greater depth. The particularized exploration of a room and a desperate state of affairs becomes animated when the voice adopts a tone registering the possibility of a human existence that supplies us with background as well as psychological texturing. These scenes are, then, crucial: they expand the terrain the reader and the protagonist traverse in the course of this story. They also offer us a powerful inducement to read this work autobiographically. For the scenes of memory have about them a highly charged emotional impact, a deeply "felt" disposition, that appeals to a reader's inclination to identify a heart behind the mind we have so often encountered:

> You stand at the tip of the high board. High above the sea. In it your father's upturned face. Upturned to you. You look down to the loved trusted face. He calls to you to jump. He calls, Be a brave boy. The red round face. The thick moustache. The greying hair. The swell sways it under and sways it up again. The far call again, Be a brave boy. Many eyes upon you. From the water and from the bathing place. (P. 18)

But autobiography is always a trap; Beckett denies its certainty. His text repeatedly reminds us that these vignettes contain "creatures" that are an integral part of the emerging "fable," the long dissolution that is every Beckett hero's life. However much they may conform to the known or suspected details of the author's life (the Irish names of roads and stores, the birth on Good Friday, the suggestion of upper-middle-class affluence in the make of a fancy car), the personal flavor imparted in these very moving scenes does not escape their role in the structured and highly self-conscious work of art. For like the origin of the voice itself, these scenes provide a problematic dimension to *Company* and remain inextricably tied to everything else in the text. Isolating them at the expense of the more intellectual reflections by "one on his back in the dark" (p. 7) succeeds only in altering the work. An autobiographical explication of *Company*, like one of *Malone Dies*, which in this respect it so closely resembles, will be, necessarily, reductive.

The situation, to borrow a phrase from *Murphy*, is "less Words-worthy": these vignettes present no "spots of time," but offer instead the "limits to part's equality with whole."[6]

Autobiography has therefore been a fiction, like everything else in this tale, for "saying" is inevitably "inventing." The scenes culled from the past bring not memory but a construct in the guise of memory to the shape that Beckett's narrativity assumes. They also impart a special movement to the text, for unlike the rhythm of reason, constantly backtracking on itself to amend a phrase, repeat it with minor variation, or take up yet another possible alternative, the rhythm of memory, even when fabricated by a voice in the dark, is swift, incisive, and direct. It is also honest, at least as candid as any made-up memory can be. Yet this too is necessarily imagined. Some of these memories have even been given to the voice secondhand, things told to him by others and then passed off as his own:

> You first saw the light in the room you most likely were con-ceived in. . . . The midwife was none other than a Dr Hadden or Haddon. Straggling grey moustache and hunted look. It being a public holiday your father left the house soon after his breakfast with a flask and a package of his favourite egg sandwiches for a tramp in the mountains. There was nothing unusual in this. But on that particular morning his love of walking and wild scenery was not the only mover. But he was moved also to take himself off and out of the way by his aversion to the pains and general unpleasant-ness of labour and delivery. Hence the sandwiches which he relished at noon looking out to sea from the lee of a great rock on the first summit scaled. . . . When he returned at nightfall he learned to his dismay from the maid at the back door that labour was still in swing. . . . He at once hastened to the coachhouse some twenty yards distant where he housed his De Dion Bouton. He shut the doors behind him and climbed into the driver's seat. . . . Though footsore and weary he was on the point of set-ting out anew across the fields in the young moonlight when the maid came running to tell him it was over at last. Over! (Pp. 12–14)

Company's so-called memory plays tricks with imagination: things told to us are sometimes indistinguishable from events we actually remember on our own. To amplify this point, Beckett follows the scene of birth with a much less personalized one of a child in a nursery: "A mother's stooping over cradle from behind. She moves aside to let the father look. In his turn he murmurs to the newborn. Flat tone unchanged. No trace of love" (p. 47). The presence of Beckett's *Proust* hovers everywhere in the background. For there we read how memory shapes the past: "It presents the past in monochrome. The images it chooses are as arbitrary as those chosen by imagination, and are equally remote from reality."[7] To remember in *Company* is therefore to imagine. And despite the text's disclaimer of imagining "ill" from time to time, the memories we get here are as fluid as Proust's—or as our own. In the vignette of the summerhouse, for example, the voice will make a double journey into the past before returning us to the present. Freely moving "to and fro," as in *Rockaby*, the voice moves from distant past, to more distant past, to less distant past, mixing an encounter with his lover and her pregnancy ("She is late" [p. 39]) with a memory of his father reading *Punch* with yet another memory of the touch of two naked bodies in bed. Time is all at once set free, as though the distinct voices of A, B, and C in *That Time* now meet in one. Memory can work wonders, especially when it has been so explicitly crafted to do so.

In *Company*, moreover, Beckett gives rapid rhythm to the voice of memory and slow rhythm to the voice of reason, then lets them play against one another in vigorous counterpoint. This technique brings much finesse as well as enormous vitality to the whole, setting in motion a dynamic conflict of styles within the writing of the fiction itself. Mind and heart wage a war of words in two competing tempos. We never know for sure just when one will intrude its distinctive presence on the other. Emotion fights with reason, and the as yet unidentified narrator will make clever use of the latter to recover from the devastating effects of the former, which, despite his valiant attempts, he does not appear likely to control.

What makes *Company* a special edition in the Beckett canon is the risk he now takes with the dualism he has balanced so delicately in this work: heart wins hands down in the end. Despite the reason-ridden intellect, emotionally charged memories, no matter how formulated, recast, and patched up, shine through in the end in the shape of haunting images that will quite simply not go away. Their successful battle with what *Molloy* calls "the falsetto of reason" makes them avoid any taint of sloppy sentimentality. All that remains for Krapp, too, after all is said and done and taped, is one essential image from the past: "the eyes—like chrysolite." As we sit in the theater and watch Krapp with our own eyes, all that exists for us is an image too: an old man isolated on stage space is suddenly not alone. Staring into the void, he is actually staring at us. The image has offered us an unexpected instance of communion with a private world in the public forum that is theater. *Company* will similarly offer us reminiscences in the form of images, and even though they represent loss, they provide the reader with powerfully drawn scenes that effectively counter and enrich the narrator's diminished state. "Now I'll wipe out everything but the flowers," the narrator of *Enough* intones near the end of his quite different fictional journey. Everything disappears but the words and the images they can be depended on to create.

Consider some of these images: a mother scolds a young boy for no apparent reason after he asks a question, typically, about depth and perception; a small boy teeters on the limb of a tree or contemplates a jump into deep waters and into his waiting father's arms; a youth finds a hedgehog and imposes his will upon it, ending in death and a loss of innocence; a young man meets his lover and confronts his culpability in her pregnancy, if such is indeed the case; a grown man now walks by himself in the fields near his childhood home but recollects in tranquility his beloved father's "shade"; an old man finds he moves unsteadily, suddenly conscious of the fact that he has been deserted forever by the warmth of his once youthful vigor—these scenes evoke the arbitrary pattern of loss in one man's existence. Everything "falls" and soon fades away. Any renewed effort of mathematics or science to define or locate the voice that broadcasts these images pales by comparison with the striking quality of such sharp visual stimulation. For the company Beckett keeps is strictly with these words and the metaphors they have been made to create. They will never leave us "alone," for they constantly return us to the initial charge of this text, which was, we should remember, to "imagine." For even in the midst of memory, Beckett's *Company* has been asking us to "imagine" along with it. "You may imagine his thoughts before and after as he strode through the gorse and heather" (p. 13), the voice states of a father anxiously awaiting his child's birth, an appeal to the reader soon to be echoed by another as the same man is discovered alone in his De Dion Bouton: "You may imagine his thoughts as he sat there in the dark not knowing what to think" (p. 14). So imagination is not quite dead, at least as far as the narrative strength of *Company* is concerned. Like the sun in *Murphy*—there is another image—it shines through once again, having no real alternative. Imagination therefore becomes the only possibility for company, for it is always full of potentiality. Time hangs "heavy already on our hands" (p. 29), it is true, but even the movement of two hands on a watch provides "variations and constants" (p. 59) ripe for narrative exploration. And when this story ends, there still remain many "matters yet to be imagined" (p. 27), "form and dimensions yet to be devised."

The "fable of one fabling . . . in the dark" (p. 63) has therefore not left us in the dark at all. This fiction may have set out to expose the limits and mechanisms of its own fictivity, but in the process of its reasoning—which in this text "reasons ill" (p. 12)—we recognize that the voice that has all along been dripping inside this character's head is nothing less than a human heart. "A heart, a heart in my head," cried out Beckett's Hamm long ago. And as long as Beckett's characters have the miniaturized tenderness of these words, this company, the present fable seems bent on reassuring us, can never be entirely in vain. Mixing memory and desire, the voice of *Company* gives shape to memory and in so doing offers us lies like truth. The last word of this text, set by itself in a lonely little paragraph, is "Alone" (p. 63). But that too is a word we have seen before in the Beckett canon, and that too presents us with an intimate image we can only encounter on our own. For we are never really alone once we hold Beckett's text in our hands. Devised allusions to the past and to past works have therefore fostered a magnificent new illusion where we may have least expected it: just who is the narrator and who is the company really does not matter when the reader's regular guest is Beckett's unnamable voice.

1. Quotations in this paragraph are from Beckett's "Dante . . . Bruno. Vico . . Joyce," in *Our Exagmination Round His Factification for Incamination of Work in Progress* (Paris: Shakespeare and Co., 1929), pp. 1, 4, 8.

2. *Company* (New York: Grove Press, 1980), p. 49.

3. *Malone Dies* (New York: Grove Press, 1956), p. 98.

4. Several critics have noticed the Shakespearean echoes in Beckett's work. See, for example, Ruby Cohn, *Just Play: Beckett's Theater* (Princeton, N.J.: Princeton University Press, 1980), pp. 22, 36, 70, 78, 84, 143, 179; Enoch Brater, "Fragment and Beckett's Form in 'That Time' and 'Footfalls,'" *Journal of Beckett Studies*, Summer 1977, p. 70–81.

5. Letter from Samuel Beckett to Martha Fehsenfeld dated 18 November 1980. My thanks to Martha Fehsenfeld for calling my attention to this mistake in the printed text of *Company*.

6. *Watt* (New York: Grove Press, 1969), p. 247.

7. *Proust* (New York: Grove Press, 1957), p. 19.

Nicholas Zurbrugg

Beckett, Proust, and Burroughs and the Perils of "Image Warfare"

The points of intersection are very important. . . . In cutting up
you will get a point of intersection where the new material that you
have intersects with what is there already in some very precise
way, and then you start from there.[1]

As this quotation from the novelist and professional wicked
uncle of postmodernism, William Burroughs, suggests, one of
the central concerns of the twentieth-century writer is the function of those "points of intersection" where different clusters of
words and images interact. Burroughs's work may best be introduced anecdotally, in terms of French poet Henri Chopin's
observation that when visiting Burroughs one finds that "the
television is characteristically switched on, with the sound
turned off, while images flicker by." Chopin perceptively adds
that Burroughs is "above all an observer, who subsequently
imagines cut-ups, thanks to this flood of images."[2]

Burroughs has himself discussed the attraction of flickering
"old movies," avowing that "when talkies came in and they
perfected the image, the movies became as dull as looking out
the window."[3] This fascination for the ambiguous flickering
image, as opposed to the "perfected" image, is by no means as
eccentric as it might appear. In precisely the same way, pioneer
film-maker Sergei Eisenstein insisted upon the "distinct non-
synchronisation" of sound and visual imagery, arguing that

"only a contrapuntal use of sound in relation to the visual montage piece will afford a new potentiality of montage development and perfection," and that "every adhesion of sound to a visual montage piece increases its inertia."[4] In his very last interview, Eisenstein elaborated these ideas, remarking: "Art begins the moment the creaking of a boot on the sound-track occurs against a different visual shot and thus gives rise to corresponding associations."[5] Briefly, both Burroughs and Eisenstein appear preoccupied with the ways in which discordant combinations of images, words, and sounds generate what Eisenstein terms "corresponding associations." In Burroughs's terms: "I've been interested in precisely how word and image get around on very, very complex association lines. . . . Cut-ups establish new connections between images, and one's range of vision consequently expands."[6]

In the context of this comparison of Beckett's, Proust's, and Burroughs's use of the image, it is essential to make a fundamental distinction between Eisenstein's and Burroughs's responses to "contrapuntal" images. Both agree that such images augment art's development and perfection; in Burroughs's opinion, "cut-up . . . enriches the whole esthetic experience, extends it."[7] To this extent, Eisenstein's and Burroughs's experiments simply confirm the modernist creator's infatuation with surprising links between disparate sensations, which is best expressed by "Breton's law": "The value of the image depends upon the beauty of the spark obtained; it is consequently directly proportional to the difference in potential between the two conductors."[8] Put another way, in symbolist rather than surrealist terms, the value of the image is directly proportional to the sensitivity of the "superior man" who alone

> can walk as master in the fantastic temple
>> whose living pillars
>> sometimes give forth indistinct words
>
> while the imbecile human flock, duped by the appearances that lead them to the denial of essential ideas, will pass forever blind
>> through forests of symbols
>> which watch him with familiar glances.[9]

These lines from Aurier's "Symbolism in Painting: Paul Gauguin" (of 1891), with their quotation from Baudelaire's poem "Correspondances," clearly assert that the poet *may* make sense of "indistinct words" and "forests of symbols," in a world in which "Les parfums, les couleurs et les sons se répondent [Perfumes, colors, and sounds answer one another]."[10] Eisenstein's reference to "corresponding associations" resulting from contrapuntal images and sounds similarly implies that his materials finally "answer" one another in what he termed "'synthetic' combinations of tonal and overtonal montage."[11] The crucial distinction between this predominantly modernist response to the contrapuntal and Burroughs's essentially postmodern response resides in Burroughs's preoccupation with disparate words, images, and sounds that *refuse* to answer one another, and that rather than resolving their differences in "synthetic combinations," clash all the more violently in states that might perhaps be thought of as *image warfare*.

In other words, whereas such modernists as the symbolist poets, the surrealist poets, and Eisenstein combined contrasting images in order to generate new dimensions of artistic *unity*, Burroughs seems most interesting as an author exploring the social and political potential of the word and image as a "virus" propagating chaos. Burroughs has set forth his ideas on this subject in his book entitled *Electronic Revolution* and in his interviews with Daniel Odier collected in *The Job*.[12] The latter volume reprints Burroughs's early essay entitled "The Invisible Generation" (1966), in which Burroughs introduces his theories, first, in terms of experiments with one's own responses to words and images, and second, in terms of the potential public application of these experiments. The essay begins:

> what we see is determined to a large extent by what we hear you can verify this proposition by a simple experiment turn off the sound track on your television set and substitute an arbitrary sound track prerecorded on your tape recorder . . . you will find the arbitrary sound track seems to be appropriate and is in fact determining your interpretation of film track on screen people running for a bus in picadilly with a sound track of machine gun fire looks like 1917 petrograd.[13]

With these admittedly somewhat dubious propositions in mind, Burroughs speculates:

> you want to start a riot put your machines in the street with riot recordings move fast enough you can stay just ahead of the riot surfboarding we call it no margin for error recollect poor old burns caught out in a persian market riot recordings hid under his jallaba and they skinned him alive raw peeled thing writhing there in the noon sun and we got the picture do you get the picture.14

With the entry of the anecdote about "poor old burns," Burrough's theories drift into fiction and back again, as Burroughs proposes that this picture of "poor old burns" might itself be used subversively in an analogous context. Consistently illustrated and exemplified by the most grotesque fictions, Burroughs's ideas tend to defy credibility, especially when uttered by such freaks as the "death dwarf" from *Nova Express*, who informs his captors:

> "Images—millions of images—That's what I eat—Cyclotron shit— Ever try kicking *that* habit with apomorphine?—Now I got all the images of sex acts and torture ever took place anywhere and I can just blast it out and control you gooks right down to the molecule."15

Although the comic genius of Burroughs's writing resides precisely in the death dwarf's subsequent antics: his repetition of the words "My Power's coming—My Power's coming—My Power's Coming," and his duplication of "a faith healer routine rolling his eyes and frothing at the mouth" (antics made all the more explicit in Burroughs's reading of this passage),16 the most interesting factor here seems to be the emphasis upon the way in which images of sex and violence may disorient the dwarf's victims when "cut" into their habitual lifestyles, and thereby "control" them "right down to the molecule." For Burroughs, such "control" inevitably implies the provocation of some sort of humiliating and disordered reaction. Thus *Electronic Revolution* suggests that

> A mike secreted in the water closet and all his shits and farts recorded and scrambled in with stern nanny voices commanding

him to shit, and the young liberal shits in his pants on the platform right under Old Glory.[17]

Burroughs's undeniably idiosyncratic visions of image "warfare" offer a remarkable model for the kind of confusion experienced by the Beckettian hero, a coincidence that is best introduced in terms of the distinction that Burroughs made between their respective concerns when reflecting:

> What I want to do is to learn to see more of what's out there, to look outside, to achieve as far as possible a complete awareness of surroundings. Beckett wants to go inward.[18]

At the risk of indulging the intentional fallacy, this statement may be read as a valuable indication of Burroughs's interest in the role of images in the context of the "outside" of problems of *social control*, as opposed to Beckett's "inward" preoccupation with conflicting images of the self. To extend this distinction, it might be argued that whereas Burroughs enthusiastically contemplates ways of precipitating image "warfare" within society (by causing riots, for example), Beckett's characters seem the reluctant victims of the rioting images within their own minds—rioting images, moreover, that they would do anything to calm.

Malone Dies thus depicts the torments of Lemuel, who is "flayed alive by memory, his mind crawling with cobras, not daring to dream or think and powerless not to," whose only solution is to strike his head with a hammer.[19] Malone himself is similarly tormented. Describing his anguish in terms remarkably reminiscent of those of Burroughs, he comments:

> Words and images run riot in my head, pursuing, flying, clashing, merging endlessly. But beyond this tumult there is a great calm, and a great indifference, never really to be troubled by anything again.[20]

Malone's complaint, and that of the majority of Beckett's heroes, is that they seldom attain, let alone retain, this ideal calm. This essential dilemma utterly subverts the ideals that most Beckettian critics associate with Beckett's heroes.

The greatest confusion in Beckettian criticism almost certainly results from the repeated identification of Proustian virtues with Beckettian virtues. Nowhere has this identification been more misleading than in the case of Beckett's suggestion, in his study of *A la recherche du temps perdu* entitled *Proust*, that:

> The artist is active, but negatively, shrinking from the nullity of extracircumferential phenomena, drawn in to the core of the eddy. He cannot practice friendship because friendship is the centrifugal force of self-fear, self-negation.[21]

Taken in tandem with Beckett's subsequent reference to the Proustian artist's contempt for "the grotesque fallacy of a realistic art—'the miserable statement of line and surface,' and the penny-a-line vulgarity of a literature of notations" (p. 76), the above statement has persuaded critics that Beckett's heroes similarly probe the "eddy" of the self, reject the "extracircumferential," and despise the superficiality of "line and surface." It is arguable that these ideals inspire certain Beckettian heroes, such as Murphy, at the beginning of their careers. But it is equally evident that by the end of their respective books, Beckettian heroes suffer so intensely from introspective "words and images run riot" that they retreat from what *Murphy* terms the "fly in the ointment of Microcosmos" to the relative safety of macrocosmic mathematics, such as Molloy's sucking-stone calculations.[22]

By the end of *Murphy*, Murphy confronts what he terms a "spool" of disturbing autobiographical images, or rather fragments, as "scraps of bodies, of landscapes, hands, eyes, lines and colours" rise in front of him; yet instead of descending to the "eddy" of these images, he decides that his experience "should be stopped . . . before the deeper coils were reached."[23] Both Beckett's subsequent *Film* and the more recent *A Piece of Monologue* dramatize this retreat from deep autobiographical reality even more explicitly, the former depicting the "scene of inspection and destruction of photographs," the latter depicting the "Speaker" red-handed, as it were, at the scene of the completed crime, avoiding all photographic and verbal "intersections" between his present condition and his past, and relating "Pictures of . . . he all but said of loved ones. . . . Down one after another. Gone. Torn to shreds and scattered. Strewn all over the floor."[24] Far from avoiding friendship, in order to facilitate introspective centripetal activity, most Beckettian heroes, such as the narrator of *Company*, deliberately evade centripetal introspection by following the centrifugal impulse to acquire the fictional friendship—or "company"—of imaginary, nonautobiographical data. Thus the narrator of *Company* expressly defines his dilemma as that of "the craving for company . . . In which to escape from his own."[25] This is, of course, the very reverse of the Proustian strategy of composing fiction to assist self-knowledge; and it is perhaps no coincidence that Beckett annotated Marcel's final wish to offer his readers "le moyen de lire en eux-mêmes" or "the means of reading themselves" with the incredulous, and doubtless disapproving, rejoinder: "Balls."[26]

This curious hostility to introspection seems especially bizarre, coming as it does from an author who quite plainly admires the Proustian hero's rejection of the "nullity" of habitual, macrocosmic reality. What made Beckett reject the Proustian virtues? The answer would seem to be: the Proustian vices. Or more accurately, Beckett's preoccupation with modes of intolerable "image warfare" in Proust's novel appears to have been far more enduring than his dutiful account of the way in which involuntary memory transforms image warfare into perceptual victory asserting the positive permanent reality of the self. Beckett's analyses of moments of image warfare in *A la recherche du temps perdu* are especially rewarding, for they not only point to a neglected dimension of Proust's novel but also indicate the way in which Beckett's critical priorities define his vision as being substantially different from that of Proust.

The two most interesting sections of Beckett's *Proust* concern incidents in which Marcel's images of others and himself cause considerable anguish, rather than resolving themselves and harmoniously responding one to the other, as terms of the symbolist salvation of involuntary memory. Beckett tellingly dubs the first of these—the incident when Marcel, leaning to unbutton his boots, both remembers his dead grandmother, and suffers excruciatingly from her absence—as "perhaps the greatest passage that Proust ever wrote" (p. 39). Diagnosing this as a "poisoned" variant of involuntary memory, Beckett comments: "This contradiction between presence and absence is intolerable" (p. 42), and in identical terms analyzes the way in which Marcel's hopelessly infatuated and hopelessly jealous responses to Albertine constitute "a multiplicity in depth, a turmoil of objective and immanent contradictions over which the subject has no control" (p. 47).

Few phrases could better describe the perceptual chaos afflicting Beckett's subsequent heroes. And with but a shuffling of negatives, few phrases could better describe the Beckettian hero's antidote to such profound perceptual torment: the antidote of "a multiplicity *without depth*, a turmoil of objective and immanent contradictions over which the subject *has control*"—in Molloy's terms, *"dutiful confusions."*27 Beckett's analysis of Marcel's agonizingly *un*dutiful confusions focuses upon its key crisis: the occasion when, having associated Albertine both with the beauty of the sea, and with a disquieting vision of lesbian love glimpsed at Montjouvain, Marcel not only can no longer differentiate between these conflicting versions of Albertine, but also can no longer enjoy the sea as an object of beauty in its own right, since it has become permanently associated both with Albertine and with her disturbing lesbian proclivities. A victim of his own associations, Marcel has—to use Burroughs's terms—inadvertently "cut up" a "sex" image and a maritime image, finding that "the sea is a veil that cannot hide the horror of Montjouvain, the intolerable vision of sadistic lubricity," and envisioning his subsequent life as "a succession of joyless dawns, poisoned by the tortures of memory and isolation" (pp. 52–53).

The concept of memory as a source of "intolerable vision" and of something "poisoned" duplicates the key adjectives in Beckett's analysis of the previous incident, and partially anticipates his surprising subsequent suggestion that the perceptual miracle of Proust's novel—involuntary memory—is notable as a source of *"intolerable* brightness"* (p. 70).28 This passage also describes Marcel's revelation more positively, as a source of "felicity." But the suspicion that Beckett would imply that *all* intense introspective perceptions—poisoned or unpoisoned— are intolerable is substantially confirmed by Beckett's avowal that Proust's wisdom consists of "the ablation of desire" (p. 18), and "in obliterating the faculty of suffering" (p. 63). At the beginning of *Proust*, Beckett quite properly distinguishes between the Proustian notions of the habitual and the inhabitual, or in Beckett's morose formulas: the "boredom of living," and the "suffering of being"—a state in which man experiences the "free play of every faculty" (pp. 19, 20). To achieve the supposedly Proustian ideal of obliterating the faculty of suffering, man must therefore obliterate "being," halt the free play of every faculty, and limit existence to the very "boredom of living" constituted by the "nullity of extracircumferential phenomena." This is certainly not the wisdom of Proust's heroes, who employ their every faculty during the triumphant existential struggles that Elstir defines as "un combat et une victoire" (1:864)—a combat and a victory. The ablation of desire, and self-immersion in the extracircumferential *is*, however, the negative wisdom of such nihilistic Proustian characters as Marcel's *tante* Léonie, who cherishes "l'inertie absolue [absolute inertia]" (1:50); and it would also appear to be the wisdom of such Beckettian archetypes as Estragon and Vladimir, who find the habitual "a great deadener."[29]

Despite the fact that Marcel suffers from the intolerable and poisoned memories and confusions that Beckett analyzes so impressively in his *Proust*, his experience does not culminate in the Beckettian wisdom of the ablation of desire. Rather, in the face of considerable evidence to the contrary, Marcel finally concludes that man's desires *are* worthy of realization. A key phase in the evolution of his conclusion occurs when Marcel meditates upon some pear trees and cherry trees, finding them to symbolize:

> Custodians of memories from the golden age, witnesses to the promise that reality is not what we suppose it to be, and that the splendour of poetry and the marvellous radiance of innocence may shine within it, and may be the reward that we should make every effort to merit. (2:161–62)[30]

As Beckett himself implied, when admiring the "dualism in multiplicity" of the "Proustian equation" (p. 11), Proust's vision is perhaps most impressive of all in terms of the ways in which it elaborates the "dual," or positive and negative, potential of every experience. Although perceptual salvation in Proust's novel results from the symbolist aesthetic of sensations that both correspond and respond to one another, Proust's exemplification of "poisoned" memories and associations also probes the reverse of such perceptual felicity. If few critics apart from Beckett have elucidated this neglected dimension of Proust's novel, few authors apart from Beckett have created a life's work based primarily upon such "poisoned" perceptions. The disadvantage of this elaboration on the "poisoned" is, of course, that Beckett cannot (and indeed does not) make any claim to emulate the extraordinary *multiplicity* of Proust's *dualistic* vision. Few trees blossom in Beckett's fiction, and even those that do cause disgust or confusion. Perched under a hawthorn (Marcel's favorite flora), Molloy grimly comments: "The white hawthorn stooped towards me, unfortunately I don't like hawthorn."[31] Waiting next to their solitary tree, Estragon and Vladimir bicker over its identity, finding it both "a bush" and "a shrub."[32]

It may be argued that Beckett's vision *is* nevertheless dualistic, since works like *Waiting for Godot* abound in binary oppositions of words and characters. This is undeniable, yet at the same time the *content* of the binary oppositions in Proust's fiction and those in Beckett's fiction is immensely different. Proust's binary oppositions operate on three distinct levels— between the habitual and the unpoisoned inhabitual; between the habitual and the poisoned inhabitual; and between the poisoned and the unpoisoned inhabitual. Beckett's binaries inhabit a world without unpoisoned inhabitual experience. His characters fluctuate between the boredom of the deadeningly habitual and the intolerable anguish of almost invariably poisoned inhabitual perceptions. At best they occasionally lose consciousness altogether before inevitably boomeranging back into boredom or intolerable anguish.

Caught between the ever increasing perceptual disadvantages of the perceptual frying pan of habit and the perceptual fire of the inhabitual, it is scarcely surprising that Beckett's characters attempt to avoid introspection by absorbing themselves in the ritualistic pastimes of gestures, dialogues, and endlessly invented fictions. At most, their recognition of identity occurs in carefully censored fragmentary monologues, such as those of *Not I, Company,* and *A Piece of Monologue,* in which every effort is made either to avoid the expression of autobiographical data or at least to minimize the anguish accompanying its expression by repetitive and circumambulatory narration. Considered collectively, these recent variations on autobiographical fragments occasionally add to the reader's knowledge of Beckett's own biography. For example, *Company* alludes to a childhood game of jumping from the top of pine trees: an odd passtime only mentioned previously by secondary sources in Deirdre Bair's biography of Beckett.[33] One might surmise that, almost despite himself, Beckett is gradually revealing, and perhaps thereby nullifying, painful autobiograpical details, a tendency akin to that which Allen Ginsberg has attributed to William Burroughs's cut-ups. Ginsberg comments:

> In fact, the cut-ups were originally designed to rehearse and repeat his obsession with sexual images over and over again, like a movie repeating over and over and over again, and then re-combined and cut up and mixed in; so that finally the obsessive attachment, compulsion, and preoccupation empty out and drain from the image. . . . Finally, the hypnotic attachment, the image, becomes demystified. . . . *He can finally look at it at the end of the spool;* he can look at his most tender, personal, romantic images objectively, and no longer be attached to them.[34]

Although the specific content of Burroughs's and Beckett's "most tender, personal . . . images" are very different, it is perhaps not too wild a suggestion to propose that such Beckettian heroes as Krapp might be deemed to be repeating, cutting up, and demystifying certain highly tender and personal images so as to defuse their painfully explosive content. In other words, Krapp's repeated reference to his taped account of his haunting moments with a girl in a punt might be interpreted as his attempt to come to terms with his poisoned memory of love that he ironically rejected for a career he now no longer cares for. In Ginsberg's terms, Krapp is trying to reach the point when he can relatively painlessly "look at it at the end of the spool."

Ginsberg's statement not only provides a helpful model for an understanding of the introspective strategies of such Beckettian heroes as Krapp but also places Burroughs's writings in a wider context. Despite Burroughs's suggestion that he is primarily interested in "outside" reality, it seems clear that to some extent at least his cut-ups reiterate "inward" imagery, be this to demystify and placate sexual obsessions, as Ginsberg suggests, or to provoke sexual stimulation (a possibility that, as Harold Beaver remarks, Burroughs himself implies in his maxim "Any writer who has not masturbated with his own characters will not be able to make them live on paper").[35] Whether Burroughs's texts serve or served Burroughs personally as a pornographic intoxicant or disintoxicant is perhaps beside the point, or at least very secondary to their decisive difference from pulp pornography in terms of their exploration of the cut-up both as a literary device and as a subversive weapon for the verbal-visual urban guerilla. To acknowledge this function of Burroughs's writing is neither to deny its pornographic content nor to blindly accept the frequently eccentric formulations and exemplifications of its variously convincing theories. It is, however, to suggest the shortsightedness of such evaluations of Burroughs's ideas as George Steiner's reference to their "childish conceit of a loose-leaf book—to be put together at random or at the reader's will,"[36] and to argue for Burroughs's validity as a theorist who has fascinatingly explored the subversive potential of *contrapuntal* intersections of words and images, and whose work additionally evokes the perfect concept for the confusion of Beckett's heroes: the concept of *image warfare*.

Located in the perceptual context of rioting words and images, the Beckettian hero's retreat from painful centripetal confusion to relatively painless centrifugal confusion is much easier to understand. For too long, critics have misleadingly attempted to interpret Beckett by *comparing* instead of *contrasting* Proust and Beckett. Beckett is not Proust (and is not Burroughs), nor was meant to be. But when considered halfway, as it were, *between* Proust and Burroughs, as a writer whose concerns are partially Proustian, insofar as they examine poisoned (but not unpoisoned) involuntary memories, and as a writer who is partially Burroughsian, insofar as he examines inward (but not outward) manifestations of image warfare, Beckett can at least be approached within the general parameters of his *own* priorities. This contextualization plainly takes no account of the different qualities of Beckett's, Proust's, and Burroughs's writing, but it does perhaps avoid the prevailing myth that Beckett's and Proust's responses to the autobiographical image—or the image of the self—are somehow susceptible to the same "law."[37] This is patently not the case; indeed, it is arguable that writers such as Beckett, Proust, and Burroughs are most fascinating and most satisfying precisely in terms of the ways in which they elaborate and explore diverging—and at times incompatible—approaches to the image of the self.

Proust, for example, provides an exemplary instance of the predominantly optimistic literary experiments of the modernist writer, both in terms of his confident, all-inclusive, telescopic sentences, and in terms of his belief in the perceptual salvation of involuntary memory. By contrast, the respectively "inward" and "outward" texts of Beckett and Burroughs both bear the two hallmarks of the postmodern writer: a pessimistic obsession with incoherent, confused, fragmentary observations, and a more optimistic approach to the creative potential of the new technology of the recording studio, television, and cinema.[38] The originality of Proust, Beckett, and Burroughs lies not so much in any apparent overlap between their ideas in such texts as Beckett's *Proust*, as in the *differences* between their pre-technological and part-technological verbalizations and dramatizations of complex "intersections" between different images of the self. To reduce their originality to any single "law" is to lose sight of their contrasting achievements, and yet to juxtapose their ideas is a useful means of revealing their individuality. As Beckett warned the reader some fifty years ago, "The danger is in the neatness of identifications."[39]

1. William Burroughs, *The Job,* interview with William Burroughs by Daniel Odier (London: Jonathan Cape, 1970), pp. 16–17.

2. Henri Chopin, *Poésie sonore internationale* (Paris: Jean-Michel Place, 1979), p. 136. My translation . ("Il est caractéristique en allant chez lui de voir la T.V. branchée, mais muette, tandis que l'image défile. . . . Burroughs est d'abord un regardant, il imagine ensuite, grâce à ce flot d'images, des *cut-ups.*"

3. William Burroughs, "The Art of Fiction XXXVI," interview with William Burroughs by Conrad Knickerbocker, *Paris Review,* No. 35 (Fall 1965), p. 42.

4. S. M. Eisenstein, V. I. Pudovkin, and G. M. Alexandrov, "A Statement," in Sergei Eisenstein, *Film Form: Essays in Film Theory,* edited and translated by Jay Leyda (New York: Harcourt, Brace & World, 1949), p. 258. First published in Leningrad in *Zhizn Iskusstva,* 5 August 1928.

5 . Sergei Eisenstein quoted by Ilya Veissfeld, "Mon dernier entretien avec Eisenstein," *Cahiers du Cinéma,* No. 208 (January 1969), p. 21. Translated by Stephen Heath in Roland Barthes, *Image Music Text,* Essays selected and translated by Stephen Heath (Glasgow: Fontana, 1977), pp. 61–62. ("L'art commence à partir du moment où le craquement de la botte (au son), tombe sur un plan visuel différent et suscite ainsi des associations correspondantes."

6. Burroughs, "The Art of Fiction," pp. 21, 25.

7. Ibid., p. 27. Burroughs defines the cut-up process in William Burroughs and Brion Gysin, *The Third Mind* (New York: Viking, 1978), pp. 25–33. Walter Veit has interestingly noted that a variation of the cut-up, the cross-reading (or the process of interlinking lines in consecutive columns), served eighteenth-century newspaper readers as a means of "connecting wittily the unconnected" ('Intellectual Tradition and Pacific Discoveries of The Function of Quotations in Georg Forster's *Voyage Round the World,*' in *Captain James Cook Image and Impact: South Seas Discoveries and the World of Letters,* II, *The Pacific Syndrome: Conditions and Consequences,* ed. Walter Veit [Melbourne: Hawthorn Press, 1979], p. 117).

8. André Breton, "Manifeste du surréalisme" (1924), in *Manifestes du surréalisme* (Paris: Gallimard, 1966), p. 51; my translation. ("La valeur de l'image dépend de la beauté de l'étincelle obtenue; elle est, par conséquent, fonction de la différence de potentiel entre les deux conducteurs.")

9. G.-Albert Aurier, "Le Symbolisme en peinture: Paul Gauguin," *Mercure de France* (Paris) 2 (mars 1891): 161. Translated by H. R. Rookmaaker and Herschel B. Chipp in *Theories of Modern Art: A Source Book by Artists and Critics,* ed. Herschel B. Chipp (Berkeley: University of California Press, 1968), p. 91.

("L'homme supérieur . . . seul sait . . . se promener en maître dans ce temple fantastique

Où de vivants piliers
Laissent parfois sortir de confuses paroles . . .

alors que l'imbécile troupeau humain, dupé par les apparences qui lui feront nier les idées essentielles, passera éternellement aveugle

A travers les forêts de symboles
Qui l'observent avec des regards familiers.")

10. Charles Baudelaire, "Correspondances," *Les Fleurs du mal*, collected in *Oeuvres complètes*, ed. Marcel A. Ruff (1857; rpt. Paris: Les Editions du Seuil, 1968), p. 46.

11. Eisenstein, "The Filmic Fourth Dimension," *Film Form*, p. 68.

12. William Burroughs, *Electronic Revolution*, collected in *Ah Pook Is Here and Other Texts* (1971); rpt. London: John Calder, 1979), pp. 123–57.

13. "The Invisible Generation," collected in *The Job*, pp. 159–60.

14. Ibid., pp. 165–66.

15. William Burroughs, *Nova Express* (1964; rpt. London: Panther, 1968), p. 43.

16. Burroughs reads from this section of *Nova Express*, subtitled "Inflexible Authority," pp. 42–46, on the phonograph recording *Call Me Burroughs* (Paris: English Bookshop, 1965). Burroughs's impressive readings are more readily available on the double recording *William Burroughs/John Giorno* (New York: Giorno Poetry Systems, 1975), GPS 006-007, from Giorno Poetry Systems, 222 Bowery, New York, N.Y. 10012.

17. *Ah Pook Is Here*, p. 135.

18. "The Art of Fiction," 23.

19. Samuel Beckett, *Malone Dies* (London: John Calder, 1956); collected in *Molloy, Malone Dies, The Unnamable* (London: Calder and Boyars, 1959), pp. 268–69.

20. *Molloy, Malone Dies, The Unnamable*, p. 198.

21. Samuel Beckett, *Proust* (1931; rpt. London: John Calder, 1970), pp. 65–66. All subsequent page references to this edition are given in the text.

22. Samuel Beckett, *Murphy* (1938; rpt. London: Calder and Boyars, 1970) p. 124. *Molloy* (Paris: Olympia, 1955). Collected in *Molloy, Malone Dies, The Unnamable*, pp. 68–74.

23. *Murphy*, p. 172.

24. Samuel Beckett, *Film* (1969; rpt. London: Faber and Faber, 1972), p. 36; *A Piece of Monologue*, *Kenyon Review* N.S. 1 (Summer 1979): 2.

25. Samuel Beckett, *Company* (London: John Calder, 1980), p. 77.

26. All references to Marcel Proust's *A la recherche du temps perdu* refer to the three-volume edition edited by Pierre Clarac and André Ferré (Paris: Gallimard, Bibliothèque de la Pléiade, 1954). Beckett's annotated copies of *A la recherche du temps perdu* (1917–27; rpt. Paris: Gallimard, Editions de la Nouvelle Revue Française, 1925–29), are located in the Beckett Collection of the University of Reading Library, England. Beckett's annotated comment "Balls" appears in *Le Temps retrouvé*, 36th ed. (1927; rpt. Paris: Gallimard, Editions de la Nouvelle Revue Française, 1929), p. 240 (3:1033).

27. *Molloy, Malone Dies, The Unnamable*, p. 15. My italics.

28. My italics.

29. Samuel Beckett, *Waiting for Godot* (1956; rpt. London: Faber and Faber, 1977), p. 91.

30. My translation. ("Gardiens des souvenirs de l'âge d'or, garants de la promesse que la réalité n'est pas ce qu'on croit, que la splendeur de la poésie,

que l'éclat merveilleux de l'innocence peuvent y resplendir et pourront être la récompense que nous nous efforcerons de mériter.")

31. *Molloy, Malone Dies, The Unnamable*, p. 27.

32. *Waiting for Godot*, p. 14.

33. Deirdre Bair, *Samuel Beckett: A Biography* (London: Jonathan Cape, 1978), p. 15.

34. Allen Ginsberg quoted by Harold Beaver, "Saint William of Tangier," *Times Literary Supplement*, 22 July 1977, p. 893. My italics.

35. Burroughs quoted by Beaver, ibid.

36. George Steiner, *Language and Silence* (1967; rpt. Harmondsworth: Penguin, 1969), p. 343.

37. See John Fletcher and John Spurling, *Beckett: A Study of His Plays* (London: Eyre Methuen, 1972), p. 28. Here Spurling maintains that Beckett's *Proust* functions as "a table of the law for any student of either Proust, or Beckett."

38. Both Beckett and Burroughs have worked with most of these new technological genres. Burroughs has made such films as *Towers Open Fire* (1963) and *The Cut-Ups* (1967) with Anthony Balch, and has also made recorded texts such as "Valentine Day Reading," available on Revue-Disque *OU*, No. 40–41 (Ingatestone 1972). Beckett has made *Film* (1964), with Alain Schneider; plays involving tape-recorded monologues for the stage, such as *Krapp's Last Tape* (1958) and *That Time* (1976); as well as radio plays such as "All That Fall" (1957), and television plays such as "Ghost trio" (1977).

39. Samuel Beckett, "Dante . . . Bruno. Vico. . Joyce," in *Our Exagmination Round His Factification for Incamination of Work in Progress* (1929; rpt. London: Faber and Faber, 1972), p. 3.

Appendix

Ohio Impromptu Holograph, Typescripts, and
Production Script

Transcription of the
Ohio Impromptu Holograph

EDITORS' NOTE. Bracketed words and phrases indicate deletions by S.B.; a blank space enclosed in parentheses within brackets indicates an indecipherable deletion.

[VERSO OF LEAF 1]

I am out on leave. Thrown out on leave.
Back to time, they said, for 24 hours.
Oh my God, I said, not that.
Slip [into] on this shroud, they said, lest you catch your death of cold again.
Certainly not, I said.
This cap, they said, for your [death's-head] skull.
Definitely not, I said.
The New World outlet, they said, in the State of Ohio. We cannot be more precise. *Pause.*
Proceed straight to [Lima] the nearest campus, they said, and address them.
[Address] whom? I said.
The students, they said, and professors.
Oh my God, I said, not that.
Do not overstay your leave, they said, if you do not wish it to be extended.

Pause.
What am I to say? I said.
Be yourself, they said, [you're (   )] stay yourself.
Myself? I said. What are you insinuating?
[Yourself before, they said.]
Pause.
[And after.]
[*Pause.*]
[Not during? I said.]

[LEAVES 1–3]

Little remains to be told.
In a final effort to—
Knock.
Little remains to be told.
Pause & knock
In a [final] last effort to obtain relief he moved from (the house) where they had [lived] been so long [together alone] alone together to a small furnished room on the [right] other bank. From its single window he could just see the downstream extremity of the Island of Swans [where as a young man he had sauntered dreaming] wandered [dreaming of things to come.]
[*Pause. Sip*]
[Little remains to be told.]
[In its extreme emptiness and] Relief he—
[*Knock*]
[Little remains to be told.]
[*Pause. Knock.*]
[In its extreme unfamiliarity (strangeness) the room held some hope of help. The narrow bed. Small table. Two? chairs. No books. No pictures. Nothing ever shared.]
Relief he had hoped wd. flow from [the strange] unfamiliarity. Unfamiliar room. Unfamiliar scene. [neighborhood] To go out to where nothing ever shared. To come back to where nothing ever shared. From this he had once half hoped some small measure of relief might [would] flow.
Pause. Sip.

192

[Those days were rare]

Rare were the days when he was not to be seen slowly pacing the island. In his long black coat no matter what the temperature & [a sort of] old world Latin Quarter hat. At the tip he would pause to observe the receding [waters flood] stream. How [its two arms parted by the slit of land in (   )] in joyous [(   )] eddies its two arms conflowed and flowed united on. Then turn & his slow steps retrace.

In his dreams—

Knock

Turn turn & his slow steps retrace.

Pause. Knock

In his dreams (many a time) he had been warned against this change. Seen the dear face and heard the unspoken words, Stay where you are, [Aloysius] Mortimer, [(   )] my ghost will comfort you.

Blows nose.

Could he not now turn back? Acknowledge his error & return to where they had [been] lived so long [together] alone together. [Shared so much] alone together so much shared. No. The answer was no. What he had done alone [there was no undoing] could not be undone. Nothing he had ever done could ever be undone. By him.

[Sip] Refills glass.

It was in this extremity that his old terror of night laid hold [of] on him again. After so long a lapse that as if never been. (*Pause. Looks closer.*) Yes, after so long a lapse that as if never been. Hm. Now with redoubled force the [same] fearful symptoms [as] described [on page (   )] at length [on] page forty [(   )] paragraph four. (*Starts to turn back the pages. Gesture stops him. [Returns to] Resumes present page.*) White nights again his lot. As when his heart was young. No sleep no [facing] braving sleep till [morning light] dawn of day.

Drinks

Little remains to be told. [Just one last] One night—

Knock

Little remains to be told.

Pause. Knock.

193

[[Just one last event, incredible as that may seem, and its [consequences] outcome. It happened thus. One moonlit night as [(   )] in his [vain] [search of] [for] vain quest of calm he [walked] roamed the streets, in his long black coat and old world Latin Quarter hat, he heard himself hailed by name. He who since his flight [(   )] had gone his ways unknown. He turned to face the intruder. A small old man. Long white hair. Ravaged face. Wretchedly attired. [(   )] In the long look exchanged slowly a name: White. See appendix 4. (*Turns pages forward to ap. 4*) White:]]

One night as he sat trembling head in hands from head to foot a man appeared to him and said, I have been sent by—and here he named the dear name—to read to you. Drawing then a vol. from [his long black] the pocket of his long black coat he sat and read till [morning light] dawn. Then [went] disappeared without a word.

Some time later he reappeared [again] with the same volume as before this time without preamble sat and read [the] it through the long night through. Then [went] disappeared without a word.

So from time to time unheralded he would appear to read the old tale through & night away, then disappear without a word.

Till the night came when having [ended] closed the book and [daylight] dawn at hand [(   )] he did not disappear without a word but sat on a little while [in silence] without a word. Finally he said, I have had word from—and here he named the dear name—[not to come again] that I am not to come again. I saw the dear face & heard the unspoken words, No need to go to him again, even were it in your power.
Pause
Nothing—
Knock
I saw the dear face & heard the unspoken words, No need to go to him again, even were it in your power.
Pause. Knock
Nothing remains to be told.

Pause.   Pause
Look   Closes book.
Curtain   Pause
                              Simultaneously they [(   )
                              right] lower their right hands to
                              table, raise their heads and look
                              at each other. Expressionless.
                              Five seconds.
                              Fade out.

L: Listener
R: Reader
As alike in appearance as possible,
Light on table mid-stage. Rest of stage in darkness.
Plain white deal table say 8' × 4'. Two plain armless white
deal chairs.

L seated facing [audience] front towards [with audience
right] end [end (his left)] of long side audience right. Bowed
head [resting] propped on right hand, face invisible, [Long
black coat. (   )] Left hand on table. Long black coat. Long
grey hair.

R seated in profile short side audience right, bowed head
[resting] propped on right hand, left hand on table, book on
table before him open at last pages. Long black coat. Long grey
hair.

Fade out on table.
Pause
R. turns page.
Pause
[So a last time the sad tale unwound]
So the sad tale a last time told They sat on as though turned
to stone. Through the single window dawn gave no light. From
the streets no sound of toil renewed. Or was it that buried in
who knows what thoughts they gave no heed? To light of
dawn. Sound of renewing toil [renewed]. Who knows what
thoughts. [Thoughts?] No, not thoughts. [No.] Profounds of
mind. Buried in who knows what profounds of mind. Of mindlessness. Whither no light can reach. No sound. So sat on. As
though turned to stone. The sad tale a last time told.

195

Pause
Nothing remains to tell.
Pause.
R [closes book] makes to close book.
Knock, Book half closed.
Nothing remains to tell.
R closes book
Pause. Knock.
Silence. 5".
Simultaneously etc.

[SIGNED:]
Samuel Beckett

Turn page halfway

L = Listener.
R = Reader
As alike in appearance as possible.

Light on table midstage. Rest of stage in darkness.
Plain white deal table say 8' x 4'.
Two plain armless white deal chairs.

L seated facing front towards end of long side audience right. Bowed head propped on right hand. Face invisible. Left hand on table. Long black coat. Long grey hair.

R seated in profile centre of short side audience right. Bowed hair propped on right hand. Left hand on table. Book on table before him open at last page. Long black coat. Long grey hair.

Fade up on table.

Pause.

R turns page.

Pause.

R   (reading). Little remains to be told *tell*. In a last - (*with left hand* L knocks on table.) Little remains to be told. (Pause. Knock.) In a last attempt to obtain relief he moved from where they had so long alone together to a ~~small furnished~~ room on the other bank. From its single window he could just see the downstream extremity of the Isle of Swans. (Pause.) Relief he had hoped would flow from unfamiliarity. Unfamiliar room. Unfamiliar scene. To go out to where nothing ever shared. To come back to where nothing ever shared. From this he had once half hoped some ~~small~~ measure of relief might flow.

Pause.

~~Most days he was~~ *daily he could* to be seen slowly pacing the island. *Hour after hour.* In his long black coat no matter what the temperature and old world Latin Quarter hat. At the tip he would ~~pace to observe~~ *always* *unworried at* the receding stream. How in joyous eddies its two arms conflowed and flowed united on. Then turn and his slow steps retrace.

pause to dwell / on

Pause.

In his dreams -

Knock.

Then turn and his slow steps retrace.

Pause. Knock.

In his dreams he had been warned against this change. Seen the dear face and heard the unspoken words, Stay where ~~we were, Lorimer, my ghost~~ *we were* will comfort you. ~~Could he not -~~

Pause: Could he not -

Pause.

Could he not now turn back? Acknowledge his error and return to where ~~they had lived~~ so long *alone* together. Alone together so much shared. No. What he had done *alone* could not be undone. Nothing he had ever done *alone* could ever be undone. By him ~~alone~~.

*Knock
Seen the dear face & heard the unspoken words, stay where we were so long alone together, my ghost will comfort you.
Pause. Knock*

Pause.

(It was) in this extremity his old terror of night laid hold on him again.
After so long a lapse that as if never been. (Pause. Looks closer.) Yes,
after so long a lapse that as if never been. Now with redoubled force the
fearful symptoms described at length page forty paragraph four. (Starts to
turn back the pages. Checked by ~~gesture from L.~~ Resumes abandoned page.)
White nights again his lot. As when his heart was young. No sleep no braving
sleep till/dawn of day.

by L's left hand
- (turns page) -

Pause.

teel
Little remains to ~~be told~~. One night –

knock.

tell
Little remains to ~~be told~~.

Pause. Knock.

One night as he sat trembling head in hands from head to foot a man appeared
to him and said, I have been sent by – and here he named the dear name – to
read to you. Then drawing a *worn* volume from the pocket of his long black coat he
sat and read till dawn. Then disappeared without a word.

Pause.
                                        this time without preamble sat and
Some time later he reappeared at the same hour with the same volume and/read
it through *again* the long night through. Then disappeared without a word.

Pause.
With never a
word unchanged
they came to be
as one soul.

Pause.
                                                                    again
At length So from time to time unheralded he would appear to read the sad tale through
and/night away. Then disappear without a word.

Pause.
                fell at last
~~Till~~ The night ~~came~~ when having closed the book and dawn at hand he (did not
disappear but) sat (on) awhile without a word. Finally he said, I have had word
from – and here He named the dear name – that I shall not come again. I saw
the dear face and heard the unspoken words, No need to go to him again, even
were it in your power·

Pause.
So ~~Nothing~~ *sad*

~~Knock~~ Knock.

Saw the dear face and heard the unspoken words, No need to go to him again, even
were it in your power.

Pause. Knock.
tell
Nothing remains to ~~be told~~.

Pause.
R closes ~~book~~ book.
Pause.
Simultaneouly they lower their right hands to table, raise their heads and look
at each other./Expressionless.
~~Five~~ seconds.
Fade out.

unblinking !

Black wide-brimmed hat at centre of table

L = Listener.
R = Reader.
As alike in appearance as possible.

Light on table midstage. Rest of stage in darkness.
Plain white deal table say 8' x 4'.
Two plain armless white deal chairs.

L seated at table facing front towards end of long side audience
right. Bowed head propped on right hand. Face hidden. Left hand
on table. Long black coat. Long ~~grey~~ hair. *white*

centre / R seated at table in profile ~~extra~~/of short side audience right.
Bowed head propped on right hand. Left hand on table. Book on
white table before him open at ~~third~~ last page. Long black coat. Long
~~grey~~ hair.

Fade up ~~on table~~.

Ten seconds.

R turns page.

Pause.

R (reading). Little remains to tell. In a last – (L knocks with left
    hand on table.) Little ~~remains~~ to tell. (Pause. Knock.) In a last
    attempt to obtain relief he moved from where they had been so long
    alone together to a single room on the far bank. From its single
    window he could just see the downstream extremity of the Isle of
    Swans. (Pause.) Relief he had hoped would flow from unfamiliarity.
    Unfamiliar room. Unfamiliar scene. Out to where nothing ever shared.
    Back to where nothing ever shared. From this he had once half hoped
    some measure of relief might flow.

Pause.
Day after day
~~Daily~~ he could be seen slowly pacing the islet. Hour after hour. In
his long black coat ~~xx~~ no matter what the weather and old world ~~Latin~~
slouch ~~Quarter~~ hat. At the tip he would always pause to dwell on the receding
stream. How in joyous eddies its two arms conflowed and flowed united
on. Then turn and his slow steps retrace.

Pause.

In his dreams –

Knock.

Then turn and his slow steps retrace.

Pause. Knock.

In his dreams he had been warned against this change. Seen the dear
face and heard the unspoken words, Stay where we were so long alone
together, my shade will comfort you.

Pause.

Could he not –

Knock.

Seen the dear face and heard the unspoken words, Stay where we were so long alone together, my shade will comfort you.

Pause. Knock.

Could he not now turn back? Acknowledge his error and return to where they were once so long alone together. Alone together so much shared. No. What he had done alone could not be undone. Nothing he had ever done alone could ever be undone. By him alone.

Pause.

In this extremity his old terror of night laid hold on him again. After so long a lapse that as if never been. (Pause. Looks closer.) Yes, after so long a lapse that as if never been. Now with redoubled force the fearful symptoms described at length page forty paragraph four. (Starts to turn back the pages. Checked by L's left hand. Resumes relinquished page.) White nights now again his portion. As when his heart was young. No sleep no braving sleep till – (turns page) – dawn of day.

Pause.

Little remains to tell. One night –

Knock.

Little remains to tell.

Pause. Knock.

One night as he sat trembling head in hands from head to foot a man appeared to him and said, I have been sent by – and here he named the dear name – to read to you. Then drawing a worn volume from the pocket of his long black coat he sat and read till dawn. Then disappeared without a word.

Pause.

Some time later he reappeared at the same hour with the same volume and this time without preamble sat and read it through again the long night through. Then disappeared without a word.

Pause.

So from time to time unheralded he would appear to read the sad tale through again and the long night away. Then disappear without a word.

Pause.

With never a word exchanged they grew to be as one (soul)

Pause.

Till the night came at last when having closed the book and dawn at hand he did not disappear but sat on without a word. Finally

he said, I have had word from - and here he named the dear name - that
I shall not come again. I saw the dear face and heard the unspoken words,
No need to go to him again, even were it in your power.

Pause.

So the sad -

Knock.

Saw the dear face ~~again~~ and heard the unspoken words, No need to go to
him again, even were it in your power.

Pause. Knock.

So the sad tale a last time told they sat on as though turned to stone.
Through the single window dawn shed no light. From the street no sound
of renewing toll. Or was it that buried in who knows what thoughts they
gave/no heed? To light of day. Sound of renewing toll. What thoughts who
knows. No, not thoughts. Profounds of mind. Buried in who knows what
profounds of mind. Of mindlessness. Whither no light can reach. No sound.
So sat on as though turned to stone. The sad tale a last time told.

Pause.

Nothing ~~remains~~ to tell.

Pause. / ~~Rxxxx~~/R makes to close book.

Knock. Book half closed.

Nothing ~~remains~~ to tell.

Pause. R closes book.

Knock.

Silence. Five seconds.

Simultaneously they lower their right hands to table, raise their heads
and look at each other. Unblinking. Expressionless.

Ten seconds.

Fade out.

L = Listener.
R = Reader.
As alike in appearance as possible.

Light on table midstage. Rest of stage in darkness.
Plain white deal table say 8' x 4'.
Two plain armless white deal chairs.

L seated at table facing front towards end of long side audience
right. Bowed head propped on right hand. Face hidden. Left hand on
table. Long black coat. Long white hair.

R seated at table in profile centre of short side audience right.
Bowed head propped on right hand. Left hand on table. Book on table
before him open at last pages. Long black coat. Long white hair.

Black wide-brimmed hat at centre of table.

Fade up.

Ten seconds.

R turns page.

Pause.

R   (reading). Little is left to tell. In a last –

L knocks with left hand on table.

Little is left to tell.

Pause. Knock.

In a last attempt to obtain relief he moved from where they had been
so long together to a single room on the far bank. From its single
window he could see the downstream extremity of the Isle of Swans.

Pause.

Relief he had hoped would flow from unfamiliarity. Unfamiliar room.
Unfamiliar scene. Out to where nothing ever shared. Back to where
nothing ever shared. From this he had once half hoped some measure
might /   of relief ~~would~~ flow.

Pause.

Day after day he could be seen slowly pacing the islet. Hour after
hour. In his long black coat no matter what the weather and old world
Latin Quarter hat. At the tip he would always pause to dwell on the
receding stream. How in joyous eddies its two arms conflowed and flowed
united on. Then turn and his slow steps retrace.

Pause.

In his dreams –

Knock.

Then turn and his slow steps retrace.

205

Pause. Knock.

In his dreams he had been warned against this change. Seen the dear
face and heard the unspoken words, Stay where we were so long alone
together, my shade will comfort you.

Pause.

Could he not –

Knock.

Seen the dear face and heard the unspoken words, Stay where we were so
long alone together, my shade will comfort you.

Pause. Knock.

Could he not now turn back? Acknowledge his error and return to where
they were once so long alone together. Alone together so much shared.
No. What he had done alone could not be undone. Nothing he had ever done
alone could ever be undone. By him alone.

Pause.

hold /   In this extremity his old terror of night laid/held on him again.
After so long a lapse that as if never been. (Pause. Looks closer.)
Yes, after so long a lapse that as if never been. Now with redoubled
force the fearful symptoms described at length page forty paragraph four.
(Starts to turn back the pages. Checked by L's left hand. Resumes relinquished page.) White nights now again his portion. As when his heart
was young. No sleep no braving sleep till – (turns page) – dawn of day.

Pause.

Little is left to tell. One night –

Knock.

Little is left to tell.

Pause. Knock.

One night as he sat trembling head in hands from head to foot a man
appeared to him and said, I have been sent by – and here he named the
dear name – to comfort you. Then drawing a worn volume from the pocket
of his long black coat he sat and read till dawn. Then disappeared without
a word.

Pause.

Some time later he appeared again at the same hour with the same volume
and this time without preamble sat and read it through again the long
night through. Then disappeared without a word.

Pause.

So from time to time unheralded he would appear to read the sad tale
through again and the long night away. Then disappear without a word.

Pause.

With never a word exchanged they grew to be as one.

Pause.

Till the night came at last when having closed the book and dawn at hand he did not disappear but sat on without a word.

Pause.

Finally he said, I have had word from - and here he named the dear ᴍᴀᴍᴇxᴨ name - that I shall not come again. I saw the dear face and heard the unspoken words, No need to go to him again, even were it in your power.

Pause.

So the sad -

Knock.

Saw the dear face ᴀɢᴀɪɴ and heard the unspoken words, No need to go to him again, even were it in your power.

Pause. Knock.

So the sad tale a last time told they sat on as though turned to stone. Through the single window dawn shed no light. From the street no sound of reawakening. Or was it that buried in who knows what thoughts they paid no need? To light of day. To sound of reawakening. What thoughts who knows. Thoughts, no, not thoughts. Profounds of mind. Buried in who knows what profounds of mind. Of mindlessness. Whither no light can reach. No sound. So sat on as though turned to stone. The sad tale a last time told.

Pause.

Nothing is left to tell.

Pause. R makes to close book.

Knock. Book half closed.

Nothing is left to tell.

Pause. R closes book.

Knock.

Silence. Five seconds.

Simultaneously they lower their right hands to table, raise their heads and look at each other. Unblinking. Expressionless.

Ten seconds.

Fade out.

Notes on the Contributors

H. PORTER ABBOTT teaches at the University of California, Santa Barbara, and is the author of *The Fiction of Samuel Beckett: Form and Effect*, as well as of criticism on a diversity of novelists and auto-biographers. The working title of his current project is *The Kinetic Text*.

PIERRE A. G. ASTIER teaches twentieth-century French literature at the Ohio State University. He is the author of *La Crise du roman français et le Nouveau Réalisme: essai de synthèse sur les nouveaux romans*, and of *Ecrivains français engagés: la génération littéraire de 1930*.

MORRIS BEJA teaches modern literature and film at the Ohio State University. He is the author of *Epiphany in the Modern Novel* and *Film and Literature*, and he has edited an anthology, *Psychological Fiction*, as well as volumes of critical essays on both James Joyce and Virginia Woolf.

ENOCH BRATER teaches modern drama at the University of Michigan, Ann Arbor. He has published many essays on Beckett, Pinter, Stoppard, Arthur Miller, Ionesco, Brecht, Peter Nichols, Noel Coward, Andy Warhol, Dürrenmatt, and contemporary art and film.

RICHARD N. COE is currently in the Department of French and Italian at the University of California, Davis. He has also taught in various fields of French, Russian, and comparative literature at the Universities of Leeds, Warwick, Queensland, and Melbourne. He has published extensively on Ionesco, Morelly, Genet, and Stendhal, as well as on Beckett. At present he is engaged on a study of childhood autobiography.

RUBY COHN teaches in the Department of Dramatic Art at the University of California, Davis. She is the author or editor of such books as *Dialogue in American Drama, Currents in American Drama,* and—on

Beckett—*Samuel Beckett: The Comic Gamut, Back to Beckett, Casebook on "Waiting for Godot,"* and *Samuel Beckett: A Collection of Criticism.*

JUDITH E. DEARLOVE, associate professor of English at Duke University, is the author of several articles on Beckett and other twentieth-century authors. Her book *Accommodating the Chaos: Samuel Beckett's Nonrelational Art* is published by Duke University Press.

S. E. GONTARSKI is an associate professor at the Ohio State University at Lima and has written essays and reviews on Samuel Beckett and D. H. Lawrence for numerous journals and various anthologies. He is the editor of the *Journal of Beckett Studies* and the author of *Beckett's "Happy Days": A Manuscript Study,* published by the Ohio State University Library Publications.

EDITH KERN has taught at many institutions in both England and the United States, and she is currently on the faculty at the New School for Social Research, in New York. She has also served as president of the Modern Language Association. Among her books are *Existential Thought and Fictional Technique: Kierkegaard, Sartre, Beckett,* and *The Absolute Comic.*

JAMES KNOWLSON holds a Personal Professorship in French Studies at the University of Reading, England. He is the author of *Universal Language Schemes in Britain and France 1600–1800* (University of Toronto Press, Toronto, 1976); *Samuel Beckett: An Exhibition* (Turret Books, London 1971); *Light and Darkness in the Theatre of Samuel Beckett* (Turret Books, London 1972), *Frescoes of the Skull: The Later Prose and Drama of Samuel Beckett,* (John Calder, London, 1979; Grove Press, New York, 1980); and a bilingual critical edition of Beckett's *Happy Days* (Faber & Faber, London, 1978).

ANTONI LIBERA is a major figure in Beckett studies in Poland; he has translated into Polish both criticism in English and Beckett's own work.

KRISTIN MORRISON, associate professor of English at Boston College, is coauthor of *Crowell's Handbook of Contemporary Drama.* She has also published articles on both modern drama and modern fiction in many journals, and she has completed a study on the use of narrative in the plays of Beckett and Harold Pinter.

RUBIN RABINOVITZ is a member of the Department of English, the University of Colorado, Boulder.

FREDERIK N. SMITH is associate professor of English at the University of Akron. He has published essays on Pinter, Beckett, Swift, and the teaching of composition. In 1979 the Ohio State University Press published his book *Language and Reality in Swift's "A Tale of a Tub."*

YASUNARI TAKAHASHI, professor of English at the University of Tokyo, has translated into Japanese the collected plays of Beckett as well as *Watt, Malone Dies,* and *Poems in English.* His own books include an analysis of the clown-figure in Beckett and a study of Lewis Carroll and Nonsense. He was Visiting Professor at the University of Toronto in 1981.

ALLEN THIHER teaches French literature and film at the University of Missouri, Columbia. His criticism includes essays on various French writers, and two books: *Céline: The Novel as Delirium* and *The Cinematic Muse: Critical Studies in the History of French Cinema.*

HERSH ZEIFMAN, associate professor of English at York University, Toronto, has published a number of articles on Beckett and contemporary drama. He is currently writing a book on the plays of Tom Stoppard.

NICHOLAS ZURBRUGG is lecturer in comparative literature, the School of Humanities, Griffith University, Brisbane.

Index of Beckett's Works

"Alba," 42
"All Strange Away," 126, 127, 128 n.
    11, 164
All That Fall, 46, 49, 162

Breath, 13
. . . *but the clouds* . . ., 136, 160

Come and Go, 137–43, 162
Comment c'est, 46, 107, 118. *See also*
    "How It Is"
Company, 13, 126, 157–71, 178, 182

"Dante . . . Bruno . Vico . . Joyce,"
    123
Dépeupleur, Le, 43, 46. *See also* "Lost
    Ones, The"
Dream of Fair to Middling Women, 122.
    See also "Text"
"Drunken Boat" (Beckett's transla-
    tion of Rimbaud's "Bateau ivre"),
    37–38

"Echo's Bones," 42
Echo's Bones and Other Precipitates, 42,
    45
Eh Joe, 104, 105, 136
Eleuthéria, 3–4
En attendant Godot, 54, 55. *See also*
    "Waiting for Godot"
Endgame, 5, 16, 28, 34, 91, 93–95, 103,
    107, 141, 158, 170

"Enough," 160, 164, 169
"Enueg I," 42–47
"Enueg II," 42, 43, 45, 47

"Female Solo," 20. *See also* "Happy
    Days"
Film, 46, 129–36, 160, 177
"Fingal," 46, 48
First Love, 160
Footfalls, 8–11, 13, 14, 48, 132, 160–62,
    164
From an Abandoned Work, 162

Ghost Trio, 136
"Good Heavens," 139, 140. *See also*
    "Come and Go"

Happy Days, 16–23, 46, 49, 138, 161,
    162. *See also* "Oh les beaux jours";
    "Female Solo"
"Home Olga," 42
How It Is, 107–19, 124, 125, 160. *See
    also* "Comment c'est"

Ill Seen Ill Said, 164
"Image, L'" (A fragment from *Com-
    ment c'est*), 118, 121 n. 23
Imagination Dead Imagine, 153, 161, 164

"Kilcool," 132
Krapp's Last Tape, 48, 103, 105, 132,
    135, 161, 162, 165, 169, 182, 183

"Lessness," 125

Lost Ones, The, 43, 145–56, 161, 162. *See also "Dépeupleur, Le"*

Malone Dies, 31, 71–79, 83, 107, 108, 141, 158, 159, 164, 166, 176

Mercier and Camier, 141

Molloy, 26, 54, 55, 83, 141, 160, 169, 181

More Pricks Than Kicks, 48, 66, 162

Murphy, 46–49, 58–67, 67 n. 5 (French version), 70 n. 28 (French version), 161, 164, 167, 170, 177

Not I, 8, 103–5, 135, 160, 164, 182

Ohio Impromptu, 10, 14, 15, 46, 105, 106, 189–207

Oh les beaux jours, 17. *See also "Happy Days"*

Old Tune, The (Beckett's translation of Robert Pinget's *La Manivelle*), 37

Piece of Monologue, A, 10–14, 138, 162, 177, 178, 182

Ping, 38

Play, 7, 8, 46, 49, 50

Poems in English, 42, 45

Proust, 20, 64, 123, 168, 177–81, 184

Residua, 125

Rockaby, 105, 106, 168

"Smeraldina's Billet Doux, The," 48, 49

"Sounds," 125–27, 128 n. 11

"Still," 160

"Still 3," 125, 126

"Text" (extract from *Dream of Fair to Middling Women*), 122, 123, 127 n. 2

Texts for Nothing, 130

That Time, 8, 91, 92, 105, 135, 160, 162, 168

Theatre I, 48

Theatre II, 48

Unnamable, The, 80–90, 124

Waiting for Godot, 4–7, 10, 26–29, 31–34, 37, 46, 48, 50, 54, 55, 91, 95, 96, 98 n. 12, 99–102, 138, 160, 181. *See also "En attendant Godot"*

Watt, 15, 30, 31, 46, 48, 50–54, 59, 141

"Wet Night, A," 46

Whoroscope, 42, 45

General Index

Admussen, Richard L., 24 n. 5, 120 n. 3, 136 n. 2, 143 n. 8
Aeschylus, 100–101
Albee, Edward, 8
Alvarez, A., 59, 67 n. 3
Amiel, Henri-Frédéric, 75
Aristotle, 26, 101
Asmus, Walter, 92
Aurier, G.-Albert, 174

Bacchus, 32
Bair, Deirdre, 57 n. 21, 138, 182
Bakhtin, Mikhail, 30
Balch, Anthony, 187 n. 38
Barnard, G. C., 120 n. 11
Barth, John, 108
Baudelaire, Charles, 7, 31, 174
Beaver, Harold, 183
Beethoven, Ludwig van, 41, 51, 53
Berenson, Bernard, 56 n. 6
Berkeley, George, 130
Bernanos, Georges, 79 n. 2
Bernard, Tristan, 23
Bible, 12, 19, 43, 91–97, 108, 140, 162, 164; Christ, Jesus, 6, 7, 9, 30, 31, 43; David, King, 162; Esslesiastes, 6, 164; Evangelists, 28; Genesis, 108; Gospel, 6; Judas, 43, 56 n. 14; Luke, St., 6, 7, 92; Mark, St., 92; Matthew, St., 6, 92, 93, 94, 97 n. 9, 98 n. 12; Psalms, 140, 162; Satan, 76; Solomon, King, 43

Bosch, Hieronymus, 31
Bouvier, Jean-Baptiste, bishop, 58, 67 n. 1
Brecht, Bertold, 8, 99
Breton, André, 173
Breuer, Rolf, 34 n. 1
Browning, Robert, 17, 19
Burnet, John, 70 n. 28
Burroughs, William, 172–76, 129, 182–84

Calder, John, 118
Campanella, Tommaso, 58
Cervantès, Miguel de, 108
Chekhov, Anton, 4
Chopin, Henri, 172
Clark, David R., 136 n. 7
Claudel, Paul, 99
Cocteau, Jean, 20
Cohn, Ruby, 17, 18, 21, 67 n. 1, 97 n. 5, 143 n. 4 & 6, 144 n. 12
Coleridge, Samuel, 75, 100
Compton-Burnett, Ivy, 52
Copeland, Hannah, 67 n. 1
cummings, e. e., 45

Dante Alighieri, 19, 43, 58, 63, 141, 147, 151, 161, 162; *Divine Comedy, The*, 63, 162; *Inferno*, 19, 43, 48, 63, 141; *Purgatorio*, 48, 147, 161
Defoe, Daniel, 19
Democritus, 44

Derrida, Jacques, 79, 83, 88
Descartes, René, 44, 82
Diogenes, 126
Donne, John, 51
Doré, Gustave, 43
Driver, Tom F., 125
Duhamel, Georges, 76, 77

Edwards, Oliver, 17, 19, 24 n. 24
Eisenstein, Sergei, 172–74
Elbow, Peter, 109, 115
Eliot, T. S., 45, 96, 143
Emig, Janet, 111, 112

Farjeon, Eleanor, 56 n. 6
Fehsenfeld, Martha, 171 n. 5
Fielding, Henry, 108
Fitzgerald, Edward, 17
Fletcher, John, 58
Foreman, Richard, 8
Foucault, Michel, 83
Francis of Assisi, St., 97 n. 9
Freud, Sigmund, 104
Frisch, Max, 79 n. 8

Garapon, Robert, 27
Gatti, Armand, 46
Gauguin, Paul, 174
Gessner, Niklaus, 37
Gibson, Susan, 120 n. 19
Ginsberg, Allen, 182, 183
Goethe, Wolfgang von, 49, 75
Goldman, Richard M., 97 n. 8
Gontarski, S. E., 18, 24 n. 2, 24 nn. 12–14
Gray, Thomas, 17

Hall, John Clive, 56 n. 17
Harvey, Lawrence E., 30, 56 nn. 11 & 13
Heidegger, Martin, 80, 82–85, 87–89
Herm, Klaus, 92
Herrick, Robert, 17
Hippasos, 65
Hölderlin, Friedrich, 82
Holinshed, Raphael, 139
Hopkins, Gerard Manley, 45
Huffer, Charles M., 68 n. 17

Hugo, Victor, 24 n. 5, 79 n. 2
Huizinga, Johan, 28, 34

Ibsen, Henrik, 4
Ionesco, Eugène, 17, 28

Jacob, Max, 45
Jacobsen, Josephine, 97 n. 9
James I, 92, 93
Janus, 6
Johnson, Dr. Samuel, 17
Joyce, James, 30, 45, 56 n. 14, 96, 123, 124, 162; *Finnegans Wake*, 30; *Pomes Penyeach*, 45; *Portrait of the Artist as a Young Man, A*, 56 n. 14; *Ulysses*, 162
Jung, Carl, 104

Kafka, Franz, 125
Keaton, Buster, 133, 134
Keats, John, 17
Kenner, Hugh, 57, n. 23, 104, 124, 142, 143
Kettle, Arnold, 37

Laforgue, Jules, 45
Lanham, Richad, 115
Lermontov, Mikhail, 73
Lessing, Doris, 79 n. 8
Lewi, Grant, 68 n. 14

Maeterlinck, Maurice, 23
Magritte, René, 14
Mallarmé, Stéphane, 23, 86
Mansfield, Katherine, 22
Manton, Irene, 56 n. 5
Marcel, Gabriel, 40
Marot, Clement, 32
Mauriac, François, 79, n. 2
Mercier, Vivian, 93
Michelangelo, 143
Milton, John, 17, 19, 20, 75, 76, 162
Mitchell, Breon, 143 n. 1
Molière, Jean-Baptiste Poquelin, 15, 33
Montaudon, Monk of, 42
Mood, John, 59, 67 n. 4

Moravia, Alberto, 79 n. 8
Mueller, William, 97 n. 9

Nabokov, Vladimir, 108
Napoléon I, 39
Neumann, Frederick, 13
Nietzsche, Friedrich, 29, 30

Odier, Daniel, 174

Parnell, Charles Stewart, 47, 56 n. 14
Péret, Benjamin, 45
Pinget, Robert, 37
Pinter, Harold, 23
Plat, 34
Poe, Edgar Allen, 79 n. 2
Pound, Ezra, 45
Prometheus, 18
Proust, Marcel, 15, 48, 75, 123, 134,
   168, 173, 177–81, 184
Pudovkin, V. I., 131

Queneau, Raymond, 40, 90

Rabelais, François, 30
Racine, Jean, 17
Raffles, Sir Thomas, 44
Reverdy, Pierre, 45
Richardson, Samuel, 72–74
Rimbaud, Arthur, 37, 38, 45
Robbe-Grillet, Alain, 108
Ronsard, Pierre de, 17
Rousseau, Jean-Jacques, 79

Sartre, Jean-Paul, 38, 53, 75, 77, 78
Saussure, Ferdinand de, 80, 82
Sayers, Dorothy L., 52
Schlegel, Friedrich von, 75
Schneider, Alan, 8, 17, 97 n. 2, 136
   nn. 4 & 7, 187 n. 38
Schopenhauer, Arthur, 19, 63
Schubert, Franz, 136 n. 7

Shakespeare, William, 3, 7, 13, 16–
   19, 28, 63, 138–43, 162; *Hamlet*, 18,
   19, 140–42; *King Lear*, 142; *Macbeth*,
   28, 138, 139, 141; *The Merchant of
   Venice*, 138; *A Midsummer's Night
   Dream*, 3, 7, 13; *Romeo and Juliet*, 19,
   63; *The Tempest*, 16, 138, 143
Sitwell, Edith, 56 n. 16
Spurling, John, 187 n. 37
Stein, Gertrude, 56 n. 16
Steiner, George, 183
Stendhal, 39
Sterne, Laurence, 108
Swift, Jonathan, 58
Synge, John Millington, 23

Tennyson, Alfred, 75
Thomas à Kempis, 97 n. 9
Turgenev, Ivan, 79 n. 2
Tyutchev, Fedor, 39

Valéry, Paul, 127
Veit, Walter, 185 n. 7
Venus, 32
Verlaine, Paul, 17, 18
Vico, Giambattista, 155
Vildrac, Charles, 23

Wall, Max, 136 n. 7
Walton, Izaac, 51
Warrilow, David, 11, 15 n. 3
Watt, Ian, 77
Whipple, Fred L., 68 n. 16
Whitaker, Joseph, 68 n. 16, 69 n. 27
Winterowd, W. Ross, 120 n. 7
Wittgenstein, Ludwig, 56 n. 10, 80–
   82, 85–89
Wodehouse, P. G., 52
Wolfe, Charles, 17, 19
Wordsworth, William, 58
Wyatt, Stanley, 69 n. 27

Yeats, William Butler, 16, 17, 99

Zeno of Elea, 158
Zola, Emile, 50